The Villages of Aberdeen
Old Aberdeen
Volume 1

'It is interesting to contemplate that Cluny and his desperadoes, having laid waste the Lands of Hilton, could later be found sitting about St Machar's Cathedral discussing the price of oatcakes like douce bodies.' With her usual high readability, in-depth research and dash of humour, Diane Morgan presents the first volume of her two-part study of the village and cathedral city of Old Aberdeen whose charm and beauty belies its vivid and turbulent past. The canvas stretches from St Machar's time (did he exist?) to the outbreak of the Covenanting Wars, (when things could only get worse), and is peopled with kings, queens, knights, bishops, bailies, scholars and the ordinary thrawn folk of the Aulton. Intriguing questions are asked for the first time, and answers attempted: Why, for example, did Bishop Elphinstone establish his university, not in Aberdeen, the largest and most prosperous town in his diocese, but in a bleak and empty marshland to the north? Like its four predecessors in the award-winning 'Villages' series, *Old Aberdeen* is profusely illustrated and attractively presented.

By the same author

'Villages of Aberdeen' series

Footdee
and her Shipyards

Round About Mounthooly

The Spital

The Spital Lands
from Sunnyside to Pittodrie

Front Cover
King's College from the south. An adaptation of the vignette from Parson Gordon's Plan, 1661.
From the original watercolour by J A Sutherland

The Villages of Aberdeen

Old Aberdeen

Volume 1

Diane Morgan

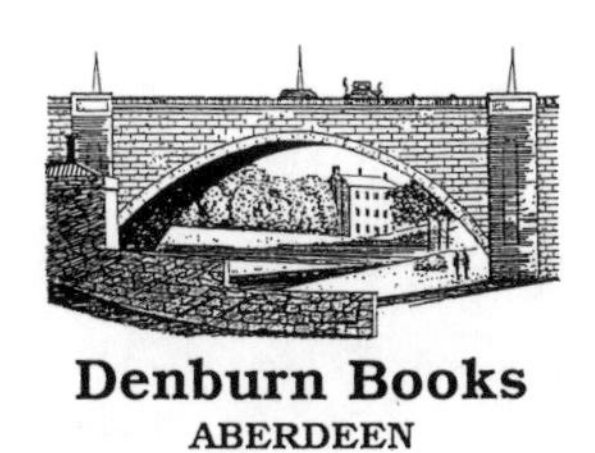

Denburn Books
ABERDEEN

First Published 2000

British Library Cataloguing in Publication Data
A catalogue record for this book is available from the British Library

ISBN 1 898645 05 1

Design and Layout by
Jimmy and Pat Sutherland

Produced by Printagraph, Aberdeen

Acknowledgements

I owe a great debt of gratitude to all those who have helped with *Old Aberdeen*, Volume One, and responded to my queries: ; Ian B D Bryce for tackling the puzzling west front of King's College Chapel and for contributing his findings thereon in Appendix 2; Mrs C G W Roads, Lyon Clerk, and Charles J Burnett Esq, Ross Herald of Arms for casting light on problems relating to the heraldic ceiling of St Machar's Cathedral; Professor Alexander Fenton for identifying some arcane Old Aberdeen occupations; the Rev Richard Frazer of St Machar's Cathedral for access to relics and the loan of illustrative material; George Gordon for material on the Earls and Marquises of Huntly; Dr Leslie Macfarlane for responding to a number of my queries with great kindness and erudition; Professor Bill Nicolaisen on place names of the Donmouth; Professor Nicholas Bogdan on the great palace at Fetternear and the Bishop's Loch (Loch Goul); Dr Ian A G Shepherd on the Seaton Stone, and Mr and Mrs Vic Booth for showing us the former sites of Mortlach and Kinkell Manses and their hospitality at Tillydrone House. The late Edward S Massie, who took much interest in this series, provided background material on Parson Gordon's Plan.

Many people have kindly shared their reminiscences of Old Aberdeen with me, and there are more to come. These all belong to the modern era and will be individually acknowledged in Volume Two. For the moment, my thanks and appreciation of their interest.

I am grateful as ever to the staff at Aberdeen City Archives, Aberdeen City Libraries and the Special Collections, King's College, University of Aberdeen for their assistance in finding material on various aspects of this work; and to Stuart Thain of Aberdeen Art Gallery and Museums for producing the very beggar's badge we sought, and permitting illustration.

A special thanks to my husband David I Morgan who has accompanied me on numerous forays to 'Auld Aberdeen and places round about' to use a favourite phrase of the chroniclers. There are less frustrating things to do on a Sunday afternoon than search in vain for traces of vanished medieval wynds in the Aulton or seek out the course of the long gone 'auld wattergang', the old Donmouth, around the Broad Hill and Urquhart Road.

My production team deserve special mention. Frank Donnelly has yet again come to my assistance with his camera and with sterling advice on a range of subjects. At Printagraph Lynn Forbes has again done excellent work. My warmest appreciation goes to Pat and Jimmy Sutherland who have worked hard over a long period to prepare this book for publication. As I have said before, so much of the success of 'The Villages of Aberdeen' series is due to their enthusiasm, dedication and professionalism.

Reproduction of illustrative material outwith the author's collection is by courtesy of the following institutions and individuals: Aberdeen University (43, 62), St Machar's Cathedral, (8, 20, 40), Professor Nicholas Bogdan, (25), Dr John Smith, (79). The line drawings are by J A (Jimmy) Sutherland.

Diane Morgan, 2000

Contents

	Part One: In the Beginning	
	Introduction	1
	The Mote Hill of Tillydrone	4
1	St Machar: Myth, Meadow or Holy Man?	6
2	Cathedral and Chanonry	15
3	William Elphinstone Founder of Aberdeen University	42
4	The Pearl of Knowledge	64
5	The Chapel	84
6	Gavin Dunbar The last great medieval Bishop	101
7	The Riddle of the Crown Tower	121
8	The End of an Era	129
	Part Two: Beyond the Bishops	
9	Dark Days for Kirk, Queen and College	150
10	The Hilton Land Raid and the Stocket Compromise	168
11	The Governance of the Burgh	172
12	The Great Fairs	189
13	College Bounds	193
14	William Gordon, Mediciner	204
15	High Street	211
16	The Market Cross	230
17	School and Tolbooth	236
18	The final Flowering of the old Chanonry	249
	Appendix 1	264
	Appendix 2	266
	Bibliography	270
	Index	271

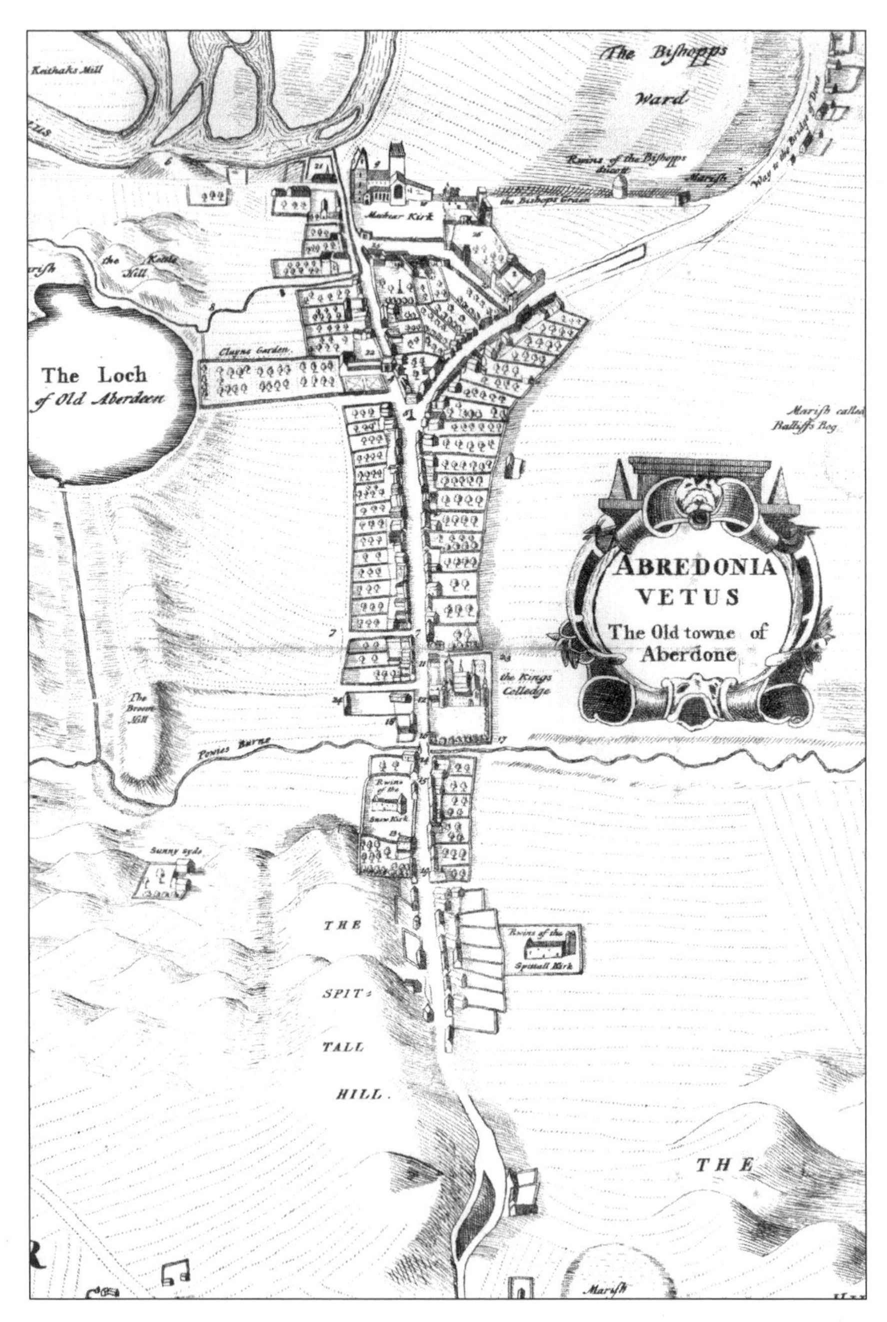

The unmistakable shape of Old Aberdeen is clearly shown on this detail from Parson Gordon of Rothiemay's Plan of 'New and Old Aberdeen', 1661.

Introduction

In the last book in this series, *The Spital Lands*, we got as far as the start of College Bounds. Now at last we are ready to embark on an exploration of Old Aberdeen, burgh of barony, university town, cathedral city. Thanks to its links with church and state, it had an enterprising and turbulent history that was quite remarkable (whisper this) for what was really a wee village.

A dilemma now confronts me. It is not appropriate to continue the story exactly where we left off. 'The colledge boundis' did not come into existence in their own right until the early sixteenth century by which time they had a college to bound. Until then along with their continuation, the Middle Toun or High Street, they formed an unpromising stretch of the King's Highway, the *via regia* of the early charters, threading northwards through a flat skelp of marshland. Since there is nothing to report there for several centuries, our investigation of Old Aberdeen must leap northwards to the Chanonry which had start-up by the twelfth century. The fascinating comings and goings there are dealt with in Part One along with the remarkable foundation of King's College.

By Part Two we have reached the early seventeenth century and return to College Bounds to stroll through Old Aberdeen from south to north to find out how the area was developing and what the ordinary people were doing. This volume therefore takes us from earliest times to the seventeenth century and sometimes a little beyond. Hopefully, its successor, Volume Two, will reach the present. Such bifurcation will come as no surprise to the readers of this series. If all goes well, at the end of the day, we will have five books covering the journey to Old Aberdeen starting with *Round About Mounthooly*, where only one was originally intended.

After descending the Spital Hill an early traveller north would encounter the Powis Burn. The Scots word *pow* meant a slow-flowing stream or a marshy place and the burn was both. It meandered through what are now the grounds of Crombie and Johnston Halls of Residence and crossed the future College Bounds. In years to come, the bog it created there would cause difficulties for the building of King's College. It then flowed along the present line of University Road to reach the Links where it changed its name to the Tile Burn.

After fording the burn (it had acquired a bridge by the sixteenth century), our traveller would find two sandhills on his left, the Broom Hill and a little further north, the Glebe Hill. On his right, to the east, were marshes and benty braes, the reed-covered hillocks that were scattered across the links. Beyond that lay the sea. Corseted between this Scylla and Charybdis of hill and marsh, the expansion of Old Aberdeen beyond the High Street was inhibited for centuries to come.

About three hundred yards north of the Powis Burn, the highway divided. At this point, any thought of St Machar's Drive must be banished from the mind. The right-hand fork, Don Street, the Seatongate in those days, took the traveller, as its name implied, to the Lands of Seaton, climbing slowly to what is now Hillhead before descending to Balgownie whose Brig had been completed by 1320. Beyond the river the road forked again, one branch going off to Oldmeldrum and Banff, a second to Udny, and a third to Ellon and beyond. The left-hand fork, the Chanonry, the approach to St Machar's Cathedral, was virtually a continuation of the High Street though its character was very different. Here Old Aberdeen had its origins. The shape of the Chanonry, like that of the High Street, was dictated by natural features. The canons' glebes ran behind their manses, but their boundaries were curtailed on the west side by a vast stretch of water, the Loch of Old Aberdeen, from whose southern shore a burn escaped to join the Powis Burn at the Broom Hill. The site of the Loch is now covered by the Tillydrone Roundabout and neighbouring playing fields. Immediately north of the Loch were the Kettle Hills whose vestiges survive in the back gardens which replaced the old glebes.

The Chanonry turned eastwards at St Machar's, passing the south front of the cathedral. The glebes of the great manses opposite ran south towards the High Street, but were curtailed by the ancient Seatongate. The Chanonry itself had turned south-east to meet with the Seatongate. Parson Gordon's Plan, 1661, opposite page 1, shows this area. The canons had gone but the lie of the land is the same .

St Machar's Cathedral commanded the ground above the Don. This volatile river has shifted its course down the years, and until the late eighteenth century flowed much closer to the cathedral than today. It has moulded the shape of the present Seaton Park, and possibly caused the land north of the cathedral to silt up. West of St Machar's were the lands of Tillydrone, the ridge of the hillock from the Gaelic, *Tily*, a small hill, and *druim*, ridge. A more ancient name is Donydronis, the ridge of the Don. At the west side of St Machar's kirkyard, a narrow path 'the common passage that goes to Donydronis hill', led westwards away from the Chanonry, to the Lands of Cruives, and eventually linked up with the ancient highway to Inverurie. The 'common passage' in modern form is that part of the present Tillydrone Road which skirts Seaton Park. The Tillydrone ridge is still there, visible on the south side of the road. On the north side, a few hundred yards from the cathedral and lying within Seaton Park stands Donydronis Hill itself, the ancient Mote Hill of Tillydrone. Such then was the difficult terrain of Old Aberdeen and 'places round about'.

And so from the topographical to the etymological evolution of 'Old Aberdeen'. This knotty problem has caused copious amounts of ink to flow. More flows in Appendix 1. It is enough to say here that by the seventeenth century the irritating phrase 'New' Aberdeen had come into use to distinguish the royal burgh from its northerly neighbour, though 'New' Aberdeen was older than Old Aberdeen. 'New' Aberdeen dropped out of use by the nineteenth century and so it remains here, unless it forms part of a quotation. I have simply referred to Aberdeen as Aberdeen, adding 'royal burgh' if there is likelihood of confusion. I have also used Old Aberdeen's other name, the Aulton, which is simply the Auld Toun as it was so often called in the burgh records.

A sprinkling of the robust North East Scots of the seventeenth and eighteenth century is retained, from the burgh records and the chroniclers. It is easy to read and modern English is anaemic in comparison. Very occasionally the spelling has been simplified, the odd comma added. Plurals were often 'is' rather than 's', 'qu' is the Scots form of 'wh'. Neither spelling nor capitalisation were standardised, and words were rarely spelt the same way twice in the one sentence. Sums of money quoted are Scots value unless indicated otherwise. A merk was worth 13s 4d. References to the Bridge of Don are to the Brig o Balgownie but to avoid confusion I have added (Balgownie) which came into use only after the present Bridge of Don was built in 1831.

The Mote Hill of Tillydrone

Not a great deal is known about the Mote Hill of Tillydrone or Donydronis Hill to give its ancient name. According to tradition, it is a motte, the earliest form of castle, a man-made earthwork that would have had a timber lodging or fortalice erected on its flat top. The motte theory is supported by research carried out in the 1990s, revealing that it may have been revetted, (covered with masonry), at least in part. Moreover, it was excellently sited to command the Don and the north and north-eastern approaches to Aberdeen.

At Tillydrone, the purpose of the wooden lodging on the summit may not have been military. It could have served as the palace of the Bishops of Aberdeen, who first emerge in the twelfth century, the heyday of the motte. However, a fourteenth century structure on or near the hill did exist, and its role was ecclesiastical, serving as a chapel and later as the bishop's courthouse. However, no trace of any timberwork remains and an encircling ditch, noted in the 1920s by the Aberdeen historian and archaeologist, Dr W Douglas Simpson, has likewise vanished. The Mote Hill now finds itself within the curtilage of Seaton Park, and though a scheduled ancient monument, its fine, sandy soil has been eroded over the years, thanks to the efforts of wind, weather, rabbits, sledgers and cyclists. Partly tree-covered, and conical in shape, its vital statistics in 2000 AD were: diameter at base 97ft (30m): oval summit, 28 x 16ft (9 x 5 m): height on east 24ft (7m) and on west 16ft (5m), the disparity due to the slope of the ground. It continues to diminish.

The Mote Hill, left with a cluster of houses at its base and the Kettle Hills in front of it. St Machar's Cathedral is to the far right with the fleche of Gavin Dunbar's Hospital visible to its left. Detail from 'Old Aberdeen' from Slezer's 'Theatrum Scotiae', 1693.

Part One

In the Beginning

The twin towers of St Machar's

Chapter 1

St Machar: Myth, Meadow or Holy Man?

> What little is known of St Machar is so riddled with myth and historical incongruity as to be almost worthless.
>
> *E S Towill, Saints of Scotland, 1983.*

The name of St Machar is a familiar one in Aberdeen and its hinterland. The Cathedral of Old Aberdeen is dedicated to him and several schools and a pub bear his name, Salvation, Education and Damnation, as it were, allowing the saint single-handedly to provide a riposte to Rosemount Viaduct's famous trio. Two parishes, Oldmachar and Newmachar were also named in his honour. Nevertheless, hard facts about his life are non-existent. He makes an appearance in *The Saints of Scotland* quoted above, only 'in deference to the prestige of the great cathedral' which bears his name. There is even a view that no such person ever existed, and that the name of the church comes solely from the Gaelic *machair*, flat, sandy meadow land near the sea, the 'links' in Scots. Tradition has it that the original church stood in such terrain, lower than its present site, in what is now the Seaton Park area. I do not belong to that camp. The famous legend of St Machar founding a church where a river curved like a shepherd's crook or a bishop's staff is one of the earliest tales I recall being told, and despite the justified scepticism of scholars, I still like to believe it.

Assuming that he existed, Machar would have been one of the pioneering missionaries who brought Christianity to what is now Scotland in the fifth and sixth centuries. Miraculous tales grew up around these holy men, but more often than not, hundreds of years elapsed before they were written down. But by the twelfth century King David I's zeal to build churches and abbeys inspired the hagiographers among his churchmen to collect the old traditional tales about the saints to whom these churches were dedicated. It was not the concern of these writers to purvey historical fact, which in any case had become hazy over the centuries, but to edify, to entertain and to amaze their flocks with tales of wondrous miracles and visions. Even Bishop Adomnán's biography of St Columba, written only a century after his death in 597, is a mixture of fact and miraculous events, in spite of the fact that Adomnán had held converse with aged monks who remembered Columba.

It was around 1125 that King David established the diocese of Aberdeen, with its seat in Old Aberdeen, at St Machar's Kirk, and it was fitting that a Life of St Machar should be written to extol the church's founder. Though it has not survived, this Latin 'Life', was the source for three later versions, all extant, all slightly different. The earliest of the three, the longest and most vivid is a late fourteenth century anonymous poem in Scots, *Saint Machor*, believed at one time to have been the work of John Barbour, Archdeacon of Aberdeen and author of the famous epic, *The Brus. Saint Machor* was found in a manuscript containing the legends of fifty saints, though St Ninian is the only other Scot. After passing through various hands, this manuscript was presented to Cambridge University by George I in 1715. The second version is a Latin one, found in the *Aberdeen Breviary*, which was printed in 1510 under Bishop Elphinstone's supervision. The third version forms part of a Gaelic life of St Columba written in 1532.

The poem *Saint Machor* tells us, by way of a preamble, of the greatness and merits of this saint 'of Aberden' though, 'in this land we ken hym nocht'. Even then, there was a shadow of uncertainty about his existence. Machor, we are told was an Irish prince, born in the sixth century to a Christian family and called Mo Chuma in those early days. (Celtic saints were often given familiar or 'pet' names which began with *Mo* meaning 'my'). Machar would acquire three different names, plus variations on each, in the course of his career, indicating perhaps that three separate legends had been cobbled together to create his 'Life'..

His childhood was suitably miraculous. 'Bricht angels' hovered round his cradle, filling the house with 'melody and angelsang'. He brought his younger brother who was stillborn into life, and was himself miraculously unscathed when his nurse, 'sitand and had him on her kne', let him fall into the fire. Nor was he drowned when a vat into which his nurse had placed him was inadvertently filled with water. She had only intended to use it briefly as makeshift playpen to prevent him crawling away. Little wonder the poor woman 'ruggit of hyr heid the hair'.

He was sent to St Columba to be educated and the great man gave him his best known name: 'Thou sal be callyt Machor'. Machor or Machar sailed with Columba from Ireland, (historically, the latter's voyage was in 563 AD), one of his twelve companions, reflecting the number of disciples, who

The Crombie Memorial window in the south-west aisle of St Machar's was designed by Dr Douglas Strachan and dedicated in 1908. Inspired by medieval church windows which portrayed episodes from the Bible, it relates the legend of St Machar.

later created a community in Iona. Machar subsequently crossed to Mull, preaching Christianity and healing lepers, then returned to Iona, where he continued to pray and to study. One night as he was copying Scriptures the light failed. He blew on his finger ends and a light leapt forth, burning until his work was done. His remarkable powers had already aroused jealousy among the less saintly of his brethren. Now 'they were inflammit of the fire of envy' says our poet, and attempted to poison his drink. Machar made the sign of the cross, poured out the poison which had conveniently risen to the top of his goblet and drank the rest, enraging his enemies even more. Columba diffused the situation, sending Machar and seven companions off to convert the Picts to Christianity, kitting him out with staff, belt, books, food, and clothes and a coracle which sailed round to the North East of Scotland in a surprisingly quick three days. On disembarking the companions were welcomed by a wealthy local chieftain, Farquhar, by good luck already a Christian. He invited them to settle in any part of his lands they chose. Machar found a place:

Besyd a watyr bank, that rane,
Into the se(a), and lyk was thane
As it a biscopis staf had bene.

Here, at the spot told of by Columba, they established a settlement, then built, with the help of:

... crafty (skilful) *men, a costly kyrk*
And that man callis yet
Of Sancte Machore the seg or set
(that men still call St Machar's seat.)

This is the famous legend of the founding of St Machar's Cathedral.

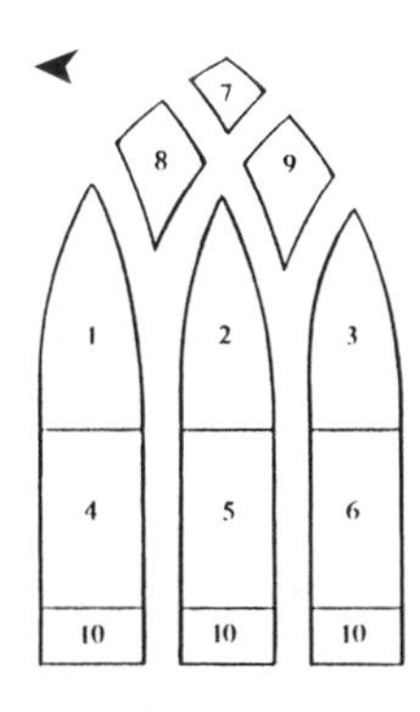

1. St Machar contemplates in his cell on Iona, while two jealous brethern scowl outside. 2. St Columba bids him leave the island, and tells him of a new mission. 3. Equipped by Columba, Machar with his shepherd's crook and his companions leave Iona. Columba, on the shore gives them his blessing. 4. On the banks of the Don, Machar is welcomed by a Christian chief. 5. Machar finds the place where the river curves like a shepherd's crook. 6. A simple Cathedral of wattle walls and a thatched roof is built there. 7. At the top of the window, the Holy Spirit in the form of a dove. 8. An urn decorated with the arms of Aberdeen University. The thistle growing from it symbolises the development of Scottish genius and guardian angels tend it. 9. The bough pot with the arms of Old Aberdeen. 10. The dedication at the foot of the window reads: In loving memory of J W Crombie, born March 4th 1858, died March 22, 1908.

Machar's first miracle among the Picts was to slake his workers' thirst by producing a spring, though presumably he could as easily have told them to get a drink from the nearby 'watyr bank' of the Don. In the ensuing years, he wrought many more marvels. He struck a bear that had been ravaging crops with his staff, turning it into what sounds very like a standing stone. He gave sight to a blind man, bathing his eyes with holy water. He resurrected a kinsman of St Columba and caused a fish bone, which had stuck in the throat of one of his enemies, to leap out. In return the enemy, now a grateful convert, granted Machar land on which he built 'a cumly kyrk'. There are no further details on this second foundation. He made contact with other holy men, St Devenick and St Ternan, who were also proselytising among the Picts. The elderly Devenick subsequently went off to convert the heathens of Caithness, while Machar remained in the North East. After Devenick's death, Machar buried him, as he had promised, at his 'bangorie' or mission centre:

Men callis the place whare he lay
Banchory Devenick to this day.

Ternan, a native of the Mearns and a follower of St Ninian had also founded a 'bangorie', at what is now Banchory Ternan. The poet tells us how Machar having ploughed a 'mekill feild' discovered he had nothing to sow. He sent messengers to Ternan to borrow a sack of seed. Ternan sent a sack of sand instead, but when scattered on the field it sprang up as corn. This story is also told in the account of Ternan in the *Aberdeen Breviary*. Later, Ternan and his followers visited Machar and a great religious rally was held.

After Machar had spent many years in Pictland and converted most of its inhabitants, Columba sent for him and together they made the pilgrimage to Rome. Here Pope Gregory the Great ordained Machar a bishop and changed his name again:

And callit hym Morise, that befor
Lang tyme to name had Machor.

On their return journey, Columba and Machar-Morise arrived in Tours whose local saint, Martin, enjoyed a great cult in the early British church. The people of Tours invited Columba to remain with them, but he declined and Machar stayed instead, vouched for personally by St Martin, who appeared in a vision. Machar, as Bishop Morise of Tours, ministered there with great success for over three years. At his death he made the miraculous exodus reserved for top class saints. Jesus, the twelve apostles, Saint

Columba and St Martin of Tours stood by his bed, and a host of angels bore him to heaven, accompanied by sweet music.

The poem *Saint Machor* has drama, pace, colour. It is the very stuff of legend and Machar is given substance by association with Columba, Devenick and Ternan who did exist. Unfortunately it contains not a shred of proven fact. The theory, first propagated by the Venerable Bede, and popular in the nineteenth century, that Columba was instrumental in the conversion the Picts, has been discredited by modern scholars. Columba did visit Bridei, King of the Picts near Inverness, but this was a diplomatic undertaking rather than a Christian mission. Indeed Columba had his hands full in the west of Scotland. He never went to Rome, with Machar or anyone else, though that legendary visit is an interesting piece of propaganda. By the twelfth century, when the original 'Life' was written, the Celtic church was losing ground to Rome. The Scottish hagiographers, alarmed least their saints were being sidelined, endowed them with political correctness by showing involvement with the Pope, and with a Premier Division saint like Martin of Tours. Nor did these writers concern themselves over the discrepancy of a century or two. Of Machar's colleagues, Devenick has been placed variously in the fifth, sixth or seventh centuries while Ternan was roughly contemporary with Ninian who used to be placed in the fifth century. Modern scholarship now puts Ninian, and consequently Ternan, in the sixth century, making them contemporary with Machar.

St Martin of Tours presented as a young soldier dividing his cloak with a beggar who was seeking alms on a cold winter's night. Christ appeared to him later that night wearing the divided cloak whereupon Martin, born of heathen parents, converted to Christianity. He became Bishop of Tours in 371.

We have a second candidate to be St Machar. In *The Origins of Christianity in Aberdeenshire*, (1925), Dr W Douglas Simpson dismissed the Columba connection, equating Machar, though he does not say on what grounds, with a St Mochrieha or Muchriecha, though he admits: 'Few authentic details are known about his life; the later medieval versions are

St Machar's Cross, Aboyne.

hopelessly garbled'. Muchriecha makes an appearance in the *New Statistical Account* of Aberdeenshire of 1843 where, in the Aboyne and Glentanar section, the Rev R M Miller describes a stone with a cross cut in it on a hill north-west of Aboyne. Nearby was St Machar's or Muchrieha's Well. The story goes that the stone with the cross was wrongfully removed and Muchrieha, the guardian of the well, miraculously brought it back to its original site. The saint rested from his labours in what became known as Muchrieha's chair, a huge stone where a hollow for a seat, had been roughly cut. 'About thirty years ago, some masons, unawed by Muchrieha, split his chair into pieces to assist in the building of a neighbouring farm-house', comments the Rev Miller. Of the stone with the cross Douglas Simpson writes: 'It is one of the most interesting relics of primitive Christianity in Aberdeenshire. It is an equal-armed cross ...incised on a glacial boulder in the heart of Balnagowan Wood'. Much of that wood has vanished since Simpson's time but the Class IV Pictish stone, now known as St Machar's Cross, is still there. The land it sits on is privately owned, but access can be obtained by arrangement.

Simpson also notes that the presence of Mochrieha-Machar on Donside is commemorated by chapel sites at Kildrummy and at Corgaff where there is another St Machar's Well. There is a legend that in time of famine the saint responded to the local priest's prayers, allowing three salmon at a time to be drawn from the well as required. Three symbolised the Holy Trinity, while the fish was the secret sign for Christ. There are also Mochrieha-Machar sites on the Ythan near Logie Buchan where there was a Macharford and there is still a Macharmuir.

There remains a third candidate to be St Machar. He is St Kentigern, patron saint of Glasgow, and known as Mu Nghu by the Britons of Strathclyde which became Mungo in English and in Gaelic, Mo Cha, which is much the same as Machar. Kentigern-Mungo-Mo Cha was primarily associated with Glasgow, with Cumbria which included Strathclyde at that time, and with the Britons of Wales. He died around 612 and was roughly contemporary with Columba with whom, according to legend, he exchanged pastoral staffs. He was also the patron of Glengairn to the south of Ballater where, until the second half of the nineteenth century, there was a feast of St Mungo at the Foot o Gairn. There was also a St Mungo's Well in the area. A fair held on the hillside near Abergairn, was called in Gaelic *Fel McCha,* or *Macha,* Mo Cha's Fair. The ruined church of Glengairn, its cemetery, and a nearby well bear both versions of his name in Gaelic, *Cill Macha* the church of Macha and *Fuaran Mungo,* Mungo's Well. He is also commemorated at Kinnoir near Huntly with a St Mungo's Hill and Well and an ancient church.

We can never know exactly how, when, or by whom St Machar's Cathedral was established, but there is a tradition that a kirk was either founded by Machar or dedicated to him in the Seaton Park area, which was *machair* or meadow land near the sea. From the early days of the Christianity in Scotland until the twelfth century, when Gaelic was spoken in and around Aberdeen, churches were given either the name of the missionary who founded them (churches named in honour of the disciples was a later fashion), or simply took the name of the place where they stood. In St Machar's (or Mo Cha's) case both elements could have prevailed, the name of the founder merging with the name of the terrain where the church was built.

But given the vagueness about the holy man's existence, why not accept the word *machair* as the origin of the cathedral? Because, as already noted, there are many Machar and Machar-related place-names on Deeside and Donside, where the terrain is not that of a *machair.* They were more likely to have taken their names from the missionary who brought Christianity to that area. And while there is no proof that Machar founded a church where the Don bends like a shepherd's crook, there is no proof that he did not. The fertile mind of a hagiographer could have seized on the kirk's picturesque setting, and so created the legend, portraying the mighty Columba as instigator of the directive to build where the river bends.

We can be reasonably sure that there was a Christian presence in the Seaton Park area by the seventh century, following St Machar's putative era. A boulder dating from that time, the Seaton Stone, a Class III Pictish

The Seaton Stone with its hollowed-angled cross and shaft in its original position in the dyke at Hillhead.

The Seaton Stone, left, in its cage at the east end of King's College Chapel and right, in its present position at St Machar's Cathedral.

stone incised with a cross, though different in shape and style to the Aboyne stone, was long ago built into the dyke at Hillhead on the Seatongate, today's Don Street. That dyke is now replaced by the entrance to Hillhead Hall of Residence. Fortunately, the Seaton Stone was preserved when Aberdeen University acquired the site. It was confined to a cage beside the apse at the east end of the chapel, just a couple of yards from the Library, where Dr Douglas Simpson presided so memorably. In 1995, this Christian-Pictish boulder returned 'home' to St Machar's Cathedral, on indefinite loan from the University and it can be seen, suspended on the north side of the west wall.

These days, the question of who converted the Picts, and brought Christianity to the North East is debated as hotly as ever. Dr Simpson's theories are attacked and Bede's words shown to be inaccurate; the rival supporters of Columba and Ninian slog it out. For our part, we can now put speculation aside, quit the ever-shifting sands of the saints' lives and examine the glorious if chequered 'modern' history of St Machar's Cathedral, which begins with the emergence of written records in King David I's reign in the twelfth century.

Chapter 2

Cathedral and Chanonry

The prebends or canon-regulars had large lodgings, yards, and gleibs or little taills at the end of their yards. They were the bishop's chapter or council; he could do nothing without them; therefore they were obliged to live near him, that they might be ready on all occasions to go about church affairs.

William Orem, A Description of the Chanonry, Cathedral etc, 1751.

St Machar's Cathedral is one of the most familiar landmarks in North East Scotland, a redoubtable edifice that looks equally fitted to withstand a siege as to glorify God. But the cathedral we know today was by no means the first on the site, nor did it ever quite receive its completion certificate.

Its history begins in the twelfth century. King David I who reigned from 1124-53, 'illuminated the land with kirks and abbeys', as behoved the son of Malcolm Canmore and St Margaret. She had brought English and continental influences to Scotland and though by no means hostile to the Celtic Church, was anxious to reform what she considered to be its archaic traditions. David I continued his mother's work, reorganising the native church, bringing it closer to Rome, redding up existing dioceses, the areas where a bishop exercised control, and establishing new ones, among them Aberdeen, which in the fullness of time would occupy an area a little larger than the historic county of Aberdeen. For some years, Nectan, 'a man of learning and dignified character' according to Hector Boece's *Lives of the Bishops,* had the charge of a monastery that followed the old Celtic rites at Mortlach near Dufftown where St Moluag had established a Christian presence in the sixth century. Around 1125 Nectan was translated, that is 'relocated', to the headquarters of the new diocese. This was not, as one might expect, Aberdeen itself, but the place we know as Old Aberdeen almost two miles to the north, which the legendary presence of St Machar centuries earlier had endowed with a special sanctity. It could have had little to offer apart from a Pictish kirk and a few simple dwellings scattered in the neighbourhood.

Nectan successfully transferred from the Celtic to the continental style of worship, and none the waur of this mild apostasy, remained as Bishop of Aberdeen for seventeen years, until his death in 1152. There is speculation that he may have had a wooden lodging on the Mote Hill of Tillydrone as his palace.

With the creation of the new diocese came the erection of a cathedral, that symbol of the bishop's authority, marking his headquarters or seat. The first St Machar's Cathedral was probably built in Nectan's time or a little after, in stone, in the contemporary Norman or Romanesque style. While the old Pictish kirk may have been located in what is now Seaton Park, the cathedral was built on or near the same prominent site overlooking the River Don where its successor now stands. Unfortunately all that remains of this first cathedral is a tiny part of an abacus or flat stone from the top of one of its columns, ornamented by a ridge of 'dog-tooth' pattern. It is preserved in the room above the south porch of the present St Machar's.

A fragment from the twelfth century Norman cathedral showing part of an abacus decorated in dog tooth pattern.

The revenues of Mortlach had been 'very slender' says Boece, but David I endowed the new bishopric generously. He was, as James I later remarked in exasperation, 'ane sair sanct for the croun', a sore saint as far as the sovereign was concerned, impoverishing the monarchy at the expense of the Church. Grants of revenue by Malcolm Canmore, David I and Malcolm IV to the Bishop of Aberdeen, were confirmed in 1157 to Bishop Edward, Nectan's successor

The Great Seal of David 1, 'ane sair sanct for the croun'.

by Pope Adrian IV (the English pope, Nicholas Breakspear) in a bull, a papal charter with a lead seal or *bulla,* These included the whole town of Old Aberdeen and St Machar's Cathedral, both mentioned by name for the first time in this charter; half the North Water (the Don), the revenues of Sclattie, Goul, (Goval then Parkhill, were later names), Petsprottis (perhaps Dilspro, later Grandhome), the lands we now know as Hilton, the teind (tenth part or tithe) 'of the ships called snows which arrive at Aberdeen', indicating the commmercial nature of the port even in those early days, the teind of the fish caught there, and of the grain there, the king's own teind of the rents in the burgh of Aberdeen, the teind of the fishings of Croys (the Cruives), of the mill of Aberdeen, with one net in the South water (the Dee), the teind of the fish caught there, the teind of the grain and fish of Baldwyniston (near Dyce?), the teind of Badfothel (Pitfodels), the teind of the royal dues between the Dee and the Spey, as well as the revenues, of Rayne, Tillygreig, Kinmundy, Mameulah, Clatt, Tullynessle, Daviot, Ellon, Banchory-Devenick, Fetternear, Oyne, Cruden, Belhelvie, Auchterless, Birse, Drumoak, with their kirks and kirktowns, and the monasteries of Clova, near Lumsden and Mortlach, itself, anciently known as Murthillach. The teinds supported the Church and its priests, and proved a remarkably versatile source of income. They could be imposed on virtually anything that was capable of being taxed.

The bull of 1157 also permitted the appointment of monks or canons at the bishop's discretion, and they appear in the records towards the end of Bishop Matthew's time. It was for the twilight years of these first canons that he founded St Peter's Hospital in the Spital. Their administrative as well as their liturgical skills must have been much in demand for the feuing out and the setting in tack (leasing) of the lands endowed to St Machar's, and the calculation and the ingathering of the revenues due to the cathedral in a variety of forms must have been a laborious task; no calculators, no writing of cheques in those days. The logistical difficulties were considerable. Even today some of the old cathedral lands near Aberdeen, the farms of Mameulah and Tillygreig for example, and Murcar with its great expanse of dunes retain a feeling of remoteness and inaccessibility.

Not that the rendering unto God the things that were God's or at least the Church's was always carried out with a glad heart. The payment of Church revenues was often met with resentment, and on occasion, violence. Richard de Pottock or Pottun was elected bishop in 1257. Boece reports on an outburst of anti-clericalism and racism which de Pottock's oath of fealty to the Scottish crown had not allayed:

> He was by birth an Englishman. This circumstance induced the mountain folk of Clova and Mortlach to be less obedient to him as being an alien and to seize

The ancient church lands of Murcar.

part of his land and buildings, at the same time beating his servants and driving them off in an ignominious manner.

The furious de Pottock excommunicated these unruly members of his flock, but in time the Christian virtues of contrition and forgiveness prevailed.

A little later, we read in Boece of the people of Scotland 'openly refusing to pay teinds of certain crops'. This developed in to a major confrontation between clergy and laity, but Hugh de Benham, who became bishop in 1272, was called on as arbiter to pour oil on troubled water at 'a meeting of notables' at Perth which he did to the satisfaction of all, or so Boece tells us. De Benham was one of our early bishops-statesmen, attending the Council of Lyons in 1274 with other Scottish bishops. After undertaking diplomatic visits to Rome and complex arbitrations on his home ground, de Benham was happy to retreat to his island palace on Loch Goul for peace and quiet. It had been gifted by a charter of David I of 1136 and lay just north-west of Scotstown Moor. Boece talks of the island where 'the old man found such delight in the pleasant groves adjoining that he sought no other retreat'. It was here that he came to a mysterious end. A List of Bishops, drawn up in 1400, notes the manner of his death: *1282. Hugo, qui suffocatus fuit in lacu de Goile,* Hugh who was suffocated at Loch Goul. Boece in his *Lives,* published in 1522, has taken this to mean that he died from a sudden attack of catarrh or a coughing fit, an unremarkable end for an old man. However the writer of the *Epistolare* or Epistle Book of Bishop Dunbar of 1527 reverts to a more violent and sinister interpretation of his end. *Hugo qui in lacu Goule insidiis occubuit 1282,* Hugh who was seized in an ambush at Loch Goul. The truth of this affair will probably never be known.

Loch Goul: The Bishop's Loch

This loch, the site of the earliest of our bishops' palaces, is some four miles north of central Aberdeen on the B977. It lay on the east side of the lands of Goul, later Goval, now Parkhill. Goul or gool was the old Scots name for the corn marigold, left, a scourge of medieval agriculture. It thrived in wet seasons, was invasive, detrimental to crops and was even legislated against by the Scottish Parliament. Perhaps this was why the name had changed to the Bishop's Loch by 1640. The palace where Bishop Hugh de Benham came for rest and relaxation was built on a promontory at the north end of the loch which became an island in wet weather. Orem, writing around 1725, described the 'palace' as 'a large hall which stood east and west, and a large office house at the east end, and also the bishop's oratory. The 'footings 'or foundations of two buildings can still be discerned when the water is low. Irregular L-shaped foundations are probably those of the 'palace', with the outline of a yard to the north-east. A rectangular foundation nearby is probably that of a chapel.

The loch was 'beautifully situated, well-wooded, of considerable extent', according to the New Statistical Account of 1843 for New Machar parish. Today the water has been invaded by reeds while the banks are covered with saplings. An unsuccessful attempt was made in 1979 to designate Bishop's Loch and its neighbours to the east, Corby and Lily Lochs as a Nature Reserve. The former path to the Bishop's Loch has since been blocked by a quarry, but a number of roadsigns on the B997 indicate its presence. The Loch is now in private ownership.

Loch Goul, the Bishop's Loch.

By 1240 the names of four senior clergy, the cathedral's dignitaries, and seven canons had appeared in the records. They formed the chapter which was responsible for electing the bishop and running the cathedral. Their income or stipend known as a prebend, came from the revenues of the parish churches within the diocese. These funding churches were said to be 'appropriated' to the cathedral, and the prebendaries, the canons maintained by these prebends took their title from the funding parish. For example, Canon Alexander Galloway, parson of Kinkell. The prebendary canon was often absent from the parish which maintained him, and the tending of his flock was carried out by a deputy for a considerably s maller stipend. It was also taken from the revenue of the parish. This system had the unfortunate effect of creating rich canons and poor parishes.

The manses of its clergy began to appear beside the cathedral and to line its approaches. Thus the Chanonry, which appears in the charters as the *via canonia,* the road of the canons, came into being. The manses of the dignitaries, the big guns of the cathedral, dean, treasurer, precentor and chancellor, stood opposite its south front, the site today of Nos 13-16 The Chanonry. All manses, like their prebendaries, took their names from their funding parishes. Moving eastwards the manse of Daviot, the treasurer's manse, was on the site of the present Chanonry Lodge, No 13, the residence of the Principal of Aberdeen University. The treasurer was responsible for the cathedral valuables, jewels, gold and silver vessels, furnishings and vestments, a task that grew over the years as the treasures gifted to the cathedral increased hundredfold on hundredfold. Next, No 14, was the dean's residence, the manse of Kirkton of Seaton of which parish he was the

An aerial view of St Machar's with Nos 13-16 The Chanonry in the foreground. The manses of the dignitaries once stood on these sites.

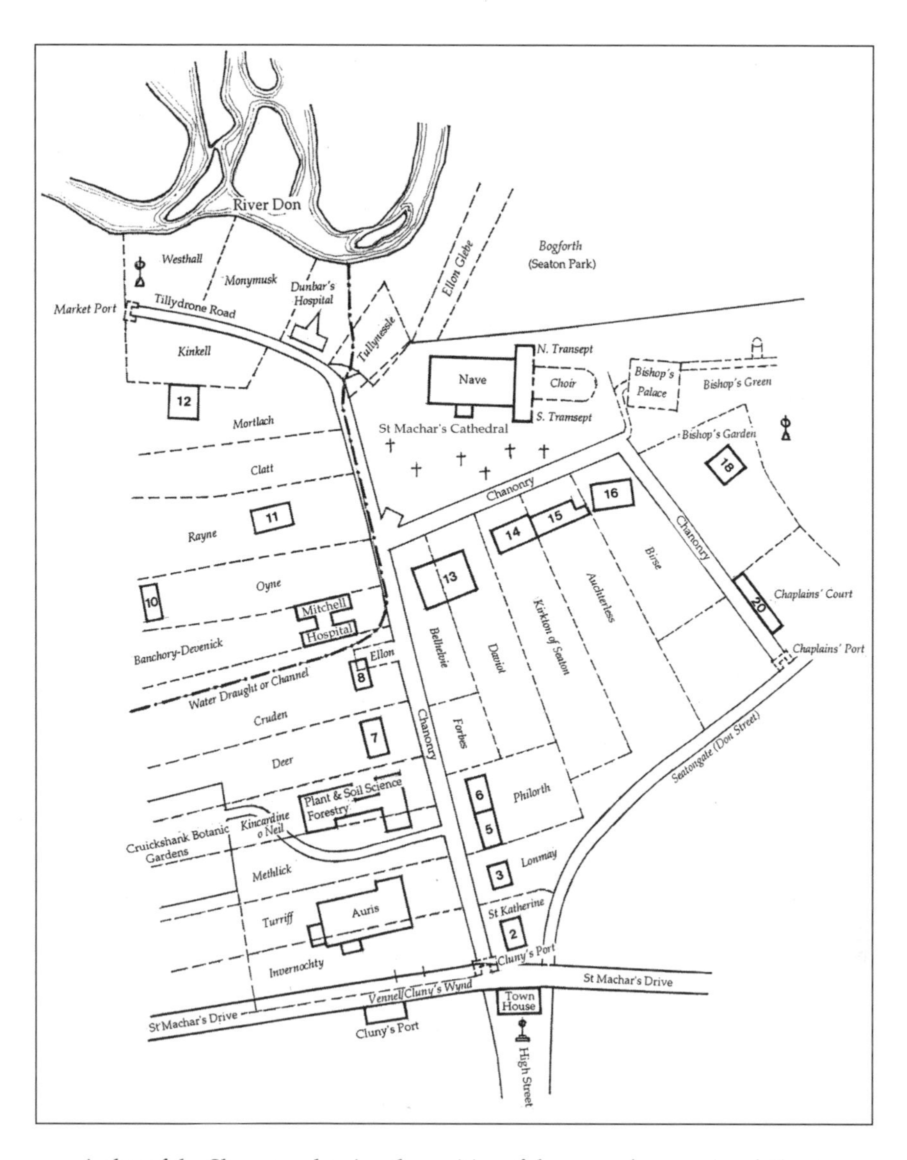

A plan of the Chanonry showing the position of the canons' manses in relation to the houses of today.

prebendary. This was the original 'home' parish of Old Aberdeen and stretched east as far as the sea. The parishioners of this sparsely populated area formed the early congregations of St Machar's. The dean, who also enjoyed the revenues of the lands of Murcar, was the administrative head of the cathedral. Immediately to the east again was the manse of Auchterless, the lodging of the precentor, responsible for music, an increasingly important part of cathedral life, and head of the sang school where the choristers were trained. Castleton House, No 15, was later built on this site. The present No 16 stands on the site of the most easterly manse, Birse, the residence of the chancellor, the cathedral's legal officer, secretary of the diocese, guardian of the cathedral seal and its librarian. Books were inspected during the first week of Lent to ensure that none 'might be lost or made worse'. The chancellor was also in charge of the grammar school. One building, even one room may have served as both sang and grammar school, perhaps to the east of the cathedral, but little is known of either.

Several other early manses occupied prime positions close to the cathedral. Belhelvie also faced the cathedral's south front, in the same line as the big four, immediately east of Daviot. Today the Principal's residence at No 13 covers the sites of both Daviot and Belhelvie. The manses of Belhelvie, Daviot, Auchterless, Seaton and Birse all had glebes, little crofts with long 'tails' or gardens, which curved down to the Seatongate, the modern Don Street. On the west side of the Chanonry, the manse of Mortlach occupied part of the site of the present No 12, Tillydrone House. Next door, the manse of Clatt stood in vacant ground between where Nos 11 and 12 now stand, while Rayne, was on the site of the present No 11, its glebe of two rigs of land backing towards the Kettle Hills. Rayne was the manse of the archdeacon, the man on the ground, who travelled round the diocese 'to correct the manners of the clergy', according to the chronicler William Orem, whose *Description of the Chanonry, Cathedral and King's College of Old Aberdeen in the Years 1724 and 1725* was published in 1791. Oyne Manse with yard and rig was sited where No 10 The Chanonry was later built. The manse of Banchory-Devenick, next door had a large yard and a glebe of arable land, 'lying towards the Kettle Hills' according to Orem. No 9, Mitchell's Hospital now occupies this site. Cruden Manse occupied the site of the present No 8. These were the earliest manses, their revenues confirmed to the bishop by Pope Adrian's bull of 1157. The revenues of the parish church of Deer were added soon after, and its manse built on the site now occupied by No 7. The glebes were cultivated, orchards planted and animals reared. All produce was happily exempt from the burden of teind and the clergy were virtually self-sufficient.

At St Machar's itself things had not stood still. The peacemaker, Hugh de Benham was succeeded by Bishop Henry de Cheyne in 1282. The first stone cathedral was now a century old and not 'glorious enough' for the new bishop who was the nephew of John Comyn, the head of one of the most important families in Scotland and nephew to King John Balliol, the Toom Tabard. Nor, more practically was this little edifice large enough for Cheyne's growing chapter of canons. He determined to have a new cathedral on the same site though built in sections, allowing services initially at least, to continue in the nave where the ordinary folk worshipped. The choir at the east end, sacred to the clergy, was to be the initial locus of reconstruction. And so in 1286, the old Norman choir was taken down and a more splendid replacement, in the Scottish style of the late thirteenth century embarked on.

But by then the Wars of Independence were underway, and Cheyne, had a difficult path to tread. He swore fealty to King Edward I of England on three occasions during the 1290s. He was said to be greatly enraged by the murder of his uncle, John Comyn by Robert Bruce in 1306 and went into exile. During this period, the revenues of the bishopric were left to accumulate. In 1309 however, he was present at the great meeting of the clergy of Scotland at Dundee which declared in favour of King Robert. Bishop Cheyne was active in running the diocese and taking part in public affairs even in the most troubled years of King Robert's reign. He witnessed various charters to which the king was a party, and in 1312, attending his parliament at Inchture. A charter of 5 December 1318, granted at Scone by King Robert, though of dubious authenticity, records a 'remission of rancour' against Henry, Bishop of Aberdeen and restoration of revenues to him. The two men were reconciled, though the relationship between king and bishop has never been satisfactorily explained.

During a progress through Scotland after the English invaders were driven out, King Robert, so Boece relates, saw the unfinished choir of St Machar's and ordered it to be completed by Cheyne from the accumulated church revenues. A similar, though apocryphal tale is told of the Brig o Balgownie; King Robert saw its unfinished state and ordered the bishop to complete it from these same monies. Given that this were true, Boece maintains an uncharacteristic silence. However the Brig was completed by the 1320s, though by whom we cannot say. St Machar's choir was not completed until 1345 over fifteen years after Cheyne's death. Only a fragment of it survives, a corbel from the inside arch of a Gothic window.

Alexander de Kininmund, Archdeacon of Lothian succeeded Cheyne in 1328. Lawyer, papal chaplain and kin to the Bishop of Brechin, this well-placed cleric enjoyed a reputation for scholarship and diplomacy. In 1320 the barons of Scotland, concerned that the papacy was dragging its feet in its recognition of Robert Bruce as King of Scots, dispatched a letter to Pope John XXII, which became famous as the Declaration of Arbroath. Kininmund, at that time parson of the parish of Kinkell in Aberdeenshire, had accompanied Sir Adam Gordon and Sir Odard de Maubuisson as emissaries to Avignon, where they delivered the letter to the Pope and pleaded the cause of King Robert. 'The Latin in which (the Declaration) is written is the work of an accomplished stylist, well versed in rhythmic prose...' states Professor Geoffrey Barrow, the distinguished Bruce scholar. Though Bernard de Linton, Abbot of Arbroath and Chancellor of Scotland, is usually regarded as author of the Declaration, Professor Barrow has argued that Kininmund, who personally accompanied the precious document to Avignon, may have written it. He remained there until September 1320, when the receipt of a safe conduct permitted his return to Scotland. Now in the pope's good graces, he was 'provided', to use the technical term, to the diocese of Aberdeen as bishop in 1328 without the formality of election by the chapter.

Our bishops had long ago evolved from being wise and holy men from whom the sovereign occasionally sought advice, into statesmen who undertook at the command of the Crown, the duties of *ad hoc* emissaries, administrators and negotiators, tasks that are now the lot of prime ministers, secretaries of state and special envoys. In 1335 Kininmund was one of the emissaries who treated for peace with England, under the mediation of the pope and King Philip VI of France.

In spite of his contacts in high places, an appeal by Kininmund to the papacy for permission to raise funds to finish the still incomplete St Machar's Cathedral made little headway. As far as his diocese was concerned, the bishop made better progress. He ministered in Mortlach in the winter and in Aberdeen in the spring where great crowds gathered in Lent. 'The summer and harvest he spent at Fetternear and Rayne', says Boece. Undaunted by the moratorium on the construction of the cathedral he organised the funding for the building of palaces in his four ports of call, to ease his journeys round his diocese. He succeeded in completing those at Fetternear and Aberdeen, the latter, just east of the cathedral where Dunbar Hall of Residence is sited, replacing the old retreat at Loch Goul which may have been abandoned after Hugh de Benham's mysterious demise.

The Fetternear palace, beside the ruins of Fetternear House, Kemnay, has been the subject of archaeological dig under the direction of Professor Nicholas Bogdan and Dr Penny Dransart. Their excavations have revealed a palace of massive proportions, comparable to the most elaborate structures of that era and type in Europe, and the first of such stature to be identified in Scotland. It is likely that Kininmund used the same masons for all four palaces and the Fetternear reconstruction, opposite, four ranges enclosing a courtyard, with a tower in each corner, indicates how Kininmund's palace adjoining St Machar's Cathedral might have looked.

A reconstruction drawing of the Bishop's Palace at Fetternear as it would have looked in the mid-fourteenth century.

Alas, Kininmund had the misfortune to be incumbent at the time of the Second War of Independence, and, according to Boece, 'was in various ways distracted by the confusion which the English, (along with Edward Balliol, son of the Toom Tabard), had thrown a great part of the country'. In 1336, in an act of reprisal against Aberdeen and the country around, an English force landed at Dunnottar and marched to Aberdeen where the defenders were quickly routed and the city 'was burnt without the omission of a single house...' Edward III personally supervised this outrage over two days, and the city burnt for six. In Old Aberdeen, the English force looted the Bishop's Palace and the sixteen canons' manses which now stood in the Chanonry, before burning them to the ground. Kininmund must have been much chagrined when his magnificent new palace was put to the torch, though according to Boece, the enemy 'had piety enough to spare the churches'. It may have been after this that the Chanonry was first fortified. 'This chanrie had high strong walls and dikes (for defence in troublesome times), whereof some part yet stands', wrote William Orem, describing the area around 1725. The palace and manses were subsequently rebuilt, the latter evolving over the years from simple mud and wattle biggings 'thekit' with divots, to handsome stone buildings, tiled with slate.

In 1355, that 'magnificent prelate', Alexander Kininmund, the second of that name, was installed as bishop. He inherited, architecturally speaking, not just a mongrel cathedral with the ancient stone nave and Cheyne's posthumous choir, but one reduced to ruin. This gloomy scenario, matched by the low morale of his clergy, worn down by the vicissitudes of the Second War of Independence, did not inhibit my Lord Bishop's lifestyle. He travelled in great magnificence, accompanied, so it is recorded, by a retinue of thirty-two horsemen and ten persons on foot. In 1363, complete with safe conduct, he made the fashionable pilgrimage to the tomb of Thomas à Becket. Although Canterbury Cathedral would be much rebuilt in the following century, Kininmund II, impressed by what he saw, made plans for a splendid cruciform St Machar's, retaining Cheyne's choir but erecting a new nave complete with aisles. Joining these two sections at right angles and thus creating the shape of the cross, would be two transepts, north and south, above whose central area, or crossing, a great belltower would soar. This, at last, was the start of the cathedral we know today.

A number of fund-raising schemes were devised. One was the setting up of a Chapel to St Thomas à Becket (the Martyr was still in vogue) on or beside the Mote Hill of Tillydrone, where candles could be lit and offerings left. In addition, Kininmund himself surrendered substantial revenues and the canons of the cathedral chapter levied themselves to the tune of £60 sterling annually, a large sum, paid to the cathedral's Master of Works, over ten years. One of those levied was the Archdeacon John Barbour, author of *The Brus*. His great masterpiece is discussed on pages 28-29.

Kininmund II created five of the ten new prebends that were established during the fourteenth century, and the Chanonry began to run out of room for manses and glebes for the new canons. The manse of Lonmay, on the present site of No 3 The Chanonry, could only be apportioned a small glebe, owing to the curve of the Seatongate, while the manse of Forbes (now also part of the Principal's garden) cut off part of the Belhelvie glebe.

Across the way, the manse of Kincardine o Neil was built just north of the present Cruickshank Botanic Gardens. This prebend derived from the revenues of the Hospital and Chapel of Kincardine o Neil, founded in 1272 by Alan Durward as an almshouse for twelve indigent men, reflecting, like Columba and his companions on Iona, the number of disciples. The revenues, sadly for the old men, were now diverted to maintain a canon at the cathedral. Orem described the manse as a 'great lodging', with an oratory at its south end, built probably by Canon John Elphinstone, Parson of Kincardine, for his 'ease and use'. The chronicler expresses surprise that permission was granted for a private chapel so near the cathedral.

The responsibility for building a manse for a newly created prebend lay with its canon, and not all had the initiative or the means to undertake this task. As a result a parish church might be 'annexed' to the cathedral years before its manse appeared in the Chanonry. Philorth (Fraserburgh), was created a prebend in 1361 but its manse, situated almost opposite Kincardine o Neil, was not built until a century later. Earlier, in 1327, Ellon was annexed but its canon had to make do with a single room chamber on the north-west side of the Bishop's Palace, next to St Machar's churchyard. There was no access from the Chanonry, and the canon had to go the long way round via the Seatongate. This was not to the liking of the prebendary in 1376, Master William Calabyr. A new manse was slotted in for him between Cruden, near the site of the present No 8 and Banchory-Devenick, the Mitchell's Hospital site, but apportionment of his neighbours' glebes was not permitted. Instead, land was provided at the 'Halch episcopi' the Bishop's Haugh, below the cathedral, later called the Bogforth, or the Bishop's Ward. It lay just beyond the south side of the Lands of Seaton which were church lands, and now forms part of part of Seaton Park. At the same time, Tullynessle manse was built into the kirkyard dyke at the north-west end of the Chanonry, beside the start of the present Tillydrone Road. Its glebe sloping down the brae, was also carved out of the Bogforth.

The growth in the number of canons in the fourteenth century was not entirely due to the increasing demands of the diocese, nor to the desire of the incumbent bishop for the status symbol of a large chapter. Absenteeism among its prebendaries was then the scourge of the Scottish cathedrals. Attendance, surprising as it may seem to us, was by no means a priority and a sizeable chapter hopefully guaranteed the presence of at least some of its canons and the continued enactment of diocesan business.

Senior clergy had bigger fish to fry. Like their bishops, they were careerists, lawyers, academics and diplomats. In *St Machar's Cathedral in the Early Middle Ages*, 1980, lan B. Cowan tells of a contemporary of John Barbour's, Malcolm de Drumbec, a chancellor of the cathedral during the 1360s and parson of Birse who was at the same time a regent (lecturer) in Arts in the University of Paris, while the treasurer, Alexander de Lindsay, divided his time between St Andrew's where he taught and the papal curia in the Vatican where he litigated. Simon de Ketenis, dean in the 1380s, was a judge and royal envoy to the King of France. According to Orem, the parson of Oyne was called Rome-raker, for he travelled continually back and forward between the Chanonry and the Holy See bearing dispatches. There was even a wandering scholar, John of Fordoun, c1320-c1387, a near contemporary of John Barbour though further down the ecclesiastical scale, a chantry priest who celebrated mass at one of the cathedral's altars, when he was there. Fordoun travelled on foot over a great part of Scotland and Ireland visiting churches, abbeys and monasteries, conversing with the clergy and making notes from their manuscripts. His work forms the first part of the Latin chronicle, *Scotichronicon*, the oldest prose history of Scotland, later completed by Walter Bower, Abbot of Inchcolm. Incidentally, Fordoun, who tells us that Malcolm Canmore spoke French and English as fluently as he spoke Gaelic, was the first to observe a great divide

John Barbour and the Brus

John Barbour, born around 1325 was briefly precentor at Dunkeld Cathedral and in 1356, soon after Bishop Alexander Kininmund II's consecration, was appointed Archdeacon of Aberdeen. He had a royal patron in Robert Stewart, grandson of Robert the Bruce, and nephew of King David II, then captive in England. Stewart, Regent of Scotland from 1346, was not anxious to see his nephew return. Terms were agreed however and the king was repatriated in 1357. As Robert Stewart's man, Barbour found it opportune to leave Scotland for the time being. He was granted safe conducts to study at Oxford, and in France, and to visit St Denis near Paris 'in company with six knights'. Robert Stewart eventually became king in 1371 as Robert II, and Barbour was able to return. He began work on 'The Brus', a long poem of over 13,500 lines, the earliest and the greatest masterpiece written in Scots.

The raison d'être of the poem may have been to flatter and bolster the ruling dynasty - Barbour had worked on a genealogy for the Stewarts throwing in mythical Trojan origins - but what emerged was a great epic, a rich and powerful narrative of the Bruce's campaigns during the Wars of Independence, a colourful canvas of combats, sieges and battles, of the clash of arms and banners waving in the wind. The might of the English army is graphically described:

Mony helmys and haberjounys
Scheldis and speirs and penounys,
And sa mony a cumbly knyvcht
That it semyt that into fycht
Thai suld vencus the warld all haile.

(Many helmets and habergeons, shields, spears and pennants, and so many magnificent knights, that it seemed that in a fight they would vanquish the whole world).

But the resolution of the Scots is also strongly conveyed. Most memorably, 'The Brus' contains some of the most famous lines in Scottish literature:

A! Fredome is a noble thing;
Fredome mays man to haiff liking;
Fredome all solace to man giffis;
He levys at es that frely levys.

(Ah! freedom is a noble thing; freedom allows man to have pleasure: freedom gives solace to man; he who freely lives, lives at ease).

Barbour retained his connections with the royal household throughout his life, concurrently with his work as Archdeacon of Aberdeen. He served as an auditor of the Exchequer in the 1370s and 1380s. In 1388 King Robert II granted him a yearly pension of £10 Scots from the burgh of Aberdeen's annual payment to the Crown, augmented by twenty shillings in perpetuity from Aberdeen's burgh mails (rents) as a token of gratitude 'for the compilation of the book of the deeds of the late king Robert the Bruce', as 'The Brus' was described. After his death in 1395 the twenty shillings was paid to his legatees, the Cathedral chapter, on condition that a mass was said annually for his soul. This was celebrated on March 23.

After two early versions in manuscript form, the epic was reprinted as a chapbook on a number of occasions in the eighteenth century. In 1997, the historian A A M Duncan edited 'The Brus' for a paperback edition published by Canongate Classics.

The memorial to John Barbour, poet and archdeacon, is on the wall in the south aisle of St Machar's Cathedral, near the probable site of his burial place. Carved by Roland Fraser, it was commissioned by the Aiberdeen Univairsitie Scots Leid (Language) Quorum and the St Machar's Kirk Session, and was dedicated on 11 November 1997. Robert the Bruce, the hero of Barbour's great poem, bequeathed land to Aberdeen which formed the basis of the Common Good Fund which, appropriately bore around half the cost of the £3000 memorial. The panels show from left, Bruce rallying his troops at Bannockburn, the Brig o Balgownie which Bruce may have ordered Bishop Henry Cheyne to complete, and Barbour at work on his epic. The famous lines on freedom are carved below.

between Scots-speaking Lowlanders, 'domesticated and cultured, trustworthy, patient and urbane' and the Gaelic-speaking, ease-loving Highlander, 'wild and untamed, rough and unbending, given to robbery'.

A comment by Orem illustrates how the cathedral's senior clergymen, with simultaneous careers to follow in the enclaves of Europe and in the chapter house of St Machar's, enjoyed a twofold system of substitution. They had a vicar out in the parish as we know, but also at least one to deputise for them at the cathedral. Discussing the lifestyle of the dean Orem says: 'He had a chaplain and a clerk (clergyman) at the cathedral to minister divine service to the parishioners, and another chaplain as a clerk at the chapel of Monycabbuck' (now Newmachar) where he had the patronage. The enactment of cathedral business was entrusted to clerics of equal status to the absentees while vicars choral took their place at the daily round of cathedral services, and with the assistance of the choristers, celebrated mass as well as the *horae canonica*, the service of Divine Office, which began early in the morning with Matins and Lauds, then continued through the day with Prime, Terce, Sext and None, concluding with Vespers and Compline in the early evening.

In 1366 Kininmund II took stern measures to curb absenteeism, fining his canons one-seventh of their prebend if they failed to keep proper terms of residence in the Chanonry. But not all canons were high-flying non-attenders. The same names appearing time and time again in the records

Monnycabbuck farm today. Part of the Dean's income came from this area, now Newmachar.

of St Machar's show that a solid core of the clergy were eident and conscientious in undertaking the cure of souls and the business of the diocese. John of Ednam, who was appointed to the new prebend of Methlick in 1376, stated that he was desirous of carrying out his residential duties at the cathedral in return for a manse and glebe. Bishop Kininmund II granted land for a toft or homestead and croft on part of the present Botanic Gardens site. His charter notes the manse of Deer to the north, and Brousterland, a brewery, to the south.

Work on Kininmund II's great scheme for the cathedral had been progressing slowly, but came to a halt altogether when King Robert II sent him as ambassador to the King of France. The walls of his crossing and the transepts were left standing *Marie Celeste*-like at nine feet on his departure. No colleague, it seems, was briefed to take over as clerk of works. The date and nature of this mission is vague, but Kininmund II returned to Scotland in 1379 and resumed fund-raising activities for the nave. That year he obtained a bull from Pope Clement VII permitting the granting of indulgences (remission of the penalties of sins) to worshippers who contributed to the erection of the nave. But the following year he died in Scone of a strangury, nothing sinister this time, only the common ailment of retention of urine. His scheme for St Machar's was much as he left it before the embassy to France. His great central tower over the crossing was unfinished, though the red sandstone piers and the springing stones of the arches at the crossing are still visible at the east end of the cathedral as if frozen by a spell as they were about to thrust through the modern gable end. The stone leaves decorating the capitals or tops of these pillars resemble curly kail rather than the traditional acanthus leaf. In *The Ancient Stones of Scotland* (1965) Dr W Douglas Simpson draws attention to the curly kail enrichment on the capitals at

The pillars of Kininmund II's crossing, their capitals decorated with curly kail are now embedded in the modern gable at the Cathedral's East end. They survive from the 1370s.

the eastern end of the nave of Melrose Abbey Church, the work of 'no one but a Scot', as opposed to the foreign craftsmen busy at Melrose. These capitals are 'strikingly paralleled' by those at St Machar's. The mason, of both, he speculates, may be John Scott who came from Melrose to work at Aberdeen, and who according to tradition, founded the oldest Lodge of Freemasons in the city.

Adam de Tyninghame who had been had a canon of St Andrew's, dean of Aberdeen, and an ambassador to the court of France, succeeded Kininmund II in 1380. The following year he held his *curia*, or bishop's court at St Thomas's Chapel at the Mote Hill (the Latin of the original charter says at the hill beside the Chanonry of Aberdon, in the chapel of the Blessed Thomas the Martyr), summoning those who claimed to hold church lands to appear there to have their charters inspected. It was a shambles. Some of his vassals failed to appear, some turned up without their charters, others with charters granted by bishops who were dead at the time, and still others with charters whose seals had been torn off.

The cathedral, though far from complete, did not engage the attentions of Bishop Adam or his successor Gilbert de Greenlaw, and it fell to the dynamic Henry de Lichtoun, bishop from 1422 till 1440, to pull things together. He was no stranger to the problems of impaired cathedrals. As Bishop of Moray he had been involved in the rebuilding of Elgin Cathedral after the depredations of that 'masterful spirit', the Wolf of Badenoch, and it was also fortunate that he was advised in a vision to restore the 'decaying house' of St Machar's. He brought in 'stonecutters from all parts', says Boece, and 'quantities of stone and lime' including yellow sandstone from Moray with which he completed the north transept. Use was made of granite boulders gathered from the surrounding fields and hewn into sturdy blocks. But yet again affairs of the realm intervened. Lichtoun was called on to settle a dispute concerning the regency of the Duke of Albany, the king's uncle. The king himself, James I, was at that time held captive at the English court whither Lichtoun subsequently journeyed to negotiate the royal ransom. There he remained for a time before returning to advise King James on the government of Scotland.

Considering the demands that state business made on him, Lichtoun's achievement was a remarkable one. It was during his era that the nave, much as we know it today, was completed with its massive pillars, small high clerestorey windows, and arcades like the cloisters of a monastery, giving access to the existing side-aisles. He completed the west front with its great window of seven long, vertical lights, and flanked it with immense twin bell towers as at Elgin Cathedral, built in military style, with machicolations and battlemented parapets. However his plans were on a more ambitious scale than Kininmund II's and their respective designs were not compatible. The twin towers of the west front did not marry with the existing design of the side-aisles whose bays, windows and buttresses were out of alignment with the piers of the arcades. As a result, a wooden 'lean-to' roof had to be designed to cover the aisles. He surmounted the twin towers with caphouses, commanding an extensive view of the surrounding countryside. The Battle of Harlaw, fought in 1411 just a decade before Lichtoun's arrival had been 'a close run thing', and the sack of Old Aberdeen and Aberdeen itself, eagerly anticipated by the Highland hordes, narrowly averted. With that episode still fresh in the memory, and given St Machar's proximity to the Brig o Balgownie, known as the Brig o Don until the mid nineteenth century and gateway to the north, such a fortress-cathedral was a wise precaution. Fortified cathedrals were by no means unusual in the unsettled Europe of the times. The French town of Elne near the Spanish border, much fought over in mediaeval times, boasts a fortress-cathedral co-eval with St Machar's, with a nave that is not dissimilar.

The earliest of the Chanonry's four ports or defensive gates, also date from this period. The Bishop's or East Port, was erected around 1429 on the Seatongate, standing just beyond the present junction with Cheyne Road. Both it and the later Tillydrone or Market Port, a little east of the Mote Hill, across what is now Tillydrone Road, significantly lay to the north of the settlement, whence attack was more likely to come, though not inevitably, as Edward III's sortie of 1336 proved.

The site of the Bishop's Port in Don Street, near the junction with Cheyne Road.

'Little' Tillydrone Road. The Market Port would have sat across this road in the distance. It was also known as 'the common passage of the canons which goes to the hill commonly called Dynydronis', (the Mote Hill). Seaton Park is to the right. The possible siting of a Girth Cross in this area is discussed on page 40.

Manses had continued to be slotted into the Chanonry during the fifteenth century. In 1412, in Bishop Gilbert de Greenlaw's time, the revenues of the Hospital of Turriff were reallocated to provide a prebend for William Lang, the priest of Turriff. Unfortunately, like Kincardine o Neil, this meant the suppression of the Hospital founded in the time of Bishop Hugh de Benham by the Earl of Buchan, the richest nobleman of his day and handsomely endowed by him for the statutory twelve indigent men. Turriff Manse was located south of Methlick. Invernochty Manse was the most southerly of all. It was built in 1431, some seventy-five years after the creation of the prebend, and lay between Turriff manse to the north and Brousterland, the brewer's land, now, somewhat eroded, to the south. In 1439 Henry de Lichtoun built a smithy and alehouse, the latter replacing the old Brousterland, by then covered with manses. Smithy and alehouse later had to go, though possibly no further than the threshold of the Chanonry. They were replaced by Philorth Manse, such was the pressure on space. Nos 5 and 6 The Chanonry now occupy this site. There would eventually be twenty-five manses. At the west side, the glebes ran down to 'our lake', the Loch of Old Aberdeen. At the north end, Monymusk and Westhall Manses were squeezed in on the north side of Tillydrone Road, 'the highway to Donnydronis hill'. Later, Bishop Dunbar's Hospital were shoe-horned in between Tullynessle and Monymusk.

Bishop de Lichtoun was 'carried off by death' in 1440, leaving Kininmund

II's great central tower over the crossing still incomplete. He was buried in 'Lichtoun's Aisle,' (or 'ile') in this sense a transept, the north, which he built and where his tomb recess remains. His effigy lies within the cathedral these days, safe from the weathering which began when the transept later became ruinous. He lies between the effigies of the anonymous little Canon X whose peregrinations will be followed at a later date, and the Cathedral's best dressed prebendary, Canon Walter Ydyll.

Today the effigy of Bishop Henry de Lichtoun, centre, rests within St Machar's, at the west end of the north aisle. In the foreground is an anonymous canon who once, minus head, occupied Bishop Dunbar's tomb. Beyond is the effigy of Walter Ydyll, prebendary of Deer and a faithful canon of Aberdeen, who died circa 1473. Over his vestments is sculpted an almuce, a garment with a hood and fur tails which he would have worn against the bitter cold of the Cathedral. Its representation in stone is unique to St Machar's.

Bishop Ingram de Lindsay, (1441-1458) was Lichtoun's successor. Like his predecessors, he was no stranger to high places, both as chaplain to Pope Eugenius IV and as a member of the General Council that met in Basle. But he was a local man, canon of Methlick, and perhaps was surprised to find himself elected bishop at a meeting of the chapter at which he was present.

Ingram appears to have been a good administrator and a 'hands on' bishop. On 27 April, 1446 we find him involved in 'debate and question' with the chaplains of St Peter's Hospital in the Spital over the boundaries between those of the Hospital's lands in the Hilton area, and the Bishop's lands of Cotton which centuries later became part of Woodside. Sir Alexander Forbes, sheriff depute of Aberdeen was appointed arbiter and called a meeting of the eldest and worthiest residents of those lands. The marches were then fixed without undue discord. A loaning going through the moor between two old stane dykes, beginning at the Market Port extending to the top of the hill (Hilton) at the south end of the dyke marked the boundary. Cotton was to be on the north side of the loaning, and the St Peter's Hospital lands on the south side, 'the loaning being common to them baith'.

By the mid-fifteenth century the cathedral had become a large business organisation. As the medieval scholar, Dr Leslie Macfarlane has pointed out, it required the services not only of twenty-eight canon lawyers, specialists in church law, but by 1445, 'a whole team of procurators, lawyers, surveyors, bailies and clerks to keep an eye on its income, collect its rents and watch for dilapidations of its property'. In December 1448 Ingram was present at a meeting of the chapter in which a number of statutes for regulating the affairs of the cathedral and improving the administration of its common property were drawn up. Complaints were made about the rundown state of the manses and their boundary walls and the canons were instructed to redd them up within the space of a year, under a penalty of 20s which would be doubled for every further year of neglect. Another statute dealt specifically with the enclosure of the canons' glebes, whose dykes were in a tumble-down state, and not for the first time. On the west side of the Chanonry from Mortlach to Invernochty, the canons and the archdeacon must all maintain their own walls, while the wall which went down to the Loch at the boundary of Invernochty Manse was a community responsibility. Ellon Manse, in the middle of the west side was not mentioned, for it had no glebe there.

Ingram also laid down, in a statute of 1456, the various household items in the manses which were to be handed on from each canon to his successor; in the public room, a substantial trestle table, a basin, washstand and hand towel, and a napkin, a silver spoon (particularly valued) and stoup with lid; in the bed-chamber, a bed and a bedcover of corresponding size, a pair of linen sheets and two blankets; in the kitchen, a copper pot, a 'sufficient' plate, mortar and pestle, a 'ketilcruke' (a chain for a kettle), a side dish, a flat plate, a charger (a large flat platter), a dublar (a large wooden plate), a sauce boat and saucer, a spit with an andiron. In the brewhouse, a brewing leid, (a large vat), a mash vat or cauldron, a trough, a gyle-vat (for fermenting wort), a bucket and a barrel.

A number of the manses were residences of substance, and would have more lavish plenishings than those items of Ingram's list. Orem reports that the dean's glebe of Kirkton of Seaton boasted three yards and an outer gate, which bore the arms of the King of Scots. The precentor's Auchterless glebe next door was large enough to contain several cottages at the south end, tenanted by those who tended the croft there. The manse of Birse nearby, large and rambling, survived to the end of the nineteenth century. Legend has it that it was linked to the Bishop's Palace by an underground passage. The manse of Belhelvie was a great house, built by its parson, who embellished it with his coat of arms, three roses and a crescent surmounted by a cardinal's hat, no less. Banchory Devenick Manse was 'a great lodging'.

Within St Machar's itself, Ingram carried out a fair amount of practical work. He paved the floor with slabs of dressed sandstone, covered the roof of the nave with stone tiles and inlaid the ceiling with panels of red fir. 'At considerable expense he placed on the entrances folding doors', recorded Boece. That must have endeared him to worshippers.

After Ingram's death, Thomas Spens, Bishop of Galloway and Lord Privy Seal was installed as Bishop of Aberdeen. A frequent attender at the Scottish Parliament and a Lord in Council, he is credited, as indeed was Bishop William de Deyn a hundred years earlier, with the restoration of the Bishop's Palace destroyed by English soldiers during the raid of 1336. In fact, the rebuilding of the palace took place in two separate phases. It had four ranges enclosing a courtyard with a tower in each corner and 'a great deep well' in the centre according to Orem. The bishop's personal apartments were in the west range, and included a hall, a great chamber, a closet,

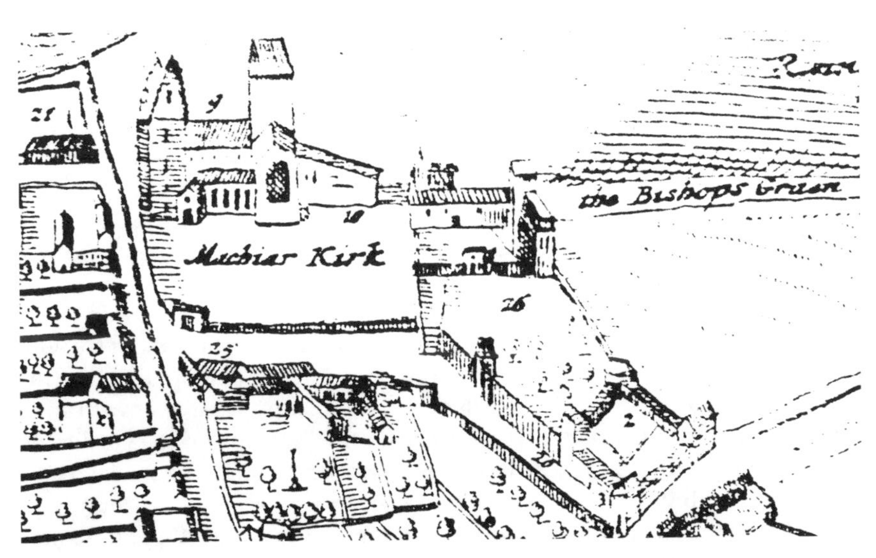

St Machar's Cathedral and the Bishop's Palace, partly ruinous to the right. The small house between the two may have been the prebendary of Ellon's chamber. The Bishop's Garden (marked 25) is below. Adjoining it (2) is the Chaplains' Chambers with its port, giving access to the Seatongate. Left of St Machar's is Dunbar's Hospital (21) and the Bogforth (Seaton Park) lies beyond it. From Parson Gordon's Plan, 1661.

study and wardrobe, a room that is, rather than a standing cupboard, with chambers above and below it. There was also a chapel and a 'chapell chaumer'. The pantry, cellar, kitchen, larder, brewhouse and bakehouse were housed in the other ranges. The bishop 'had also a passage by an iron gate, from the lodging into the chancel, and from that into the church, which was easy and convenient for him', wrote Orem.

A watergate led to the Don whence he would be rowed perhaps south to Fittie or even to Torry to embark for the continent. East of the palace, the long narrow Bishop's Green, boasted a doocot of immense proportions if Parson Gordon's Plan is to be believed, providing pigeon pie for my Lord

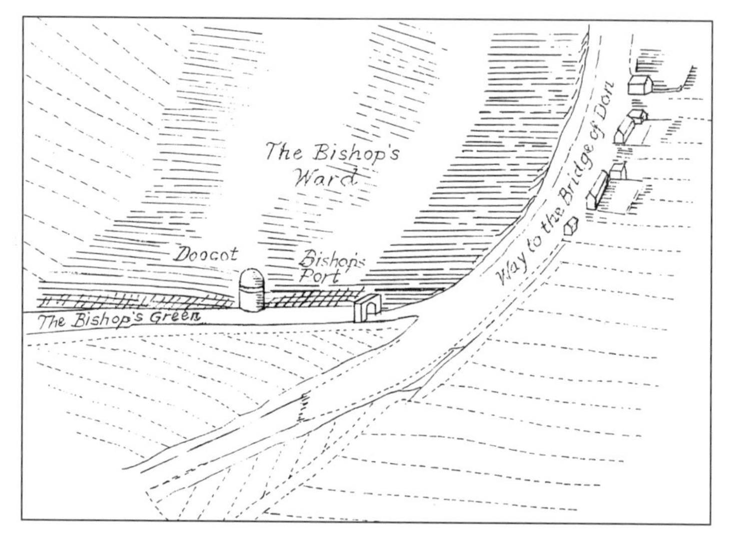

The Bishop's Doocot, centre, appears larger than the Bishop's Port to its right and the Seatongate houses, top right!

Bishop and his guests, and, according to tradition, a girth or sanctuary with a girth cross, pages 40-41. The Green gave access to the Bishop's Port, on the Seatongate. South-east of the palace lay the bishop's garden, with high dykes and slits to the north which allowed the 'good air of the garden' to circulate in his lodging. On the west dyke was a summer house, three storeys high giving a good view of the Chanonry and the fields around. To the north of the palace the ground sloped down to the Bogforth, a little estate in itself enclosed by a strong fail (turf) dyke. In the early eighteenth century Orem noted that marks where bowbuts for archery practice had stood were still visible, as was the hay-yard, a throwback to the days when Bogforth had been the parson of Ellon's glebe.

Externally, Spens did not advance the fabric of the St Machar's, but gifted paintings and statues, curtains woven with gold and cambric and rich vestments for the clergy. He replaced the old choir stalls that were 'all but worn done' with splendid new ones, and had the windows glazed, for which his flock may have considered the most welcome of his benefactions. He also gifted a bishop's throne or *cathedra* in Latin, hence the name, though he would have had little time to occupy it for he was one of Scotland's leading statesmen, and was sent on embassies to France and Burgundy by King James III. His journeys took him into danger on occasion and Boece recounts his stirring adventures with pirates, shipwrecks and the old enemy of England.

Bishop Spens enjoyed good relations with the royal burgh of Aberdeen whose pride and joy was the Mither Kirk of St Nicholas, the most important parish church in the diocese with origins going back to at least the twelfth century. Since 1256 the Bishops of Aberdeen had been prebendary canons of St Nicholas, their prebends coming from the revenues of that church. It was therefore one in which they took a special interest. Its chancel was small and Spens encouraged its replacement by a splendid new choir, though some sources credit Ingram de Lindsay with this initiative. The former East Church of St Nicholas stands on this site. Spens led the way in funding the work, making a welcome contribution of his second teinds which were drawn from range of sources due to the Crown, then granted by the Crown to the Bishops of Aberdeen. The building of the choir was very much a local effort with wealthy citizens contributing handsomely to the work in cash or kind, barrels of salmon or grilse, lentrinware or futvale, (lambskins) and others providing eight days of labour. Dues on merchandise coming into the port were also levied to swell the funds.

In 1480, Bishop Spens was succeeded by Robert Blacader. A canon of Glasgow, a privy councillor and a major player in the corridors of powers, he was Bishop of Aberdeen for only three year and was hardly ever here. There was trouble in Birse almost as soon as he arrived, and he had to bring in 'the king's troops' to quell the disturbance. He angered the people of Aberdeen by withdrawing the gift of the second teinds from St Nicholas Kirk. Building was delayed and infuriated magistrates sent a bellman to cry through the streets, forbidding citizens to pay any *firmas* or rents due to the bishop on pain of loss of freedom. This did not mean incarceration but loss of membership of their guild or trade, and the accompanying privileges. By the time he took recalcitrant Aberdonians to court, he had been translated to his new diocese of Glasgow, later elevated to archdiocese. After much involvement in the affairs of state, Archbishop Blacader died on a pilgrimage to the Holy Land. But in Aberdeen he had been succeeded by William Elphinstone. A new era was about to begin.

How Many Girth Crosses?

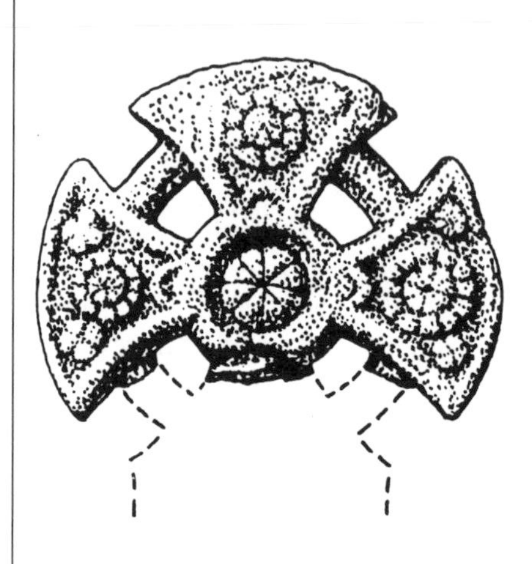

St Machar's Cathedral, in common with others, had an area of girth or sanctuary in its grounds, its limits marked by a girth cross where those accused of serious crimes could take refuge from pursuit by civil authorities. Under canon law they could not be imprisoned until their cause had been heard. Girths were first recorded in the statutes of William the Lion (1143-1214) and continued in use until the Reformation, but not every malefactor had the right of sanctuary. A number of thirteenth century charters of St Machar's denied sanctuary to highway robbers, those who laid waste to crops or vandalised churches, or were excommunicate.

The charter of 10 December 1498, in which Bishop Elphinstone set the boundaries of Old Aberdeen, takes the girth cross, as its starting point, (without saying where it was), then the line runs towards the sea. This indicates the east. Though it was gone by his time, Orem states that the girth cross stood in the Bishop's Doocot Green. It lay south-east of the Bishop's Palace and the 1867 Ordnance Survey follows Orem, indicating 'the supposed site of the Girth Cross' on the eastern edges of the Doocot Green, just west of the Bishop's Port which stood on the present Don Street, about 20 yards north-west of the junction with Çheyne Road. Once through the Port, the fugitive could reach out and cling to the cross.

Though the site of the girth cross cannot be plotted accurately, there has been speculation that the fragment, illustrated above, housed at St Machar's since the early twentieth century, may have been the cross-head. Dating from the late twelfth or early thirteenth century, it is carved in a rough-grained pink sandstone which has weathered grey, indicating that it has stood in the open for a considerable time.

Another cross however, a wooden one, may have acted as a girth cross and boundary marker on the west side. It is mentioned in several charters relating to land and buildings in Old Aberdeen. These are identified in relation to neighbouring properties, roads and local landmarks of which 'ly girtht cors' was one. A glance at the top left hand corner of the plan of Chanonry manses, page 21 will be helpful here.

First of all, in the Registrum Episcopatus Aberdonensis (Volume I pages 240-41), there is a charter of Bishop Lichtoun of 1444, in which he gifted land to Gilbert de Johnstoun on the north side of Mortlach Manse 'beside the common passage of the canons which goes to the hill commonly called Dynydronis' (the Motte) which sounds like 'little' Tillydrone Road. The boundaries are also described in relation to the stone dykes of Mortlach Manse, 'ascendendo usque ad crucem ligneam que vulgariter dicitur ly girthcorse', ascending to the wooden cross, commonly called the girth cross. I have taken this ascent also to mean 'little' Tillydrone Road, which climbs as it leaves the cathedral. A later charter in the Registrum, (Volume I page 344), records that what sounds like the identical site was sold by Alexander de Johnstoun to Canon William Mowat in 1498. Kinkell Manse was later built there. Like its near neighbour, Mortlach, Kinkell stood in what became the grounds of the present Tillydrone House, No 12 The Chanonry.

In Sir Alexander Hay's Mortification of 10 February 1574-75, (Register of the Great Seal Volume IV, pages 632-33), the positions of the crofts which provided the necessary revenues for the mortification are identified by reference to their near neighbours. For example, there is 'the croft called the tail of Kinkell Manse now belonging to Wm Seytoun in Kingseat facing the crofts and Lands of Cotton (to the west) and the way from Kinkell Manse facing the Girth Cross to the north'. Then there is 'the manse called Westhall (opposite Kinkell) with its garden, at the north boundary of the aforesaid Chanonry facing the west between the Manse of Monymusk on the east, the Water of Don to the north, the Motte to the west, the way from the Cathedral towards the girth cross to the south - 'little' Tillydrone Road ?

In the Registrum again, (same reference, page 412), there is a contract of 18 December 1537 between Alexander Kyd the subchantor and, William Myrton, master of the Cathedral's song school . Kyd infefted Myrton (assigned to him) his tenment (land holding) in Old Aberdeen, 'aforenent the cors (over against the cross) of the same on the west'. Just where was this 'tenment'? Another item from Hay's Mortification (reference as before, page 633) gives a clue, a rental from the hospital and garden on the west side of Old Aberdeen. This was Gavin Dunbar's Hospital and the Monymusk glebe next door which belonged to it at this time. This property had the manse (the 'tenment aforenent the cors'), 'formerly of Mr Alex Kid subchantor in Aberdeen' to the north, the way to New Aberdeen on the east, and the Bishop's Loch to the west. On this evidence, the westerly girth cross may have lain close to the north-west boundary of the Cathedral precincts, near the Market Port. The properties discussed had to be identified by close neighbours to be accurately located. The easterly girth cross was likely to have been too far away to be of help in pinpointing them.

Our knowledge of the easterly girth cross comes from a vague mention in the boundary charter of 1488 and Orem's hearsay, while the existence of a cross that seems to lie to the west is indicated in a number of charters. It could be that both east and west boundaries of the cathedral precincts were marked by crosses, guiding fugitives coming through the Market Port as well as Bishop's. Incidentally, the girth cross is quite different from the market cross which appears in Hay's Mortification as the 'crux foralis', the forum or market place cross.

Chapter 3

William Elphinstone:
Founder of Aberdeen University

Advocate in France and Scotland, judge, arbiter, legislator and Lord Chancellor in Scotland, student and teacher of law in the Universities of Glasgow, Paris and Orleans, Dean and Rector of Glasgow university, vicar, official of the diocese and bishop in the Church, ambassador to England, France and Austria, he had seen and studied every phase and condition of intellectual and social life, its defects and its remedies. Scotland needed such a man.

Neil J J Kennedy: 'The Faculty of Law' in Studies in the History of the University, 1906.

In April 1488, William Elphinstone, then fifty-seven years of age, was consecrated Bishop of Aberdeen at St Machar's Cathedral, in the presence of King James III. Unlike many of his predecessors and his successor Gavin Dunbar, he was not a member of a mighty or powerful family but was the leading civil and canon lawyer in the kingdom and one of the monarch's most skilled ambassadors. He was dogged, hard-working and ambitious. And unusually in those days, as the Catholic Church approached nemesis, he was both devout and incorruptible. He was born in Glasgow in 1431, the son of a young St Andrew's graduate, also William Elphinstone who was the younger son of Sir William Elphinstone of Pittendreich. His mother is something of a mystery, though she is thought to have been Margaret Douglas, daughter of a Laird of Drumlanrig. Elphinstone was subsequently dispensed from illegitimacy by the pope in 1454 to allow him to take holy orders, and by King James III in 1477.

His father was a canon of Glasgow Cathedral when William Turnbull was bishop of that diocese. Elphinstone *père* and Turnbull were old friends, having studied civil law together at Louvain University as young men. (Elphinstone later gifted his father's Louvain lecture notes to King's College where they remain in the archives). Bishop Turnbull founded Glasgow

University in 1451, and one of his first actions was to appoint Canon Elphinstone as Dean of the Faculty of Arts. They did not tread an easy path and William, brought up in his father's household, learnt at first hand the difficulties involved in establishing a university.

Bishop Elphinstone from a portrait, painted on wood, in possession of Aberdeen University. It was hinged at one time and may have been one of the folding side wings of the 'retable', the screen backing the high altar in King's College Chapel.

His career was not typical of an ambitious churchman. He ran the family estate for a time, graduated in arts at Glasgow University in 1462 at the age of thirty-one, then went on to study canon law there and pled in the consistorial court. This, the church court for the diocese of Glasgow applied the canon law and was presided over by a judge known as the official of the diocese. The court's jurisdiction in civil and criminal matters was wide, dealing with crimes such as adultery, slander and perjury, as well as civil causes relating to legitimacy, bastardy, divorce and the recovery of debts. But Elphinstone pled especially or the poor, the *personae miserabiles*, 'not for a fee but for the sake of equity and justice', wrote Hector Boece in his *Lives of the Bishops.*

He withdrew to the parish of Kirkmichael to devote more time to his studies, and to work as parish priest, but later, with a little persuading from his uncle, Laurence Elphinstone, set off for the University of Paris to resume his studies in canon law. His aptitude for legal argument caught the attention of his masters and after graduating was made reader (lecturer) in that subject. Next Elphinstone 'passed to Orleans' to study civil law, which was subject to papal veto at Paris. He returned home in 1471 after less than a year at Orleans, possibly alerted by his father, still a canon of Glasgow Cathedral, that the post of official of that diocese was about to fall vacant. He was duly appointed, then following in his father's footsteps, was presently elected Dean of Faculty of Arts at Glasgow University. He become Rector there in 1474-75, defending the privileges of the university against royal intervention. In 1478 he left Glasgow for Edinburgh and a more senior posting, that of official of Lothian within the archdiocese of St Andrew's.

James III, impressed by Elphinstone's legal abilities, appointed him privy councillor and sent him on an successful embassy to Paris, to the court of Louis XI to foster friendship and the Auld Alliance. Elphinstone, according to Boece, made an elegant speech in Latin to the French king and his council, quoting from the *Jurgurthine Wars* of the Roman historian Sallust. One phrase used, *concordia parvae res crescunt* (through friendship small matters grow great) became in a slightly different form, the motto of Old Aberdeen.

At home King James had annexed the earldom of the treasonable Earl of Ross, Lord of the Isles, and in 1481 nominated Elphinstone to the bishopric of Ross. James's reign was riven with feuding and intrigue among his powerful subjects and he saw the need to strengthen his own position in a remote and troublesome area with the support of an able and trustworthy lieutenant. But Elphinstone would not pay the tax owed to Rome by his predecessor there, and was never consecrated. He remained in Edinburgh and sat as a member of the Scottish Parliament. There, in 1482, he would have met the provost of Aberdeen, Robert Blinseile (there are several variations in the spelling of the name), its parliamentary commissioner, in modern terms, its MP. One of the ruling merchant élite of Aberdeen, Blinseile traded in high places. In 1494 he would sell James IV twelve and a half ells of satin at £4 12s to be made into a doublet.

In 1483, following Blacader's translation to Glasgow, the king appointed Elphinstone Bishop of Aberdeen. This was a more important bishopric than Ross, and comprised a hundred parishes in most of what later became Aberdeenshire, part of Kincardineshire and a portion of Banffshire. Here the same financial problems prevailed as Blacader had not paid his dues to Rome either, but King James pressed the pope to allow consecration to take place. While he awaited papal sanction Elphinstone served as judge on the committees of the Lords of Council, as an auditor of exchequer and witnessed numerous royal charters. He was chief negotiator in the peace treaties with the English kings Richard III in 1484 and Henry VII two years later. Robert Blinseile was also a member of the latter embassy. Elphinstone a little earlier had attended Henry VII's coronation as the representative of James III.

In 1488 events moved in quick succession. In February Elphinstone was appointed Chancellor of Scotland, the leading law officer in the realm, and his long-awaited consecration as Bishop of Aberdeen followed two months later. But by June James III was dead, murdered in mysterious circumstances while apparently fleeing the Battle of Sauchieburn where an army, led by rebel nobles long at odds with the king, won the day. James's eldest son, scarcely fifteen years old now became king as James IV. He had left the stronghold of Stirling Castle and joined the disaffected noblemen, but the death of his father caused him bitter regret. He would wear 'ane belt of irone' as a penance for the rest of his life. Elphinstone, as the late James III's man, was quickly deprived of the Chancellorship.

For a time it was necessary to keep a low profile, but it was not long before he was in high office again. The qualities that had impressed James III were also apparent to the nobles around the young king. Elphinstone had resumed his judicial work as a Lord of Council within months of Sauchieburn, and by 1489 was brought back to the privy council. But he had boundless energy and ambitious plans for his new diocese for which his predecessor had so little time to spare. Though in holy orders as all lawyers were, Elphinstone had been appointed, not from the ranks of the career clergy, but as a leading judge and diplomat who was loyal to James III. The diocese provided him with a *tabula rasa* and a base from which he could make considerable reforms within the Church, and remarkable advances in education.

He quickly mended the fences that Blacader had broken, restoring the gift of the second teinds to assist the completion of the choir of St Nicholas Kirk, in which as its prebendary he took a special interest. Here the wright John Fendour, (pages 92-93) carried out superb work. By the early sixteenth century, St Nicholas was one of the 'largest and noblest of the Scottish parish churches', a cathedral in all but name. Within the diocese of Aberdeen, Elphinstone 'reformed the clergy and restored the worship, which owing to the evil times had for some years had been somewhat neglected', says Boece. Indeed it had been neglected since Blacader succeeded Bishop Thomas Spens in 1480. Over the years Elphinstone embarked on numerous legal actions to recover misappropriated church revenues, necessary to maintain his churches and clergy and he succeeded in appointing, at least for six months over the course of any year, his own clergymen, who would work to implement his programme of reforms, instead of having to accept the placemen of pope or king. His re-organisation of the cathedral's finances are detailed in his Constitutions of 1506, and can be found in the *Registrum Episcopatus Aberdonensis.* At national level, he provided Scotland with a liturgy, the *Aberdeen Breviary* whose compilation, one of his major accomplishments, is discussed on pages 82-83.

The founding of King's College was greater than all his other achievements. Perhaps even before he came to Old Aberdeen he had begun to nurture a vision of a new university. St Andrew's and Glasgow Universities had been founded by the bishops of their respective dioceses, to serve the east and west of Scotland, and now Elphinstone undertook, in the words of Boece, 'the advancement of the northern parts of the country', and was

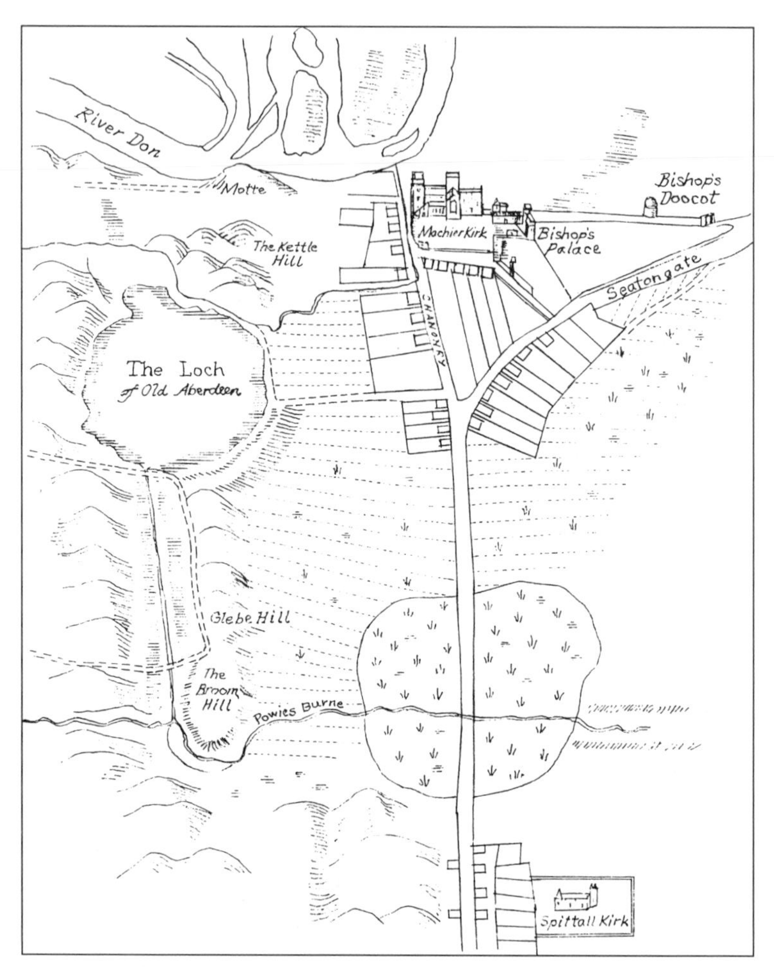

An artist's impression of Old Aberdeen before King's College was built, showing development confined to the Chanonry and the area around it.

ideally placed to do so. He was in a position to organise the necessary funding, had access to the pope, the head of western Christendom, from whom authority for such a venture had to be sought and had the ear of the bright young James IV. Thanks to his family circumstances he was aware of the considerable demands involved in setting up a university and having absorbed humanist thought and the early force of the Renaissance in Paris, he had firm ideas about the quality of teaching staff he wished to engage.

Where would the new university be located? It was the usual practice at this time to establish universities in towns which could support a community of scholars, where there was a market and where suitable buildings were cheaply or freely available. The two existing Scottish university towns were both ancient ecclesiastical burghs. St Andrews, a busy east coast port, was a cathedral town with a famous fair while Glasgow had grown from a village to a small market town with its own cross. Aberdeen, the chief town in Elphinstone's diocese and near neighbour to his seat at Old Aberdeen, had more to offer than either of these. Since the twelfth century it had been a royal burgh and its merchants traded with Danzig, Poland and the Low Countries, exporting the staples of wool, woolfells, (sheepskin), hide, salmon and trout and importing a wide range of goods, including many luxuries; cloth, soap, preserved fruit, spices, wines. Trade had also developed between Aberdeen and the other east coast ports from as far north as Orkney and Caithness to Leith and Berwick-on-Tweed in the south. The burgh enjoyed the services of skilled craftsmen and had thriving markets and an annual fair where the produce of the fertile hinterland was offered for sale. By Elphinstone's time Aberdeen had become one of the four wealthiest burghs in Scotland and with a population of around 4000 was, by medieval standards, an important centre.

A university would add to the burgh's prestige and there was no reason to suppose that the burgesses, appreciative of Elphinstone's largesse with regard to St Nicholas Kirk, would not assist financially in its funding. In the thirteenth century, townspeople had shown generosity to the Trinitarians and the Carmelites, the Red and the Whitefriars, who built their friaries near the Green, and to the Dominicans, the Blackfriars, who set up in Schoolhill. The town's grammar school could provide a continuing supply of scholars while from among the Dominicans, renowned for their scholarship, there was a ready reserve of teachers that could be tapped. Nor was the town yet so crowded that suitable accommodation for a university could not be found. Only twenty years before Elphinstone's arrival the burgess, Richard Vaus of Menie, had gifted the Franciscans or Greyfriars some derelict property in the Broadgate where Marischal College now stands. Here the Greyfriars built their monastery and planted an extensive garden that sloped down to what is now West North Street.

Elphinstone may well have considered all these advantages, then decided that Aberdeen was not the ideal base. It was dominated by a dozen or so families of the wealthy merchant-burgess class who had exclusive control of foreign trade, and whose ruling élite, the 'auld blud of the toun', the Blinseiles, Chalmers, Collisons, Cullens, Menzies, Rutherfords and Vauses, also controlled the burgh, electing from among themselves its provosts, bailies, treasurers and deans of guild. They were major property owners within the town, and some were landed gentry to boot. They married among their own kind, or with powerful local lairds. Elizabeth, daughter of Robert Blinseile, for example, had married Sir Alexander Cumine, one of the 'prood Cumines of Culter' (there are the usual numerous variations in the spelling of the name, from Comyn to Cumming), of the same family as the Cummings of Inverallochy. Some, like Blinseile, were involved in national as well as local affairs. Well disposed as the ruling élite might be towards a new university, Elphinstone could doubtless foresee problems, interference, rivalries. Even Vaus's gift to the Greyfriars came with strings attached. Given the municipal set-up in Aberdeen he would, to some degree, be beholden to its merchant princes.

To run his own show he must look to his own domain, the church lands of Old Aberdeen. What was it like at this time? The enclave of the Chanonry, part country village, part ecclesiastical close, virtually *was* Old Aberdeen. The charter creating Old Aberdeen a burgh of barony would describe it as 'the Chanonry of Aberdeen with its pertinents commonly called Old Aberdeen'. One can imagine the too-ing and fro-ing of clergy there, vicars choral and choristers processing towards the cathedral, the canons' servants, cowfeeders, and gardeners toiling in the glebes. Lawyers and litigants would make their way towards the consistorial court held in St Machar's Cathedral most week days. The sound of cattle lowing beyond the glebes would mingle with the chattering of the choristers and at intervals down the years, with the chapping of masons at the cathedral whenever a new phase of development got underway. Even so, with the high degree of absenteeism among the clergy and the bishop often away with his servitors, attending to affairs of the realm, its permanent population was small. The glebes, worked as little farms, would supply most of its needs.

The Chanonry was already a small seat of learning. According to Orem, a 'college of canons' had long been based there, where there were 'many learned men ...Doctors of Divinity, and of the Canon and Civil Laws' who taught aspiring theologians in their manses. But the spacious glebes of the canons had gobbled up much acreage and there was little room for any academic establishment that was more ambitious in scale than a small theological college. And apart from the lack of space, Elphinstone was planning his university with a secular dimension. It is likely that for these reasons he resolved to distance it from the Chanonry. To create a suitable base he had to look to the land beyond, to these 'pertinents', going roughly as far south as the Powis Brig, to the future High Street and College Bounds. This area had hitherto enjoyed little settlement apart from a brewery and probably a smithy, removed from inside to just outside the Chanonry when space within the enclave became tight.

This lack of development in the future High Street is borne out by archaeological investigation which reveals scarcely any trace of medieval development of the area, even at the north (Chanonry), end. In *Historic Aberdeen,* by E P Dennison and Judith Stones, 1997, the authors state, that at No 59 High Street 'natural levels were encountered immediately below the modern', while 'excavation at No 81 High Street' a large house and front garden near the Chanonry end, 'suggested that there may have been no pre-seventeenth-century occupation on this site'. At No 101, very near the Chanonry, 'observation during development revealed that the modern levels lay directly on the natural subsoil'. The theory, that no village of Old Aberdeen outwith the Chanonry existed before Elphinstone's time, is further reinforced by a papal bull of 20 February 1498 which noted that before the bishop's arrival there were only 'three or four houses of inhabitants' there.

While the Chanonry was a walled enclave, Elphinstone was well aware that this empty land to the south, through which the king's highway ran, was readily accessible. If the whole area were granted the status of a burgh of barony, this unpromising stretch would be given the impetus to develop as a place fit to house a university. And so in Edinburgh on 26 December 1489, just twenty months after Elphinstone was consecrated bishop and eighteen months after James IV came to the throne the sixteen-year-old monarch, in the stylised wording of the charter, in token of the bishop's work as royal ambassador, elevated 'the Chanonry of Aberdeen with its pertinents commonly called Old Aberdeen', to the status of burgh of barony. The inhabitants gained the right:

> to buy and sell within the said burgh wines, wax, cloth woollen and linen, broad and narrow, and other merchandise. To have and to hold bakers, brewers, butchers and sellers of flesh and fish, and other craftsmen in any way belonging to the freedom of a burgh in barony.

The burgh would have its own magistrates though power to choose them was vested in Elphinstone and his successors as Bishops of Aberdeen, the eponymous barons of the burgh. There would be burgesses who would have the right of a market place with a market cross, and to hold a weekly market there on Mondays. There were to be two annual public fairs, a Pasch or Easter fair on Skyre Thursday, the day before Good Friday when, traditionally, folk were shrived, that is, confessed their sins and received absolution, and an eight day long autumn fair on St Luke the Evangelist's Day, 18 October. As a burgh of barony, Old Aberdeen's 'rights, liberties and privileges' would include the same trading rights as Aberdeen itself, with the exception of the right to overseas trade which was exclusive to royal burghs.

By now demands of state were crowding in on Elphinstone. By 1492 he had been appointed Keeper of the Privy Seal, with control of royal patronage, Commissioner of Crown Lands and Auditor of Exchequer, high offices which he held for the rest of his life. That year he led the team of Scottish ambassadors who negotiated a lengthy truce with Henry VII of England. Nevertheless the university project was always in his mind and in late 1494, five years after Old Aberdeen became a burgh of barony, he travelled to Rome, bearing a petition from James IV to Pope Alexander VI, the infamous Rodrigo Borgia. Its contents, reiterated according to convention in the founding bull, state that a university was necessary to improve the condition of the people in the north of Scotland:

> considering that there are some places, separated from the rest of the kingdom by the arms of the sea, and very high mountains, in which dwell men who are rude and ignorant of letters and almost barbarous.

King James IV (1473-1513) became king at 15. Under his able and energetic leadership, Scotland took great strides forward in the administration of law and order, education, scientific experiment, medicine, dentistry, poetry and architecture. He was astute enough to enrich the crown at the expense of the church yet was a keen pilgrim and dreamt of leading a crusade against the Turks. He was a linguist, a bibliophile, enjoyed pageantry, cards, dicing and hawking. He was fascinated by the old black arts, like alchemy and by new technologies such as the printing press. He had a passion for artillery and the sea, building the largest warship of the time, the Great Michael. At time of his marriage to Margaret daughter of Henry VII he entered into a Treaty of Perpetual Peace with England which failed to prevent the tragedy of Flodden field. The bonds of the Auld Alliance were stronger.

This was good for dramatic impact, but something of an exaggeration since students from the north had until then managed to make their way both to Scottish and continental universities. 'That noble prince, King James', continued the bull :

had the utmost desire that a university should be erected in the famous city of Old Aberdeen which is near enough to the northern islands and the foresaid mountains, and in which a temperate climate prevails, and where are found an abundance of victuals, convenience of dwellings and a good store of other things pertaining to the requirements of human life.

An optimistic assessment of the marshland earmarked for the college buildings!

Pope Alexander VI, (Rodrigo Borgia) from the portrait in the Uffizi Gallery, Florence.

Pope Alexander gave his assent. His bull, the founding bull of Aberdeen University concludes: 'Given at Rome at St Peter's in the year of the incarnation of our Lord, 1494 the fourth of the ides (10th) of February'. It was long believed that 1494 was the correct year of foundation since the bull said so. However at this time the Christian year began on 25 March, the Feast of the Annunciation. By modern reckoning the correct date is 1495. Nevertheless the 'old style' date of 1494 appears on the old Library at King's (now the Visitor Centre) and the gateway to New King's, both of which were built centuries after modern reckoning was adopted.

The bull granted permission to establish a university in Old Aberdeen, with the same powers and privileges as the Universities of Paris and Bologna, and with undergraduate courses in arts and, at post-graduate level, in theology, canon law, civil law and medicine. It was innovatory in that it included laymen as well as churchmen in its remit in an era when the clergy still formed the majority of the educated classes, in its inclusion of the study of medicine and in the establishment of a civil law course. The king was determined to strengthen the administration of law and order, and in particular to curb the lawlessness of the Highlands and Islands. Earlier in the century his forebears had struggled to bring about legal reform but the judicial committees of the day were fluctuating bodies which lacked the opportunity to lay down a coherent pattern of civil law. But a permanent court of civil justice was evolving which would emerge as the Court of

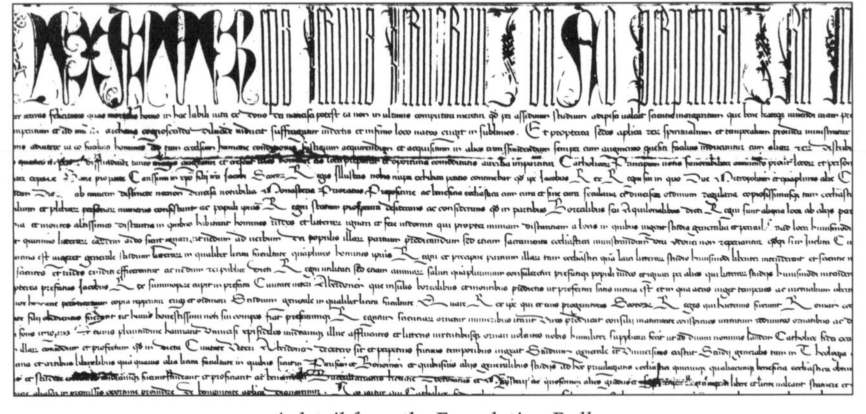

A detail from the Foundation Bull.
The original is preserved in the archives at King's College.

Session in the reign of James V. In modern parlance there would be increased job opportunities for civil lawyers.

And so the bull has a Janus quality, commending the medieval ideal of learning for its own sake, laying emphasis on the teaching of theology, yet also looking forward to the modern world of vocational education, a concept which would be reinforced by James's famous Education Act of 1496 in which we can assume Elphinstone had a hand, indeed he attended the parliament which passed the measure. That act required barons and lairds to put their eldest sons to grammar school 'fra thei be aucht or nyne yeiris of age' until they had 'perfyte Latyne', before proceeding to university. There it was arts and law, not theology, that the king ordained the eldest sons of the gentry to study.

Elphinstone did not publish the bull immediately on his return to Old Aberdeen. Inadequate income and arguments had hampered the early development of both St Andrews and Glasgow Universities, and he was determined that Aberdeen's growth would not be similarly thwarted. And in reverse of today's procedures, when mighty schemes are first announced, followed by appeals for money to get them off the ground, Elphinstone set about securing the necessary funding before making any public statement about the new university. He was a skilled revenue chaser, using his financial and legal expertise to acquire ecclesiastical and secular endowments. He secured his first endowment, the revenues of the hospital of St Germain in East Lothian, in February 1496. These included the teinds of Glenmuick and Abergerny (Glengairn) in Mar and Aberluthnott (Marykirk) in the Mearns. The following year, King James granted £12 6s annually from rents on Crown lands in Banffshire to support a mediciner, a Professor of Medicine in modern parlance. He had a genuine interest in medicine and established the Royal College of Surgeons of Edinburgh in 1506, though his own experiments in surgery and dentist may not have been appreciated by the guinea pigs among his subjects. Though medicine had been taught sporadically at St Andrew's and at Oxford and Cambridge since the early fourteenth century, this was first permanent, endowed lectureship in either Scotland or England.

The papal bull founding Aberdeen University was at last made public by Bishop Elphinstone in St Machar's Cathedral on 25 February 1497, in the presence of his canons and an invited audience of 'considerable persons', says William Orem. The bull outlined the *raison d'etre* and the functions of the university, but Elphinstone would later publish his first Foundation Charter, and subsequently draft a second, both of which, particularly the latter, gave detailed accounts of its structure and organisation. The bishop, already the ecclesiastical baron of Old Aberdeen had become, by courtesy of the bull, Chancellor of the University of Aberdeen. Though as yet town and college existed only on parchment, Elphinstone would control both.

Almost a decade had passed since the new burgh of barony of Old Aberdeen, the university's planned base, had been instituted. How were things progressing? Not too well. There had been a hiatus. Elphinstone was taken up with affairs of state, involved in discussions with the burgesses of Cologne with regard to Scottish trade, and even more demandingly, with Maximilian, the new Holy Roman Emperor, on an alliance against England, James IV having taken up the Yorkist cause, of which more anon. But now things were getting underway. Another, rather curious bull, casting light on 'the new town' and its slow development was granted by Pope Alexander at St Peter's, Rome, on 20 February 1498. The petition for the bull had been presented, doubtless at Elphinstone's instigation as baron of the burgh, on behalf of King James and 'gentlemen and inhabitants and residents of the new town within the bounds of the parochial church of St Machar, outside but near the city of Aberdeen'. The petition, repeated in the bull, stated that 'in the said place in which formerly there were three or four houses...abundance of inhabitants and residents has grown there', thanks to the blessing of God on the industry of these inhabitants. But the bull goes on to express the hope that through the king's proclamation of a weekly market (this had first been proclaimed almost ten years earlier, and would be proclaimed again in six months time), and by the building of a parish church 'men may be the more induced to live there'. Clearly growth had not been as speedy as expected. We also learn that permission to build a parish church had already been granted but not implemented.

The mighty Borgia pope was not quite certain what this petition was about. 'We, not having sure information of the circumstances...' he grumbles. However he goes on to abolish the theoretical erection of the new church and free the parishioners from any obligations they might have to it. 'Act in the circumstances at your own discretion', he tells Bishop Elphinstone, giving him *carte blanche* to push ahead again.

Next comes a new charter from King James, dated 21 August 1498, reaffirming his edict of 26 December, 1489, in short, relaunching the burgh of barony. It is no longer referred to as 'the Chanonry of Aberdeen with its pertinents commonly called Old Aberdeen', but instead 'the Village of Aberdon with the bounds and pertinents commonly called Ald Aberdon', and, more grandly, the 'Cathedral Church City and University of Aberdon'.

Now Elphinstone, using the authority delegated to him in the *carte-blanche* bull of 20 February 1498, drew up a 'public instrument', at his palace in the Chanonry on 10 December 1498, the fourth charter in this flurry of documents and complementary to the barony relaunch charter. It established once again, a parish church for the new town 'with bell-tower, bell, cemetery, place for holy things, baptismal font...' and set out the boundaries for the new parish. (Complex though modern town planning legislation is, one does not have to apply to the monarch and the pope at every turn). The Girth Cross, at its site on the Bishop's Green, was the starting point. The boundary line went eastwards towards the Tyleford, a ford across the Tile Burn, in today's terms a couple of hundred yards beyond the east end of Seaton Place East. Then the line went 'from the rabbit hill to the sea' then 'up by the old boundaries and divisions between the land of Seaton and the lands of the hospital of St Peter's, then *usque ad septa et terminos college limitum,* that is, right up to the end of College Bounds, though at that time, there was no college to bound.

There are several interesting points here. Firstly, Elphinstone's boundaries took in a considerable amount of the Old Town Links, to the east of the Old Aberdeen. There is mention of the rabbit hill here, probably man-made. Rabbits were valued for their flesh and fur. Warrens and warranders to look after them had been introduced into the Aberdeen area by the fifteenth century. The royal burgh had its own rabbit hill or Cunnigar Hill, (*cunni,* coney and *gar,* garth or enclosure), at a site later occupied by the City Hospital. Secondly, the Tile Burn, which became the Powis Burn east of the present Regent Walk, was the demarcation line, between 'the old boundaries and divisions between 'the land of Seaton and the lands of the hospital of St Peter's'. The line went along the present University Road as far as the Butchart Centre, then broke away behind the gardens of the present No 48 College Bounds, to join with Orchard Walk, and to emerge about No 10 College Bounds, as noted in *The Spital Lands.* Thus a portion of land south of Powis Brig, on the east side of College Bounds came within the boundary of the new town.

On the west side, the Powis Burn again acted as the boundary marker.

It ran from just south of the present Powis Gate in College Bounds, through the grounds of today's Johnston and Crombie Halls, to join the tributary to the Loch, which is shown in Parson Gordon's Plan. And so on to the Loch of Old Aberdeen itself, then along its margin to 'the lane between the manse of Invernochty and the land of Master Duncan Shearer, Rector of Clatt'. Invernochty Manse was the most southerly in the Chanonry, and the land of Duncan Shearer, one of the great benefactors of cathedral and university, consisted of twenty perches sold to him by Bishop Elphinstone in 1492, one of many of the bishop's land transactions. It lay just outside the Chanonry, south of Invernochty Manse. The lane between the two that is mentioned became Cluny's Wynd, and is still remembered by older folk in the area. The boundary line then crossed to run *'per murum canonicorum'*, alongside the high dyke at the rear of the glebes bounded by Seatongate.

The barony relaunch charter was silent on the Chanonry while this charter marking the boundaries of the new parish, excluded it altogether. 'The new town within the bounds of the parochial church of St Machar' of the *carte blanche* bull of 20 February 1498 was superseded. Elphinstone had re-drawn his domain, effectively disjoining the Chanonry, which he perceived exclusively as an ecclesiastical close, and creating this new host town for his university. Its residents, layfolk and scholars alike, would have no call to enter the Chanonry to worship in St Machar's, for they would have

The Chanonry or Cluny's Port would have stretched across the Chanonry from the site of the wall, left centre. The wall and adjoining cottage were demolished in the early 1920s to make way for St Machar's Drive.

their own parish church and college chapel. Indeed the new college was planned as a collegiate church with its own body of priests and choristers to sing Divine Office. It may have been around this time that the Aulton's third gate, the Chanonry Port was built, blocking off the Chanonry at Invernochty Manse. It was surmounted by an effigy of the Virgin Mary with the inscription:

Hac ne vade via, nisi dixeris
Ave Maria
Invenies veniam sic salutando
Mariam.

The same area today as shown in the picture on the previous page.

(Do not go this way without saying 'Hail Mary'. You will find pardon by thus saluting Mary). There was also a tablet affixed to the port, carved with a pot of lilies, symbolic of the purity of the Virgin which became one of the emblems of Old Aberdeen.

One suspects that the citizens of Aberdeen would have been unaware of such fine-tuning of boundaries. Though there was great pride in St Nicholas Kirk, they venerated St Machar's and this is made evident thanks to the affair of Perkin Warbeck. He was the Flemish impostor who claimed the English crown as Richard, Duke of York, the younger of the two princes in the Tower of London, and not murdered on the orders of Richard III after all, or so he would have it believed. James IV supported the Yorkist cause and Warbeck's claims, not out of conviction but hoping to get Berwick and other border strongholds out of it if Perkin were successful. He even arranged Perkin's marriage to the beautiful Catherine Gordon, daughter of the second Earl of Huntly. There were tit-for-tat cross-border sorties during 1496 and 1497 between James and the forces of Henry VII of England, with James pushing his luck in a campaign that was popular with his subjects.

Aberdeen was one of the royal burghs required to contribute to an annual allowance paid by the king to Perkin and the magistrates would have been following developments as closely as circumstances would allow. Towards the end of these hostilities, Aberdeen, though somewhat removed from the theatre of war, was put on a 'red alert'. The Council summoned the burgesses to report fully armed at Cunnigar Hill and harbour defences were to be erected. On 4 July 1497 the bailies specifically ordained that if the English proposed to land at 'the north part of the haven' that is the Donmouth, at that time not far from Cunnigar Hill, 'al manere of men' with their war carts, gunnery, artillery 'and al uther defensable wappinnis', were to head for Old Aberdeen to resist the enemy 'for the saiftie of our cathedral kirk', the Bishop's Palace, 'our maisters the chanons', their households and manses. Old Aberdeen, still undeveloped, lacked the citizens to defend itself. Nothing came of this scare, and in September 1497, Elphinstone and his colleagues negotiated a seven year truce with Henry VII who preferred to be at peace with Scotland. His daughter, Margaret Tudor, was later betrothed to James IV whom Henry had come to treat with caution and respect. As for Perkin Warbeck, he was captured and executed on Henry VII's orders.

Back in Old Aberdeen preparations for the new college were underway by 1497. With the boundaries of the new parish now clearly marked out, Elphinstone located his university as far from the Chanonry as they would allow. The college buildings were planned to stand in splendid isolation near the Powis Brig, dominating the entrance to the new town. Elphinstone met the massive financial outlay necessary to build the college from his personal resources. His account with Andrew Halyburton, 'the conservator of the Scottish Nation', our agent in the Low Countries through whom Scotland's trade with the continent was carried on, reflects building activity in Old Aberdeen. In 1497 the bishop exported salmon, trout and wool while the conservator sent him gunpowder which would be used to blast out the building stone for the new college, though the site of the quarry can no longer be identified. The following year Halyburton shipped carts and wheelbarrows to Elphinstone presumably for transporting the stone. These items were not available in the 'famous city of Old Aberdeen...' as one might have suspected, nor apparently anywhere else in the North East. The conservator also sent the Bishop a 'lytyll pok (poke, parcel) in the quilk there was a stek of ryssillis blak', a piece of black russels cloth, a mixture of woollen and cotton cord from the Flemish town of Rijssil (Lille), as well as two 'blak bonetis' and two red caps, academic headgear perhaps? Robert Blinseile, who traded in wool, salmon and 'fynans' through Halyburton, also handled goods on Elphinstone's behalf. But the charter of 1489 which created Old Aberdeen a burgh of barony had also given the Bishop of Aberdeen exceptionally wide trading rights, endowing him with:

full privilege, liberty and power to buy all sorts of victuals, wines and other merchandise brought within the port of Aberdeen, or outwith the same, by our lieges whatsoever, or by strangers from other kingdoms....and to sell again the said victuals, wines or merchandise.

This allowed him to entertain in style. His account with Halyburton for 1497 includes almonds, rice, pepper, ginger, cinnamon, mace, cloves, nutmegs, saffron, confections and a intriguingly anonymous 'troussel' or bundle. He 'kept a splendid table', wrote Hector Boece. 'He hardly ever dined without noble company, and while his table was always sumptuous, he himself amid these dainties was abstemious, cheerful of countenance and pleasant in conversation'. King James, visiting Old Aberdeen to observe the progress of the college, would have enjoyed the bishop's hospitality. When he lodged at the Bishop's Palace he slept in a four poster bed whose canopy was embellished with the royal coat of arms. As a matter of interest, the Bishop's 1498 accounts include payment for 'the mendyn of an oralag and the cais new', the repair of his horloge or clock, and a new case, indicating that there were no reliable clockmakers in Aberdeen. Elphinstone also dispatched considerable sums in Scots money which were converted to ducats and sent to Rome through Cornelius Altonitz's bank. The North East's church revenues were not only expended on the local needs but on papal dues.

Elphinstone's pursuit of funds for the maintenance of masters and scholars continued. In 1498, he endowed the university with the patronage and revenues of the Church of Slains. The second Earl of Buchan was not too happy, for the patronage, formerly his father's, had lapsed to the Crown on his death in accordance with feudal law, and the son doubtless expected to acquire it. An accommodation with the Earl was reached however. In 1500 the open-handed and devout Robert Blinseile, mortified (bequeathed) to the University the annual feu duty of twenty-three shillings Scots 'furth of a land in the Castlegate'. In return, funeral services and annual masses were to be held for himself and his family. Other welcome donations followed, and the king's munificence in endowing a mediciner had encouraged a handful of affluent Aberdonians, sympathetic to the Bishop's ambitions, to follow suit, though it is a moot point whether more benefactions would have come in had the university been based in Aberdeen.

On the college site itself, one of the first tasks was the taming of the boggy terrain. As Parson Gordon commented in his *Description of Both Touns*: 'The quholl (whole) fundatione of this colledge, being builded in a marrish ground, is underlayde with great rafters of oake'. Shades of the Athenaeum in later times! There was early subsidence at the east end of

Chapel, and the later construction of the belltower, the famous crown tower, caused problems. But systems of drainage were improving, the quagmire problem had been partially solved and an aqueduct some four feet wide was laid out from the Bishop's Loch to the College to boost the water supply. Eventually, as the 'dettoun', the motto or inscription on the west front of King's Chapel in translation from the Latin records:

> By grace of the most serene, illustrious and invincible James IV: On the fourth day before the nones of April 1500, masons began to build this renowned College.

The date, converted from the Latin style is 2 April, an auspicious one, which according to tradition, marked the start of the building of Solomon's temple at Jerusalem, though it may or may not have been the actual day that operations began.

King's College is taken for granted these days. Not so at the time of its

The inscription on the west front of King's College Chapel.

erection. The fact that it was custom-built was remarkable. Early universities tended to evolve out of existing buildings. Both St Andrews and Glasgow Universities were housed in various buildings over a number of years, as were a number of European universities. Marischal College had to make do with the buildings of the former Greyfriars Monastery at the Broadgate for a century and a half after its foundation in 1593. As the new college grew slowly, its progress would have been observed by marvelling clerics from the Chanonry, by travellers along the king's highway and by curious folk from Aberdeen itself. Hopefully something of its spectacular nature has been conveyed by the front cover of this book. In an essay on Canon Alexander Galloway, Dr William Kelly, the architect-historian, conjures up the atmosphere of those heady days:

> the clean, new wonderful chapel as it rises, at length so triumphantly crowned; the stir of stranger masons and craftsmen come to carry out the Bishop's projects at St Machar's and the College; the unpacking of the carved woodwork, glass, arras cloth and metal work just brought from 'the shore'.

The shore would develop into Trinity Quay. These precious cargoes may, however, have been disembarked at the Donmouth, which was much nearer Old Aberdeen. It took over five years to build the chapel and the principal buildings. Some took longer. Alexander Galloway, one of the earliest students, graduated before the buildings were complete.

The new parish church was also being built, for real this time, almost opposite the new college and likewise as far from the Chanonry as was possible. Indeed, part of this area was outwith the original boundaries of the new town so land had to be acquired from the rector and chaplain of St Peter's Hospital to provide a manse and glebe for the new prebendary, confirmed by a charter of 1503. Elphinstone may not have intended to build so far south but the 'marrish ground' of what is now the Powis Gate-Johnston Hall area may have been impossible to build on at that time, beyond even the help of 'great rafters of oake'. The church was a plain sturdy building, in no way detracting from the splendour of the new college on the other side of the king's highway. It had a corbie-stepped gable and a simple belfry which housed two of the cathedral's small bells, Schochtmadony and Skellat, the gift of Bishop Elphinstone. Schocht is the same word as shuggle while Madony could be Madonna. Skellat is Scots for a small bell.

In the charter of 1503, the name of the new parish and church, *Sancta Maria ad Nives*, St Mary of the Snows, appears for the first time. An account of the associated miracle which had become a fashionable cult in Europe and would be included in the *Aberdeen Breviary*, may have inspired Elphinstone to choose that name for the new parish. In the fourth century Rome, so the legend goes, a wealthy couple decided to devote their fortune to the honour of the Virgin. St Mary appeared to them and to Pope Liberius in dreams, indicating her wish to have a church dedicated to her on the Esquiline Hill. Its site would be marked out with snow. The next day, though it was August and the heat was intense, snow had fallen, marking out the site. Here in 432, the church of *St Maria ad Nives* was built. Elphinstone, a devotee of the Virgin since childhood, would have been much interested in this cult. He had already dedicated St Machar's to the

Virgin, providing the cathedral with a double dedication. Her effigy stood on guard at the entrance to the Chanonry and his new college too would be named in her honour. However local folk always called the new church the Snow or Snaw Kirk.

Elphinstone was not entirely successful in his policy of segregating the Chanonry from his new town. The annual fairs of Skyre Thursday and St Luke's, authorised by the barony charter, 'in popish times stood within the chanry and were great ones', as Orem reports. The new town was still thinly populated and the bulk of those attending the fairs would arrive from the north which explains why the gate near the Tillydrone Mote Hill was named the Market Port. St Machar's kirkyard was handy to graze beasts, and along with the cathedral made a good sales arena. The bishop would have none of this. In his Constitutions of 1506 he instructs the sacrist, among many other things, to keep pigs, horses and oxen out of the kirkyard by constructing dykes, and at the time of markets, fairs and feast days to keep kirkyard and cathedral free from merchant goods and food stalls.

The original seal of the College of St Mary in the Nativity showing the emblems of salmon, lillies and the hand of God.

By this time, the 'famous city', almost non-existent when presented to Pope Alexander VI as an ideal milieu for the new university, was developing in reality. Its barony status offered an inducement for tradesmen and craftsmen to settle there and sell their wares at the weekly markets. Cottages began to line the highway between the emerging college and the Chanonry. That stretch was known as the Middle Toun before it became the High Street. By a charter of December 1504 Elphinstone gave Gilbert Piot and his wife thirty-three roods of land to build a brewery there. If a rood, a remarkably hard-to-pin-down measurement, is roughly the fourth part of an (English) acre, this was a fair 'skelp o grun', indicating that the High Street was far from fully built up in the early days of King's College. Perhaps the famed Old Aberdeen brewery was later built on this site.

On 17 September 1505 Bishop Elphinstone formally inaugurated his university, by publishing the Foundation Charter of St Mary in the Nativity, a College for the number of thirty-six persons.

Dead Souls

The wall monument of Simon Dodds.

Who shrunk Simon Dods? This might well be one's reaction to the quaint miniature effigy clothed in mass vestments and lying in a shallow wall recess in the south aisle of the Cathedral. The inscription below the effigy is now virtually indecipherable, but it relates that he was a graduate in civil law and in the decretals, a branch of canon law and that he founded various masses in St Machar's, including one for the soul of John Earl of Mar, his predecessors and successors. Contemporary records reveal Dods to have been involved in running the business side of the Cathedral, of which he was a generous benefactor. He died in 1496. The Earl of Mar noted in the inscription was the uncle of James IV and patron of the prebend of Invernochty of which Dods was rector. Mar had met an unnatural end at his the behest of his brother, James III, who suspected him of disloyalty, even sorcery. James IV had become tutor (legal guardian) to the late earl's son, his young cousin, who had succeeded his father as patron of Invernochty of which Dods was prebendary.

A charter of James IV dated 23 January 1494 granted confirmation of an endowment by Dods to maintain a priest who would offer masses in perpetuity for the souls of James's forebears, and for the late Earl of Mar at the altar of the Haly Blude (Holy Blood) which Dods had founded at St Machar's. Dods also built accommodation for the new mass priest at the Manse of Invernochty, perhaps a little single room chamber.

The founding of an altar by Dods and the appointment of a priest to say masses for the 'decessit' Earl was the type of endowment much in vogue in the fifteenth century. Following outbreaks of the Black Death in the late fourteenth century there had been an obsession with the fleeting nature of life. Making a good death was important, and masses for souls after death was believed to ensure salvation, reducing time spent in purgatory as punishment for sins. Perpetual chantries were created and mass priests appointed to cope with the demand for masses for the dead. This preoccupation with death is encapsulated in the dirge-like refrain 'Timor mortis conturbat me,' the fear of death disquiets me, in William Dunbar's poem 'Lament for the Makaris'. The poet, once a civil servant, was certain to have know both William Elphinstone and Gavin Dunbar.

Masses for the souls of the departed or 'obits' were a welcome source of income for St Machar's. Kennedy, in his Annals, lists the obits celebrated there and the annuities paid to the Cathedral' s common funds; among them, David Lindsay, for whose obit a foundation was made by Bishop Ingram de Lindsay from the Chapel of Westhall, an annuity of £1; Thomas Trail, canon of Aberdeen, gave an annuity of 8s 2d from crofts in the Spital and Futty for his obit, and Alexander Cissor and Cicilia his spouse an annuity from the Mill of Mundurno of 13s 4d for theirs.

The Snow Kirk also had its masses for the dead. In 1503, Elphinstone ordained that there should be masses for the weal of the soul of James IV and his brothers, for Elphinstone himself and for his flock and for the rector of the Snow Kirk, James Browne, and his parents. Elphinstone bequeathed an annuity of £7 4s for celebrating a mass of commemoration on the anniversary of his own death.

At King's College Chapel, the chaplains wore chasubles of 'black and blue double worsat' to celebrate the Office for the Dead. The merchant Robert Blinseile mortified an annual feu duty of 23s to the College from a land in the Castlegate in 1500 for his obit. In his Second Foundation, in a section written before Flodden, Elphinstone ordained a requiem for the anniversary of James IV's death at the Chapel. It was to be preceded by the ringing of the greater bells and proclamations by bellmen 'throughout the towns of New and Old Aberdeen'. He could not have foreseen how soon and how tragic that death would be.

Chapter 4

The Pearl of Knowledge

Among the other blessings which mortal man is able to obtain by the gift of God in this fleeting life it deserves to be reckoned not among the least that by earnest study he may win the pearl of knowledge.

Foundation Bull, Aberdeen University, 10 February, 1495.

St Mary's' never really caught on. 'The Royal College' and soon 'the King's College' reflecting King James's personal interest became current in speech and by 1512, in writing too. By then Elphinstone, aged eighty-two, had gifted much of his library to the college, and in a volume of Nicholas of Lyra's *Commentary on the Old Testament,* Principal Boece has written: *Liber Regalis Collegii Aberdonensis ex dono Reverendissimi patris Willelmi Elphinston.* (A book of the Royal College of Aberdeen, gifted by the most holy father, William Elphinstone). The 'College of St Mary in the Nativity' appears sporadically in a number of deeds, and along with 'King's College', in a document of 1542. St Mary's makes its last appearance in 1553, in the deed which appointed Alexander Anderson as fourth principal.

The college was built in the familiar defensive style of four ranges forming a quadrangle with a well in the centre. The chapel took up the north range and part of the west, where its famous crown belltower was set back a little from the highway. The west range also contained the Principal's suite of two rooms which linked with the south-westerly tower, one of the quadrangle's two 'capitolls' as Parson Gordon called them. This tower and its opposite number, the south-easterly 'capitoll' flanked the south range which was the residential quarters of the arts and theological students, though this was not completed in Elphinstone's lifetime.

On the east range, the site of today's King's College Visitor Centre, stood a two-storey building, ninety feet in length. On its ground floor was the 'Publick School', described by Parson Gordon as a 'long low barn like place', where assemblies of the whole college were held, but it was mainly used for teaching. On the first floor was the handsome Great Hall whose barrel-vaulted oak ceiling was a companion piece to that of the chapel. Both are attributed to the master wright and woodcarver, John Fendour. The Great Hall's daily use was as a refectory with the students seated on wooden benches at long tables while the masters sat on a raised dais. Conversation was in Latin or French, the latter, since it was unlikely to have been taught at local schools, an indulgence for the old University of Paris hands among the masters. No fooling about was permitted. Before dinner and supper an arts student read a passage from the Bible, while after the meal, theology students took it in turn to read the section from Nicholas of Lyra's *Commentary on the Old Testament* on that particular passage. The commentary is set in a panel in the centre of the page with the biblical text around it in smaller print. Forks were not then in use, and little knives were used for cutting up the meat which was eaten with the fingers. Nevertheless Lyra's *Commentary* remain in the King College archives, handsomely restored and free from all traces of medieval grease.

Both Public School and Great Hall were amply endowed with windows, allowing maximum light for reading. Those of the Hall were particularly fine. Half-a dozen mullioned windows, their upper parts filled with tracery overlooked the quad, while the window with three long, elegant, round-headed lights in the corbie-stepped south gable would have provided a view not only of the college garden near the present University Road junction, but right up College Bounds.

The college gate, small and unwelcoming, shown in the lower left hand corner of Gordon's vignette overleaf, was ennobled by 'the King's armorial coat' as Orem noted, on the raised panel above. The gate closed at ten in summer and eight in winter, nor was it 'to be opened before four in summer and five in winter'. Walls nine feet high consolidated the fortress-like appearance of the quadrangle, a deterrence to enemies such as the English and Highland caterans, and distractions such as women. Elphinstone wished his youngest and poorest scholars to pursue their studies in peace and seclusion. Those students who were successful in obtaining an *exeat* had to wear their scholarly garb, differentiating them from ordinary folk; black rounded hoods for the arts undergraduates, 'cornets', long pointed hoods resembling ice cream cones for those with bachelors' degrees and round hoods for those studying for higher degrees. Security became increasingly important. The detailed Second Foundation, which Elphinstone drew up towards the end of his life, stipulated that arts students must take it in turn to guard the gate 'each for a week by himself and not by another'.

The 'thirty-six persons' referred to in the first Foundation Charter of 1505 was not a magic number but the one sustainable by the existing endowments; six masters including the principal, thirteen undergraduate

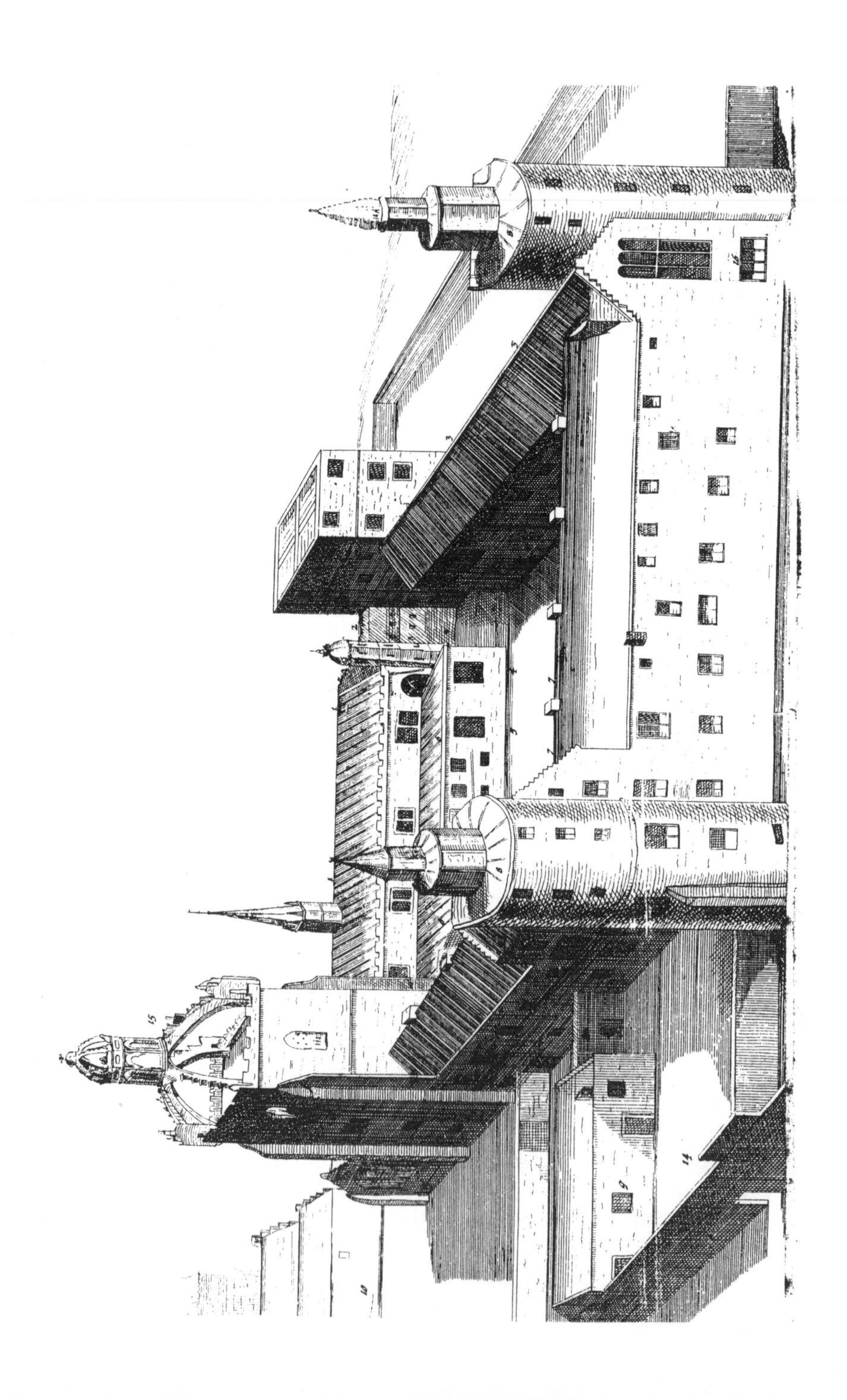

arts students, five post-graduate theological students, plus eight chaplains and four choristers whose duties were largely confined to the chapel. The Bishop of Aberdeen as chancellor was an *ex-officio* member of the university. He exercised a benevolent dictatorship, selecting the masters, controlling the admissions, and in the last resort, expelling any student 'who be found incorrigible'. His right hand man, the rector, presided over degree ceremonies and carried out an annual 'visitation', an inspection of the college, which examined the efficiency of its administration, assessed the performance of staff and students and kept a sharp lookout for 'alienation, pledging or squandering of the goods of the said college', in particular the money put aside for the maintenance of its fabric. Canon Alexander Galloway, parson of Kinkell, was rector on four occasions between 1516 and 1549. He was so highly esteemed by Elphinstone, Boece tells us, that 'hardly anything' was done by the bishop his official capacity without Galloway's guidance. We first met the versatile Galloway in *The Spital* in connection with the mysterious St Anne's Chapel. He was a canon lawyer, the official of the diocese of Aberdeen, a notary public, as well as designer of splendid sacrament houses, and what one might describe as a proto-architect.

Elphinstone had head-hunted Hector Boece, of whom he had good reports from his continental contacts, as a potential principal. A St Andrews graduate in his early thirties, a Christian humanist with a reputation as a skilled writer of Latin prose, Boece was teaching philosophy in Paris at that time. He had a minus point in that he had no degree in theology, the latter a requisite for the principalship, but a plus in that he had begun the study of medicine in Paris, the very subject that Elphinstone and King James sought to promote. Bishop Elphinstone 'chose me, all unworthy as I was for such a task', he wrote modestly. 'On my arrival in Aberdeen, I received a kind reception from the canons,' he recalls, painting a scene of academic life in full swing. 'David Guthrie, Professor of Civil and Canon Law, and James Ogilvie, Doctor of Divinity...laboured hard at expounding

Opposite: Parson Gordon's vignette of King's College, from his Plan of 'New and Old Aberdeen' of 1661. The principal's apartments are right of the Crown Tower, with the Grammar School, a later addition, in front, and the gate bottom left. The residential quarters are in the foreground between the towers, Jove, on the left, which has not survived and Scorpio, right, which remains. The corbie-stepped gable end, right, with the long windows belongs to the Great Hall with the small windows of the Public School below. Both were located in the dark building between Scorpio Tower and the New Work (Cromwell Tower), top right, which dates from 1658. The Timber Muses, a three-storey wooden residential building with a belltower, lies between the New Work and the east end of the chapel. Bishop Stewart's library building projects from the Chapel's frontage.

to crowded audiences, the one sacred writings, the other canon law.' He lists the eminent scholars who had already studied in Old Aberdeen including a group of Dominicans from the Schoolhill friary whose prior, the remarkable John Adam, later became Provincial, or head of the Dominicans in Scotland and, in the teeth of fierce opposition, reformed the Order which had become corrupt and worldly.

With learned doctors of divinity on his doorstep, why did Elphinstone lure this stranger, not yet even a bachelor of theology from Paris? It was, perhaps, part of his aim to distance his new university from the Chanonry and its 'college of canons', which was purely a theological college. Within a few years it seems that Boece had not only gained his first degree in theology but was running the university. The publication of the First Foundation in 1505 is likely to have marked his elevation to principal and the beginning of teaching in the new buildings. Boece's stipend or salary was fixed at forty merks annually or £26 13s 4d Scots, but it cannot be equated with a modern salary. It was generous for the time and accommodation was free. Additional perquisites included life tenure, freedom from all church dues and all taxes 'by whatsoever authority imposed'. Such 'feelgood' factors were by no means a *sine qua non* in academic circles of that time. At Glasgow the luxury of an academic stipend was a rarity. Boece's other sources of income, included, in his later years, a pension granted by King James V. His salary was well earned for the principal's range of duties, as detailed in the Second Foundation was remarkable :

> His duty will be to rule and govern the college, to preserve it in honour, to keep it clean, without refuse and filth in the yards, chambers and all other places, to preside over all other persons of the said college, to instruct them in morals and discipline, to visit the lectures of the regents (lecturers) and if need be reform them, to punish either personally or by deputy, those who offend in any way, to allot the rooms of the said college and assign them to masters and students when need be.

Most important of all, he had to teach theology and philosophy to his students 'and to preach the word of God to the people six times a year'. That would have been in the vernacular. The Constitutions of 1506 which Elphinstone drew up for St Machar's reveal, perhaps unusually for his time, that he considered preaching, as well as music, to be an important part of worship.

In spite of a heavy workload Boece found time to continue his study of medicine and to write two works, both in Latin, which were famous in their day, though 'infamous' might be a better description of his *History of Scotland* of 1527, which in the style of the time, was more fable than fact. The *Lives of the Bishops of Mortlach and Aberdeen,* published in 1522, was written on the suggestion of Bishop Gavin Dunbar, to honour the memory of Bishop

'He had to teach theology and philosophy to his students...' Title page of the 'Expositio Sequentarium', printed 1506.

Elphinstone. Suspect in places, it is nevertheless an invaluable source, though Boece's skill as Latinist did not inhibit James Moir, co-rector of Aberdeen Grammar School and editor of the 1894 New Spalding Club edition, from going through the text with his dominie's red pencil, correcting Boece's prose.

In 1528, Boece gained the higher degree of Doctor in Theology and on 9 September of that year, the magistrates of Aberdeen, to mark the occasion, offered him a 'propine' - a gift of a cask of wine, 'gif he will bid quhill (bide until) the new wynnis cum hayme, or, thane with twenty lib. Scottis, to help him buy him bonatis', perhaps the cap of doctor of theology. Having been carried away by their generosity, the councillors had to meet again that afternoon, 'to se and devise quhar this mony salbe esiast gottin.' We never do find out if Boece chose the wine or £20 Scots towards a bonnet.

His subprincipal and successor as principal was William Hay, who had studied philosophy with him in Paris. 'We were both native of the province of Angus, had passed our boyhood together in Dundee,' Boece recalled. Hay, who taught philosophy to the arts students, held the subprincipal's post for over thirty years. He also lived in residence, sharing the south range with the students.

No record of the first eigh-

The surviving ambo or preaching desk in King's College from which Hector Boece may have preached to the people of Old Aberdeen.

teen bursars, hopefully 'apt, docile, modest and of good disposition', survives. Thirteen of them, aged between fourteen and sixteen were studying for their Master of Arts degree and had to be, in the words of the first Foundation Charter, 'poor scholars...talented and apt for speculative sciences for whose academic education their family are unable conveniently to give assistance'. The first two bursars were to be of the name of Elphinstone, 'if such can conveniently be had', and three, if possible, were to come from the funding parishes of Glenmuick, Glengairn, Marykirk and Slains. So country lads were encouraged, but most students would have been drawn from the burgh school in Aberdeen, and the cathedral school in Old Aberdeen whose respective dominies William Strachan and Alexander Vaus, both prebendaries at the cathedral, had been among those welcoming Boece to Old Aberdeen.

The arts course followed was that of Paris, with the texts read from a manuscript or book. (Thus the term 'reader' for a senior university teacher). All teaching was in Latin the *lingua franca* of the Middle Ages, but not all students had left school with the 'perfyte Latyne', ordained by King James. It was the task of the grammarian to ensure that their Latin was of a reasonable standard before, as Boece put it, 'they attacked philosophy'. John Vaus was one of the earliest grammarians. His family were of the 'auld blud of the toun' and he was one of that rare band, like Canon Galloway, who had graduated from King's before the buildings were complete. He came back from the University of Paris, where he had continued his studies, to take up the post around 1510, probably at the invitation of Boece, whose student he had been. He brought half-a-dozen Latin text books back with him, and these are to be found in the archives at King's, his name neatly inscribed on their flyleaves. It was the norm to learn Latin from Latin at that time, a formidable task. But Vaus compiled an innovative Latin grammar the *Rudimenta* which in part uses the vernacular: *hic magister,* ane (ie this) maister, *hec musa,* ane sang, *hoc scamnum,* ane bynk (bench), and so on. Of the four editions of this work the first two were printed in Paris during his lifetime, in 1522 and 1531 respectively.

The grammarian was installed initially as rector of the Snow Kirk. Its revenues were 'appropriated' to the new university as the rector's prebend which served as his teaching stipend. It was twenty merks, the same as that of the subprincipal. He taught in his manse, which lay just south of the Snow Kirk, probably the first of the four extra-mural staff dwellings planned for College Bounds. Though this extended campus was not completed until after Elphinstone's death, it was not an afterthought, but part of his original 'package'. The layout of this area is shown as it was in 1661 on page 192. The First Foundation speaks of the canonist (who taught church law) the mediciner, the prebendary of St Mary of the Snows (the grammarian) and the legist (or civilist who taught civil law) 'who are to have their manses outwith the same college'. The grammarian's manse used to be nicknamed 'at the sign of the mitre', just like an inn, for above its gateway was a niche containing Bishop Elphinstone's shield and mitre, perhaps indicating that it was the first to be built, and certainly in Elphinstone's lifetime. The arch of the original gateway and Elphinstone's insignia were later built into the wall of Humanity Manse, No 19 College Bounds, as shown on page 196, which replaced the original manse. These few pieces of stone are the only surviving relics of the four 'manses outwith the college'. At time of writing Humanity Manse is home to the Research Institute of Irish and Scottish Studies .

Boece and Hay lectured in the Public School. Aristotle, was the staple of the philosophy course, his work translated into Latin from its original Greek. His *Logic* was taught to the first and second year students, his *Physics* to the second years along with Pliny's *Natural History*. Third year work included lectures on the *Cosmographia* of Ptolemy of Alexandria, from which the students would learn some arithmetic, geometry trigonometry, astronomy and geography. Boece's own copy, a German edition of 1482 is in splendid condition at King's. Its twenty-one maps include the famous representation of Scotland on an east-west rather than a north-south axis which includes the *Diva Fl(uvius)*, the River Don, with a settlement, *Devana*, on its north bank. In the fourth year Aristotle's *Metaphysics* was taught. For the Masters of Arts degree, students answered set questions on texts and debated in Latin propositions posed by examiners. James Melville, diarist and nephew of the great reformer Andrew Melville, later dismissed his arts course at St Andrew's as:

> Bot a few buikes of Aristotle quilk they lernit pertinatiuslie to bable and flyt (argue) on without right understanding or use therof.

Were young Melville's comments typical of standards at King's? Hopefully not. Dr Leslie Macfarlane has written that humanist reforms introduced by Boece and his colleagues to the arts courses, 'made King's College pre-eminent among the Scottish universities before the Reformation'.

The remaining five bursars, who would be chosen from the brightest arts graduates, were to study theology as their second degree under the principal. This was a lengthy course but theology was the entrée to the Church, still offering security for life. After successfully completing the first half of their course students took it in turn to preach in Latin in King's College Chapel. One of them 'of the most docile and finest bent' was also to assist with teaching of the arts students, a pupil-teacher, with the perk of free food and drink.

The principal's three senior colleagues, canonist, civilist and mediciner, like the grammarian, lived outside the quadrangle of King's in manses 'which were furnished with all conveniences as if they had been so many little colleges', according to Orem, on the land both 'on the near and the far side of the Powis Brig' according to the Second Foundation. The canonist had replaced the grammarian as prebendary of the Snow Kirk sometime before 1513, though the grammarian continued to derive a small part of his stipend from the 'fruits of Snow' and retained his manse within the kirk's curtilage. The canonist's manse also had been 'built and erected', a little north of the Snow Kirk, near the Powis Burn. Here he was to 'read in canon law in his manse or church', though the latter, *ecclesia* in the Latin of the Foundation Charter, is likely to be the Snow Kirk rather than the college chapel which was often, though not always, *templum* in the original. The singing of the Divine Office there throughout the day would not have been conducive to uninterrupted teaching. One of the earlier canonists was Arthur Boece, the principal's brother, who was also a graduate in civil law at King's. He later became the college's civilist and was among the first judges of the Court of Session after its foundation in 1532. There was a third manse within the Snow Kirk enclave, the home of the resident vicar, who had the actual cure of souls of the folk of Old Aberdeen.

The civilist's manse was on the east side of College Bounds, almost opposite the grammarian's and just north of the present Orchard Walk. He taught civil law, particularly the works of Justinian, following the course of Orleans University, whose doctoral gown he wore. The chaplains and choristers of the chapel lived between Powis Brig and the civilist's, directly opposite the Snow Kirk enclave. Elphinstone did not wish his eight chaplains to be exposed to external temptations any more than his young arts students, and the Second Foundation states:

> In order that (they) should have no occasion to roam outside the walls of the said College, especially at night, we assign to them all that land lying beyond the bridge and burn called 'Powes brig' and the land of the manse of the civilist opposite the church of St Mary of the Snows for the construction of manses and gardens there, in such wise that the precentor begins next to the burn, and after him the sacrist, each of them having twelve roods each while the remaining six chaplains going up after them towards to the said manse of the civilist, eight roods of land, for the erection of like gardens and houses.

The mediciner's manse was the last to be built and the only one on the college side of the Powis Brig. The Second Foundation speaks of 'that land newly brought into cultivation opposite the said college on the west, assigned...for the manse of the mediciner'. No 53 College Bounds now occupies this site. Because of the marshy ground around the present Powis

Gate area there was a sizeable gap between the Snow Kirk enclave and the mediciner's precinct which may not have been intended in the original planning of the external manses.

The First Foundation was pessimistic about the chances of appointing a mediciner; 'if such can conveniently be found', it stated for doctors could earn considerable amounts in private practice. However one such was found. James Cumming, at that time practising his skills on the continent, was known both to the ruling élite of Aberdeen and Bishop Elphinstone. He was one of the Cummings of Culter or Inverallochy, related to the Blinseiles by marriage and closely linked to the 'auld blud'. Dr Leslie Macfarlane tells us he had been one of the bishop's agents in the Low Countries between 1493-99, probably when he was studying medicine there, and clearly not averse to a bit of commercial dealing, for he earlier negotiated the purchase of breviaries (prayer books) for use in King's College Chapel. Now bishop and bailies mounted a joint initiative to bring him back to Aberdeen.

On 20 October 1503 the magistrates appointed him the city's first physician. He was to 'cum and vesy tham that beis seik, and schow them his medicin'. He was granted ten merks annually with the additional 'sweetener' of the rights to a hanet, that is a half-share of a net's catch during the season, at the Midchingle or the Fords of Dee salmon fishings, free of grassum, (an initial payment), though thereafter he had to pay the same rent as anyone else. The ten merks was not to be paid until he 'mak personale residence' with his 'wyf, houshalde and barnis' which seems fair enough. (Unlike their academic colleagues mediciners were not in holy orders, and free to marry). At the same time Elphinstone was able to offer Cumming a stipend of twenty merks to take up the mediciner's post at King's, made up from the king's endowment of £12 6s per annum, with the remaining 20s 8d coming from annual rents in Banff. Though not built when the Second Foundation was written, the mediciner's manse likely had been completed before Cumming's death in 1521. He and his wife and bairns may have 'held houss' there, the cries of children at play disrupting the 'lofty study' and quasi-monastic routine across the way at King's.

Hector Boece may have crossed the road to continue his medical studies under Cumming, but there were no medical bursars at King's, not even by the time of the Second Foundation which raised the number of endowed members of the university to forty-two. Revenue had been secured to fund one additional student in theology in 1506, the benefactor being William Cumming of Inverallochy, Marchmont Herald at the Court of the Lord Lyon and a relative of Mediciner Cumming. He granted the university half of his lands of Audiall near Aberdeen, and an additional six merks. Other new funding allowed the introduction of one student in canon and two in civil law, plus two additional choir boys. There was, however, an X factor.

Since its earliest days not all students at King's had been poor. The charter of 1503, relating to the Snow Kirk's manse and glebe ordains that:

> every student in our said new College shall pay to the rector of St Mary's...every year at the Paschal (Easter) feast, four pence; and with the poor the said rector shall compound amicably.

The Second Foundation states the position more clearly. The college, its members and their benefices are exempted from all church dues, indeed from all 'taxations by whatsoever authority imposed'. The only exception is the 'four pennies payable by every rich student to the prebendary of Snow' on receiving the holy sacrament at Easter. Though Elphinstone had created bursaries to fund poor but able lads, he was not averse to those who could pay their way. The Education Act of 1496, ordaining university education for the sons of barons and lairds, was specifically addressed to those 'that ar of substance'. Indeed, the Second Foundation sets forth a code of conduct more applicable to rowdy sons of the gentry than to poor students or the pious theologians who were their mentors:

> All within the said College should live honourably, the greater as much as the lesser. We prohibit and forbid that they should have public concubines, that they should carry arms swords or daggers secretly or openly...or that they should be pimps wandering by night or gallants straying abroad, but they are to be given over to good behaviour and occupied with lofty study.

No details have survived on how many rich students there were, what they were studying or where they lived. But we do know that the endowed students lodged in the south range, completed by Bishop Gavin Dunbar after Elphinstone's death and giving rise to an apocryphal falling out between Dunbar and Boece. Later known as Dunbar's Building, it looks imposing on Parson Gordon's Plan, but it was just fifteen feet wide and several yards nearer the Chapel than today's range.

Much information about this original wing survives, recorded in an Inventory of 1542, the first to note college possessions. It was made during the visitation of an early rector, James Strachan. The fourteen residential chambers in Dunbar's Building were romantically named after the planets, Jove, Mercury, Venus, and Saturn, the constellations, Corona and Hercules, the eight signs of the Zodiac, Aries, Taurus, Gemini, Cancer, Leo, Virgo, Libra, Scorpio, and Luna (the Moon). Was this Boece's idea? Or perhaps it was that of William Hay the subprincipal, who had resided in this wing from the time of its completion. Hay taught astronomy to the third year arts students, and had brought back books on cosmography from Paris, one of them containing an account of the voyages of Amerigo Vespucchi. The

Zodiac names were a useful teaching aid, helping the young students to learn the names of the heavenly bodies. These names, however, were the only exotic thing about these apartments. Most were single rooms, but Jove, Corona, Cancer and Libra were two-room suites with a *cublicum* or bedroom and a *bibliotheca* or study. The occupants of these suites did not withdraw from their studies into their bedrooms at 'lights out', for both rooms were crammed with beds. In 1542 there were twenty-eight in all.

Simple furniture, hand-made locally of oak or fir, was in general use, while a few items of quality were imported from Flanders or England. The better beds were 'standand', 'meikle' or 'sylit' - with canopy - and there was the occasional 'lang seitt bed' made from a settle. The remaining furniture consisted of benches, presses and 'lytil buirds', that is little boards or tables, where the students sat at their studies. Luna, economically had a 'buird' made from a half bed. Sometimes they had trestles, which could be folded up and the 'buird' laid against the wall when not required. Benches were the usual form of seating at that time. The ownership of a chair denoted importance and only two are found in Dunbar's Building. Gemini's study had room only for 'ane lytil buird and ane lytel cheir all off fyr'. The second chair, of oak, was in Libra where there was also 'a lytil almery' or cupboard, made at the expense of Canon Galloway, a gift to the college. Hercules had an unusual feature, an altar 'with ane bak'. Perhaps the occupant was particularly devout, or more likely, the study was used as makeshift storage space for the bed was 'biggit between the portall (door) and the studie'. The chamber called Jove was located in the south-west 'capitoll', the tower which has not survived. Its furnishings were plain; three beds, two presses and some tables. Corona next door possessed the only hanging cupboard or wardrobe in the college, while Cancer had a kist and almery belonging to the Subprincipal Hay, as well as his fir bed and

Scorpio, now known as the Round Tower.

some maps, as befitted a teacher of cosmography. The south-east tower, Scorpio, which is still extant, was not part of the sleeping quarters. It was built next to the gable-end of the Great Hall and originally served as the college library.

There is no mention of fireplaces in the Inventory but Parson Gordon's Plan shows four sets of chimney stacks in the roof of the south range, indicating a fireplace in every room. Wood was everywhere and fire danger great. The Second Foundation states:

> No one should have straw in the hearth of his chamber or anything which may easily catch fire; and that fuel should not be stacked within any house of the College.

The principal had a suite of two rooms on the west range, beside to the crown tower. They overlooked the college close and wall and commanded a good view of the highway. Boece had been in residence there, probably since the completion of the range until his death in 1536, and many of the principal's furnishings, noted in the Inventory of 1542, would have belonged to him. The outer room had a great oak cupboard locked and secured with metals bands, a great oak four-poster bed hung about with three curtains of red and green worsted with an arras or tapestry wall hanging to match; a feather bed and bolster; a long Scots 'countour' or desk, locked and bound with a metal band; a bench and a form, both of oak; 'ane lytil Flanderiss countour' with three leaves; a hanging chandelier of brass, with the image of the virgin and six flowers, at a guess, the lilies of Old Aberdeen; a map of Gaul and 'twa other breddis', two other boards; a great fir kist, with lock and band, 'keipand *ornamenta facultatis atrium* in the mongrel Scots-Latin of the Inventory, keeping the academic garb of the faculty, a few academic caps and gowns. In the inner room were an oak bed with oak canopy and curtain, an oak settle bed, and that status symbol, a Scots chair of oak. The two doors, inner and outer were of carved oak, possibly the work of Fendour or his craftsmen.

A number of items from the outer chamber are of interest. The principal at this time was the only person in college to have a 'countour' or desk, indeed two, one Scottish, kept locked, and his 'lytil Flanderiss countour', imported from Flanders. These were craftsman-made writing desks, superior to the boards on trestles of the south wing. Countours were coming into use in the early sixteenth century, taking their name from the counting board painted on to the table, an early form of calculator, to assist those who had to keep accounts. The Flanders desk had three leaves which Boece could have drawn out to give himself more space while he was writing his *Lives of the Bishops* and his *History of Scotland.* The map of Gaul, of what is now France, like the 'twa other breddis' would have been painted on wood. Boece must have brought it from Paris to remind him of the days when he strolled by the Seine with his fellow student, the great scholar Erasmus, with whom he kept up a correspondence throughout his life. Alas, this map has not survived. In the outer room there were also a long bench and form, so he may have taught there and even on occasion 'corrected' those whose aptness, docility and good disposition left something to be desired.

Rather surprising is the four poster bed and its hangings, the arras cloth, and the feather bed and the bolster, probably the mattress and pillows of the four poster. Had Boece kicked over the traces, reacting to the notoriously Spartan regime at Montague College of the University of Paris which he endured as student and teacher? No, these luxurious furnishings were in all likelihood acquired after his time, for the visit to Aberdeen by the king,

James V and Mary of Guise.

James V, and his French queen, Mary of Guise who lodged in the principal's apartments. They made a progress to the north with their court in 1541. Their two young sons had recently died, and the purpose of the royal visit, William Kennedy explains in his *Annals of Aberdeen* of 1818 was:

> to amuse the King and to remove the melancholy with which he had been seized on the loss of his sons. They visited the College and were entertained with stage comedies, and with orations both in Greek and Latin, by the students; while nothing was neglected by the principal and professors that could contribute to the amusement of the royal visitors.

A daughter, Mary, was born to the royal couple in the year following that visit, on 8 December, 1542. She became Queen of Scots six days later, on the death of her father. Sorely depressed after the defeat of the Scots at Solway Moss, James V had turned his face to the wall.

The mention of orations in Greek as part of the royal entertainment is interesting for the study of that language was introduced into Scotland in 1534. Either Boece, shortly before his death or his successor William Hay, had included it in the college curriculum. One wonders who taught it. Plays too were performed in the Great Hall from an early period. The touches of luxury that enhanced the Hall, may well have been first introduced at the time of this royal visit. Tapestries, heraldic shields, portraits of Bishop Elphinstone and his successors gradually made their appearance, and a group of pin-ups later enlivened the scene. In the words of Kennedy:

> the ten sibyls, said to be likenesses of the most celebrated beauties of Aberdeen of that age, done by Jameson, decorate the east wall.

Food for the college was provided by the provisor. It was stressed then that he should have adequate funding so that 'masters and students shall have not occasion to complain of their portions'. Originally his kitchen and larder was based at the east end of Dunbar's Building, but later kitchen, larder, granary and brewery were built behind the east range, handily sited for the Great Hall and roughly opposite the surviving tower, Scorpio. Paintings of the rear of the college show the marked contrast between the splendour of King's and the provisor's quarters, a little range of low buildings that would have originally been thatched, and which would have resembled the early cottages of the Middle Toun. In the college garden near the Powis Burn the provisor grew herbs and vegetables 'necessary for the College'.

The Inventory of 1542 describes his plain but serviceable equipment. In the kitchen itself, 'ane gret brandar of irne (a great gridiron), four great spits with racks, a small spit, mortar and pestles of stone and brass, 'five pannis, gret and small', 'sex pottis, gret and small, and later addition 'ane gret beif pot', six 'luggit' dishes (with lugs or handles), a great platter and nineteen dishes, six round trenchers, an oak cutting block and a baking board; in the bread room, a five gallon wooden pail, a five quart pail, a pint pail, and a chopin (a half pint measure): in the brewhouse, a brewing vat, a wooden tub, a cauldron, a wort tub for unfermented malt, and a vat of fermenting wort; in the larder, two meat vats, two meat bowls and two cutting blocks; in the granary two storage chests of fir with lids, one for malt, one for meal and measures and scales. The alehouse contained six ale barrels, two bowls and two stands for ale-barrels. Cupboards and locks and keys were in much evidence possibly to prevent hungry lads helping themselves.

With work on the college well underway, Elphinstone turned to St Machar's Cathedral which he now moved towards completion. He covered the roof of the nave with lead in place of Ingram de Lindsay's stone slabs, the revenue coming from the Brig o Don (Balgownie) fishings gifted to him by James IV. Next he tackled the great central tower, left incomplete since Kininmund II's time. John Fendour was called in again and a two-part contract was entered into on 18 April 1511. The first part was for the completion of the tower and the building of a lead-covered timber steeple, 'a sea mark', Orem called it, to surmount it. It was to be built according to Elphinstone's detailed specifications, and to be modelled on that of St John's Kirk in Perth which he admired. A battaline, a veranda in the style of a miniature battlement would encircle the base of the steeple whose height was to be 'as the Reverend Fadir will desire'. No nonsense about town planning regulations then. The work was to be carried out 'with all possible haist so that it may be completit and thekit betwix this and wyntir nixt following'.

An artist's impression of St Machar's Cathedral as it would have been at the end of Elphinstone's life, showing Lichtoun's caphouses, left, nave and porch centre, and Elphinstone's tower and steeple, and the south transept on the right.

Fendour was to be paid £88 18s in four instalments of £22 4s 6d, the last one payable when the finishing touches were added. This involved the 'upputting of the weddircok' again in the same style as St John's Kirk. The weathercock, as later described by Orem, was mounted on a stang (pole), five ells in length, with two crosses. A knop or knob, a great globe of brass, was placed above the first cross and above the second was a brass cock with a copper breast, an ell in length. This was a popular design. The original oak-covered spire of St Nicholas Kirk was similarly ornamented, though its weathercock was gilded. The second part of the contract was for the loft and belfry within the central tower, and for 'the hinging of the great bellis' there. There were three of them weighing 12,000 pounds, and their installation would not have been easy. But the design was practical, the need for width and space emphasised to allow for the hoisting of the bells and to provide easy access for the ringers. The fee here was £44 9s, again payable in instalments.

Elphinstone loved the sound of bells and the splendour of choral music within his cathedral and chapel. At St Machar's his twenty choral chaplains under John Malison, the master of music had to be experienced in Gregorian chant or plainsong, at the least, and if in descant, better still. His chapter now numbered twenty-nine, and the fourteenth century choir that Robert the Bruce had long ago badgered Bishop Henry de Cheyne into completing was inadequate to cope with the increased numbers of clergy. Moreover it may have looked a little shabby when compared with the splendid choir at St Nicholas Kirk. And so the bishop forged ahead with a new choir on a more extensive scale. 'No small part (of it) was finished before he departed this life', wrote Boece. The old choir was dismantled, though a fragment of it does survive.

Elphinstone's Constitutions of 1506 contain lengthy rules on the running of the cathedral. The sacrist had make sure that the bells were rung before five every morning, summer and winter, and that the vicars choral were in the choir at six, properly dressed and ready to sing matins. He was responsible for 'ruling' or regulating the clock and looking after the clergy's vestments and breviaries. He had to provide fire for kindling the candles of the high altar and fresh water for holy water and the baptismal font, probably drawn from St John's Well below the cathedral in what is now Seaton Park. One of his many responsibilities was the keeping of windows free 'from all blots' and the removal of 'all dust and mousewebs' from the walls four times a year, though the washing of altar cloths and the cleaning of brasses and the like could be delegated to an honest matron or young woman. Every Sabbath he washed the pavement 'from all rottenness' and cleared out drains and aqueducts. On Palm Sunday he had to provide palms, one wonders where from. He also earned an additional perk by 'keeping the cathedral so that doves and ravens come not in, as well in summer as in winter'.

Elphinstone was as practical as he was devout. He had acquired the timber, iron 'and all uther needful stuf' for the steeple and belfry, and for the building of the choir he selected skilful stonecutters, masons and artisans and collected great heaps of lime and stone and made other preparations on a great scale, says Boece. He had already seen to the quarrying of stone for King's College, and would initiate work on a bridge for the Dee, ingathering the materials required. As Boece put it:

> He was not wearied by all the works and labour nor by his daily employments, controversies, decisions, and consultations he undertook for the public good, but like the hundred-handed giant of the poets, turning in every direction, he performed splendid work in many different places.

By 1513 he was in his eighty-third year yet remained one of the great officers of state and a valued adviser of James IV. He had spoken out against the foolhardy policies which led to the king's defeat and death at Flodden along with the greater part of the nobility and the cream of the nation's young men. But he had been shouted down, 'by those', Boece wrote, 'who having had no experience of the horrors of war, thought war in theory desirable'. And he added; 'Never again was he seen to smile'. Called to Edinburgh to help pull the nation together, William Elphinstone died, worn down by the cares of state, just over a year after Flodden, on 25 October, 1514. 'Neither in a public nor in a private capacity did he ever live for himself but for his country and its welfare', wrote Boece in a fitting epitaph.

The Breviary, the Printing Press and Vaus's Voyage

When William Elphinstone became Bishop of Aberdeen in 1488, a form of service called the Sarum or Salisbury Use was followed in Scottish churches, though with local variations. This ritual had developed centuries earlier at Old Sarum, the cradle of Salisbury Cathedral, but the outbreak of the Wars of Independence in the late thirteenth century coupled with an increasing sense of national unity led to dissatisfaction with it. However time passed and no other form of service emerged to take its place. Elphinstone now took the initiative in creating a new prayer book, the Aberdeen Breviary, which gave the Scottish church a distinct identity and its 'ain Scottis use'. His clergymen travelled through the dioceses of Scotland, collecting material from numerous sources. The Breviary omitted some English and continental saints, replacing them with over eighty Scottish saints, and Northumbrian saints with Scottish connections. Many, like St Walloch, who 'preferred a poor little house woven together of reeds and wattles to a royal palace' were thus saved from oblivion.

The bishop was not content with having the Breviary compiled. He was determined, not only that it should be printed, and thus hold its own with imported breviaries like the Roman Breviary, but printed in Scotland where he would have the greater opportunity to inspect its progress. To this end he persuaded James IV to authorise the introduction of a press. The king saw the advantage not only in having all his subjects singing from the same hymn sheet but in having the Acts of the Scottish Parliament and law books for his lawyers printed as well. In his royal patent, granted under the privy seal in Edinburgh in 1507, the king commanded Walter Chepman, a wealthy Edinburgh merchant burgess and his associate, Androw Myllar,

B eatus vir
q non abiit
in cōsilio im
piorum: et in
via peccato
rū nō stetit
et in cathe
dra pestilentie non sedit.

An excerpt from the Aberdeen Breviary from 'Introduction of the Art of Printing into Scotland' by Robert Dickson, 1885.

a bookseller, to 'bring hame ane prent (printing press) with al stuf belangand thar and expert men to use the samyne'. At the same time James banned the sale of the Sarum Use in Scotland.

The Breviary, consisting of two volumes, the Pars Hyemalis and the Pars Æstiva was printed by 1510. The latter part ends: 'collected with special care and very great labour, by William, Bishop of Aberdeen, not only for his own church of Aberdeen, but also for general use of the whole church of Scotland'. Alas, the costliness of the new Breviary militated against its immediate adoption, and before it had time to come into its own, the Reformation had tolled the knell for popish prayer books ancient and modern. Only four copies survive, all imperfect, though a fine facsimile edition was produced in 1854.

Chepman and Myllar also printed tales of chivalry and romance, Blind Harry's famous epic, 'Wallace' and some poems of William Dunbar and Robert Henryson. After 1510 printing in Scotland virtually ceased until Thomas Davidson revived the art in 1530. That was the reason why John Vaus, grammarian at King's College, sailed in late 1521 or early 1522 for Dieppe. He bore with him certain manuscripts including Principal Boece's 'Lives of the Bishops', and a new edition of his own Latin grammar, the 'Rudimenta', first issued around 1507 and one of the earliest books to be printed in Scotland. Vaus had a dangerous voyage. The seas were patrolled by unfriendly English vessels and a great storm washed away passengers' baggage, though fortunately not the precious manuscripts. He made a safe landfall, and travelled to Paris where old friends from his university days introduced him to Josse Bade (Jodocus Badius), founder of the Ascension Press and one of the foremost printers of the age. Thus, after an adventurous journey, Boece's famous 'Lives' came to be printed. There is a neat little Latin paean by John Vaus in praise of Boece at its end:

> *'Perennial glory has been gained by thee, Hector Boece,*
> *Who in one book recordest so many great exploits…'*

This indicates that the translator, whose metres bring McGonagall to mind, pronounced Boece as 'Boyce' to rhyme with 'exploits'.

Setting up the type for Boece's 'Lives' would have caused Josse Bade no problem. The 'Rudimenta' was a different matter. 'Don't be surprised if you find mistakes', he writes at the end, explaining that he was 'Scoticae lingua imperitus', ignorant of the Scottish tongue.

Chapter 5

The Chapel

The Chapel of King's College, Aberdeen, is one of the most outstanding examples of medieval architecture and art in Scotland. Not only that, but it is the only college chapel in the whole of Great Britain which retains its original Gothic screen and canopied choir stalls.

King College Chapel, Aberdeen, F C Eeles, 1956.

It was on 21 October 1506, according to a document in the Aberdeen burgh records, that Provost Andrew Cullen, factor to Bishop Elphinstone, entered into contract with 'John Buruel an Englishman, and plumber to the King of England regarding the roofing of the church of the Bishop's new university'. Surprising though it sounds, it was quite in order to find the King of England's plumber on top of the chapel. James IV, who took great interest in the building of the college was son-in-law to Henry VII, and the plumber, from the Latin, *plumbum,* lead, was, to use the vernacular of the time, about to theik the roof with leid. Buruel undertook to find the fire and timber necessary for the work. The contract indicated that the chapel's completion was drawing near, and given its autumn date, Buruel would want to forge ahead before the winter storms began.

The chapel, sturdy, rectangular and curving to a three-sided apse at its east end, was consecrated on or about 10 October 1509 by Bishop Edward Stewart of Orkney who was in Aberdeen at that time. Those places inside and outside the chapel anointed with oil by Bishop Stewart and touched by his crosier during the ceremony, were later marked by consecration crosses. By tradition there should be twelve both inside and outside, representing the twelve apostles, and though interior crosses can sometimes be seen repainted flamboyantly on the walls of continental churches, original external consecration crosses are rare. At King's the surviving external crosses owe their preservation to the fact that they were incised into the stone. Any crosses cut on the south wall have vanished owing to later construction there, but in 1938 Dr William Kelly found five on the north wall, one in each bay, though he had difficulty in finding the most easterly. Traces of the five are still there, visible, but only just. The 'dettoun' or motto of the foundation inscription may have been completed in time for the dedication ceremony, and as Bishop Stewart solemnly processed around the chapel he must have been impressed by what he saw.

One of the five consecration crosses on the north side of the Chapel, before they became eroded.

The chapel was built of two different types of sandstone. For the lower courses, reddish stones were transported perhaps from Kildrummy in those carts ordered by Elphinstone from Andrew Halyburton. But before the walls were far up, writes Dr Kelly:

> the use of stone from this unknown quarry was abandoned, and much softer creamy-white stone from Covesea on the Moray Firth, was used. It weathers to a beautiful grey colour, and has proved to be far more durable than the hard red stone.

Dominating the north range of the chapel are the great windows. The fourth from the west, like the west window itself, round the corner, have massive central mullions and are round-headed; their companions are all pointed. They have suffered much over the years, blocking up, loss of glass, subsidence at the east end, destruction even. But they have survived or been reinstated, some original tracery remains, some has been restored and the powerful presence of the whole north range can best be appreciated from the neighbouring lawn where students now relax on sunny days. At a time when death stalked the land, even as small a college as King's had its own burying ground, 'the cemetery thereof', as noted in the Second Foundation, below this very lawn. Mourners would have made the short journey to the grave from the north door of the chapel.

The Chapel, right, from the quad. John Smith's Tudor frontage, running left from the Crown Tower, had replaced the principal's quarters by 1825.

The Chapel's north frontage, with the fleche on the roof and the round-headed window third from the left. The grassy area in the foreground was once the College graveyard.

One of the consecration crosses incised beside the north door, has above it a shield-niche that lies intriguingly empty. Above that again is the coat of arms of James IV's brother, also James, Duke of Ross and Archbishop of St Andrew's who died in 1504 while the chapel was being built. It is one of a unique royal family tableau of armorial panels. Round the corner on the west front, are the three shields which complete the tableau. The first belonging to James IV's queen, Margaret

The north door. Above the empty, canopied niche are the arms of the Duke of Ross, James IV's younger brother.

Tudor, is on the buttress beside the west door. It shows the impaled arms of Scotland, and the quartered arms of France and England, indicating England's claim to French throne. Its supporters, the Lancastrian hound and the Welsh dragon of Henry Tudor, can just be discerned. One learns from Ross Herald of Arms that it is the only complete surviving example in Scotland of the full heraldic achievement of Margaret Tudor. The magnificent arms of James IV on the neighbouring north buttress of the crown tower is the earliest carved example of the full armorial achievement of the royal arms. Inscribed with the year 1504, this is the only panel to be dated, though all are coeval. This is the least weathered of the shields. The south buttress bears the arms of Alexander Stewart, natural son of James and Marion Boyd, and a student of Erasmus's at Sienna. He succeeded his uncle as Archbishop of St Andrew's. He was a promising young man, but fell with his father at Flodden. His shield, like those of his uncle on the north wall has angel supporters who hold up the royal arms of Scotland.

The west door, where wedding guests now enter was the only access to the chapel for the people of Old Aberdeen and then only to the nave. An engraving, based on a seventeenth century painting of 'King's College as originally built by Bishop Elphinston', below, shows the crown tower and west front of the chapel open to the highway, but the rest of the college walled off on both sides. This served a dual purpose, displaying the college's most handsome architectural features to those travelling along the highway and providing an entrance for public worship which did not disrupt the seclusion of the college. Canon Galloway's visitation of 1549 specifically reinforced a ban on locals, or as his 'hit list' more disparagingly puts it, on *muliercule...rustici,* wifies and yokels, from entering the chapel through the interior gate. They must use the gate *ad extra,* on the outside.

Detail from 'King's College as originally built by Bishop Elphinston' with townsfolk entering the chapel via the gap in the dyke, left.

Bishop Edward Stewart would have seen the elegant

hexangonal flèche on his consecrational round, springing from the chapel roof, roughly marking the interior division between nave and choir. One wonders if he went into raptures as the writer Francis Douglas did during his visit of 1780. 'I went to some distance and enjoyed the prospect of it for a good while,' he enthused. 'Come and see it.' It was thought for a time that the flèche was a later addition, but Dr Kelly ascertained that its oak timbers date from the early sixteenth century, making it of an age with the chapel. It was largely rebuilt in the seventeenth century.

The fleche.

Apart from a battlemented stone parapet matching that of the tower and shown on Parson Gordon's vignette, (page 66), the chapel's south flank, which one views from the quad, was plainer in those early days than at any other time in its history. The small library range, abutting the south wall, shown by Gordon, had not yet been built, but space had been reserved. This explains the presence of the high clerestorey windows below which the library building would slot. There was a solitary great window at the east end, designed to sit beyond the library. Because of the anticipated library range it is unlikely that any exits were placed in this south façade. The north or graveyard door would have been the main entrance for members of the university.

Inside the chapel, a part of Elphinstone's legacy still remains, and Boece's own account in the *Lives of the Bishops* and the Strachan Inventory of 1542 allow us to imagine how it looked in his day. 'All the church windows', according to Parson Gordon, 'wer of paynted glas; and ther remayns as yit a pairt of that ancient bravery.' Today only two fragments of 'that ancient bravery', the original stained glass, remain. The present west window, dating from 1875 is to the left as you enter the chapel from the quad by the south-west door. And there, amid the bright, flowing nineteenth century angelic host of the high tracery are the two surviving pieces of 'paynted glas', tiny, deep golden daisies. Are these marguerites or marigolds in honour of Margaret Tudor who married James IV in 1503?

The internal dimensions of the chapel are just over 122 ft (38m) by 29 ft (9m) spacious one might think for the original university of thirty-six members. But their place of worship was the choir in the east half. The nave, the people's area, in the west half and was larger than one might have expected in a collegiate church. But remembering the First Foundation's dictum, that the principal 'preach the Word of God to the people' six times a year, it is clear that a good turnout of the folk of Old Aberdeen was anticipated on these occasions.

Two fragments of the original stained glass, depicting deep golden daisies, survive.

The nave was terminated at its east end by a great wooden rood screen, rood being the old word for a cross, running from wall to wall, elaborately carved, bisecting the chapel, separating nave from the choir beyond. The screen had a carved central door with two altars, the gift of Bishop Elphinstone, on either side of it. The north altar was in honour of the Virgin Mary, the south was dedicated to St Germain. Revenues from the East Lothian hospital named in the saint's honour helped to fund the university at its inception. The nave was otherwise bare, but if the screen door were open, worshippers could have keeked though and seen the choir and the high altar beyond.

Above the door, where these days the organ pipes look frozen at the point of blast off, was a rood loft of some depth, with galleries on either side, bounded by a handsomely carved balustrade in whose niches were statues of Christ and the twelve apostles, and at whose centre an ambo or reading desk was incorporated. It was from here that the sermon in Scots was preached to the folk standing in the nave below while the gospel and epistle were read from ambones placed on either side. Behind the central ambo, the holy rood itself towered, a great crucifix, with statues of St Mary and St John on either side and an altar and a painting of the crucifixion, the gift of John Vaus, the grammarian, nearby. Mass was celebrated in the rood loft on occasion, and the host (the consecrated wafer of the eucharist) displayed in a monstrance for the people below to venerate. The loft was also home to the chapel's original organ which was decorated with a painting of the Virgin Mary. Near roof level, an elegant and richly carved canopy stretched over loft and galleries, the central section raised to accommodate the great crucifix. After the library range abutting the south wall had gone up,

The nave as it might have looked at the time of the 1542 Inventory. The door faintly seen to the right is the one we enter by today. The carved door of the rood screen is open, showing a glimpse of the high altar. To the left of the carved door is the altar to the Virgin Mary, on the right, that of St Germain. Above the door is the carved balustrade of the rood loft with the ambo from which the sermon was delivered placed centrally. Above it are statues of St Mary and St John, the altar and the crucifix. The organ is to the left, with the carved canopy almost at roof level. From 'The Chapel and Ancient Buildings of King's College' by Norman Macpherson, 1890.

students could enter the chapel by a little door there which led through to the rood loft, whence a spiral staircase inside the screen took them down into the chapel. For young lads, this was probably the most interesting way of arriving for their devotions. The outline of the little door can still be seen high on the south side of the chapel wall.

Though the folk of Old Aberdeen were confined to the nave, they shared with the masters and students in the choir, the glories of the timber wagon ceiling. Like that of the Great Hall it is attributed to master wright John Fendour and would have been put in place some time after 1506, when the roof was completed. And like Fendour's new ceiling in the St Nicholas choir in Aberdeen, the embellishment of the chapel ceiling echoes that of

John Fendour: The Enigmatic Fleming

John Fendour, a skilled master carpenter and wood carver, thought to be of Flemish origin is first mentioned in the Aberdeen Council Register in 1495 where he appears as Johne Ferdour (and sometimes as Findour or Findon). He entered into a contract with the magistrates on 10 April of that year 'for the making of the ruff and tymmir of the queyr' (the roof and timber work of the choir) of St Nicholas Kirk. Bishop Elphinstone, as prebendary of St Nicholas, was much involved in this project, and given his continental contacts and ambitious building programme it may have been he who recruited Fendour from the Low Countries. Not to be outdone by the bishop's generosity in restoring the second teinds, 'certaine personis of thar ain fre wil', according to the Council Register, in effect the leading burgesses, raised £62 5s 4d to pay Fendour. By 1498 Fendour's work was finished for the time being, and that September Elphinstone carried out the dedication ceremony.

The interior of the East Church of St Nicholas, formerly the choir of St Nicholas Kirk .

Fendour and his men next reported at the site of Elphinstone's new college to work on the Great Hall and Chapel ceilings and to carve the Chapel stalls ready for assembly. While still busy at King's, he entered into a further contract with the Town Council on 26 December 1507: 'Johne sall, God willing, big, oupmak and finally end and complet the thirty-four stalls in thair queir with the spiris and the chanslar dur'. The work was to be completed by Michaelmas, 29 September 1508 at the latest. Fendour was to be paid £200 Scots and 'ane bontay' was on offer. According to inscriptions on a cornice, work on the ceiling of St Nicholas continued in 1510 and 1517.

In 1511 he was back in Old Aberdeen building the central steeple and belfry of St Machar's, and may have worked on Elphinstone's new choir. Boece records that the bishop had rounded up the top tradesmen but his death in 1514 curtailed the work. By 1519 the heraldic ceiling of St Machar's Cathedral was underway. The carpentry was carried out by a mystery man, James Winter from Angus according to Orem who did not always get names right. Dr Kelly assumes that Winter was Fendour. The pronunciation of the names is not dissimilar and the carpentry of the great ceiling indicates the master's hand. Having built the St Machar's belfry, Fendour may also have been involved in the final stages of the King's belfry (the Crown Tower) when the great bells finally arrived around 1520 .

Fendour's work in King's College Chapel has survived. Elsewhere he has not been so fortunate. The Great Hall was demolished in 1860. A finely carved wooden panel, thought to be by Fendour, was salvaged and later placed on the north wall of the Chapel. Below a gothic canopy of vine leaves resembling those in the Chapel are Elphinstone's arms, embraced by climbing lilies, symbolic of the Virgin. In 1835 the East Kirk of St Nicholas as the choir of St Nicholas Kirk had become, was demolished but a contemporary drawing shows that the ceiling was almost identical to that of the chapel. It is likely that Fendour used the same ceiling design for Chapel, Hall and Kirk. After the Reformation his stalls in St Nicholas Kirk were removed and Matthew Guild, 'sweird slipper' or armourer of the Hammermen's Corporation, used some of the wood for a handsome chair which he presented to the Seven Incorporated Trades. Panels from these stalls were also used in the fine provosts' desks and seats in St Mary's Chapel, the undercroft of St Nicholas Kirk, now a Third World Centre. Additionally, four canopy panels from St Nicholas Kirk are now in the Museum of Scotland.

Provost's desk and seat at St Mary's Chapel. The panels are similar to those at the base of the chapel screen, page 95.

The Fendour panel from the Great Hall, now in the Chapel.

quadripartite stone vaulting with the ribs following the same pattern. The ornate spokes of formalised carved foliage look like giant snow crystals radiating from the central bosses in alternating patterns of four and eight.

On the other side of rood screen was the choir, with its magnificent stalls, Flemish in style, companion pieces for the screen. The Second Foundation provided for forty-two endowed members of the college but Elphinstone commissioned fifty-two stalls, fifteen upper and eleven lower stalls on both sides of the chapel. Three of the upper stalls on both sides formed 'returns' at the west end. The principal and subprincipal sat on the south side here, the grammarian and canonist on the north, all facing east and doubtless keeping an eye on the choristers and arts students ranged in the 'front stalls'. A strict order of seating was laid down by Elphinstone and robing-up in the appropriate hood and gown, a *sine qua non* that is emphasised in the First Foundation, is stressed even more firmly in the Second, where students are also enjoined to appear in 'decent clean surplices'. A few dirty ones must have been sighted! That, coupled with the fact that the principal is instructed to ensure that divine service was celebrated without chattering, indicates these boys were no more saintly than their counterparts outside. The lower stalls also included two 'returns', on either side, directly below the stalls of the dignitaries, small stalls perhaps reserved for especially small and/or naughty boys.

Though the bishop was allowing for the expansion of his university and utilising the skills of the craftsmen when he had them on site, there would have been occupants for these surplus stalls, even from the early days. The Second Foundation notes, for example 'two poor scholars studying grammar until they be promoted in the arts'. These were not choristers for they had to say, or perhaps intone the psalm *De Profundis* for departed souls in the chapel every Sunday on receipt of certain monies. (The Latin *dicere* to speak is specifically used in the Foundation instead of the usual *cantare* to sing). Whatever way they did it, it must have been something of an ordeal for the two lads. They seem to have formed a pre-university 'crammer' group, having their Latin grammar polished until it shone brightly enough to allow them to embark on the arts course. The rich students, also mentioned in the Second Foundation would have required stalls, while last but not least, visiting dignitaries such as the consecrating bishop and his retinue, the rector and the chancellor himself would also have to be accommodated on an *ad hoc* basis.

The stalls, like the rood screen, are rare examples of late medieval craftsmanship and again are thought to be the work of John Fendour and his men. Just as the plumber would have a bothy where he prepared his lead, the wrights likely had a shed where they carved the stalls before bringing them into the chapel for the finishing touches. The stalls would have been

The carved choir stalls, canopy and rood screen, drawn by R W Billings in the 1840s.

set in position sometime between the roofing of the chapel in late 1506 and its consecration three years later. Apart from the end stalls, each robust and amply made stall shares arm rests with its neighbour, moulded on the edges and curving up to form a decorated band along the top of the seat. These carved pieces differ in detail from stall to stall. It is as if each craftsman had been given a general notion of what was required, then went off to carve his section in his own style. The decorated bands, in a 'vignette' or trailing pattern, have an autumnal theme of leaves, tendrils, elongated acorns, flourishing thistles and giant brambles, though the latter are said to be bunches of grapes. The wrights may have been uncertain as to how the latter actually looked and carved what they knew. The magnificent wood carving of the stall ends depicts miniature Gothic windows called fenestrated panels. The tracery is rich and each is different from the next. Two upper stall ends have 'trails' of almost identical thistles, but with differing leaves. One of these on the south side also has a pattern of fleurs-de-lis on its lower half, the two sections together symbolising the Auld Alliance .

Stall end, showing the thistle pattern.

The stall seats were designed to turn up, rather like those in the cinema, not to let others pass for there is plenty of leg room, but to provide support for infirm clergy during lengthy parts of the service when it was necessary to stand. The underside of each seat had a carved wooden panel, a misericord, from the Latin *misericordia:* compassion. It was visible when the seat was raised and terminated in a lip at the top. Seven misericords have survived, all in the 'front stalls', three on the north side and four on the south. Vine leaves and accompanying grapes (or brambles) are a popular theme, though two have thistles and roses in honour of the recent

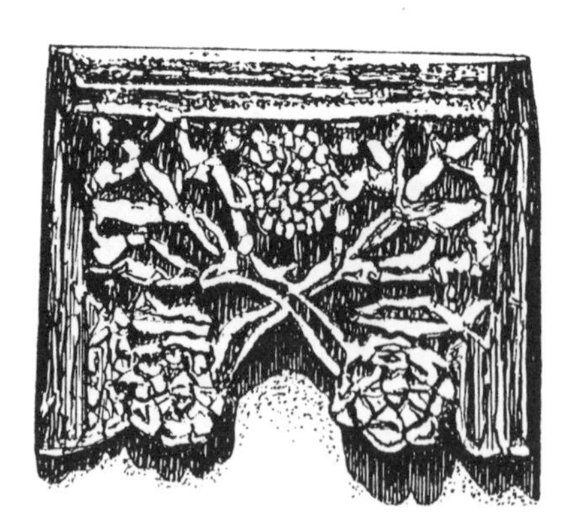

Misericord, King's College Chapel.

Stewart-Tudor marriage, which William Dunbar had celebrated in his poem *The Thrissel and the Rose.* One misericord on the south side has a crown (non-imperial), and its neighbour, the sacred monogram IHS, the first three letters of the Greek ΙΗΣΟΥΣ, Jesus.

The upper stalls once had richly ornamented back linings, but these have not survived. Above them delicate, filigree, lacy canopies remain, among the chapel's crowning glories, stretching in a continuous screen with crocketted pinnacles pointing heaven-wards. In 1846 the artist R W Billings wrote :

> The great glory of King's chapel is the wood-work of its chapel. Its main features are a double row of canopied stalls and a lofty open screen...The carving throughout is of the most gorgeous and delicate kind, and is as clean and sharp as if it were fresh from the knife...There is no wood-work in Scotland capable of a moment's comparison with the stalls of King's College nor will many English specimens rival them. Such productions are chiefly to be seen in the Flemish churches.

Strachan's Inventory of 1542 reveals a choir glowing with colour, as ornate as the nave was plain, with statues, paintings, magnificently wrought brazen chairs and ambones, altar hangings, crucifixes, lamps, gold and silver vessels, monstrances, chalices, sensers, spoons, candlesticks, 'a casket of cypress-wood set with pearls...' Most of these treasures had been gifted by Bishop Elphinstone and his kinsmen, by Principal Boece, his brother Arthur, by John Vaus, by church dignitaries and Aberdeen burgesses. Many of the sumptuous vestments were also gifts, copes, chasubles, dalmatics, tunicles, maniples, albes, orphreys, amices, stoles and apparels, different sets of these vestments for different altars, changing their

A chaplain of the sixteenth century in eucharist vestments.
a. The apparel, embroidered cloth at neck and foot.
b. The stole.
c. The maniple, a little stole worn over the left arm.
d. The chasuble, a large oval cloak, made of silk.
e. The albe, a long linen garment.

colour according to the Christian calendar or the rites being performed. Orphreys, richly embroidered border work, were woven in gold and silk with the images of saints in needlework or in red wool silk, scattered over with gold stars. The choristers who carried the tapers in procession wore 'blue tunicles of palmate silk with shining orphreys'.

The high altar was dedicated to the patron saint of the college, St Mary in the Nativity. Hung around it were four large curtains, each of nineteen square ells, Scots measure, 'made of soft wool mixed with silk thread in which the King's arms as well as those of the Founder are woven, with a variety of flowers'. Four brass columns supported the curtain rods, surmounted by four angels, with ten brass candlesticks above. On the north side of the high altar, Canon Alexander Galloway whose gifts to the chapel were 'many and costly' had designed the Altar of the Venerable Sacrament where the host was kept in a sacrament house, 'pyramidal in shape'. Galloway excelled in the design of sacrament houses, and a number survive in the North East, though much weathered, including one at his own church of Kinkell. Principal Hector Boece bequeathed funds for a third altar in the sanctuary, on the south side, opposite Galloway's, dedicated to St Catherine. The flat, 'table' slab of one of these pre-Reformation altars survives. Its story is told on pages 166-167.

The hangings of these altars must have been superb; one, for example, was of *attrabaceum*, tapestry from Arras. The carpet covering the pavement before the high altar was interwoven with flowers and Bishop Elphinstone's arms. Other soft furnishings included five cushions for some lucky people, 'the fifth being of soft wool and silk woven with the lamb of the altar'. One small piece of arras cloth was 'woven with coneys', which sounds like an example of verdure work, with foliage and flowers and little rabbits disappearing into their burrows.

Two small corbel stones set into the wall of the sanctuary, marking the parameters of the high altar, can still be seen. That on the north side has a carved M for the Virgin Mary, the other, on the south, has oak leaves for St Catherine whose altar was nearby. They were used as pedestals for small statues, but during Lent, they would have supported the veil screening the high altar.

One of the two surviving corbels. The M is in honour of the Virgin Mary.

Elphinstone believed that the singing in the choir, both in the

'A man skilled in organ playing'. A chorister works the bellows.
A medieval organ, from a fifteenth century manuscript.

chapel and at St Machar's should rival the magnificence of the buildings themselves. His First Foundation of 1505 appointed eight chaplains who had to be well versed in Gregorian chant, as well as 'priksinging,' figuration and 'farburdon' that is the more elaborate polyphonic styles with descant. One chaplain had to be 'skilled in organ playing'. He received two merks in addition to the basic annual stipend of sixteen merks, £10 13s 4d. Initially the chaplains had to provide their own surplices, long gowns, gathered at the neck, and their black furred hoods, in winter, but the Second Foundation gave a clothing allowance of half a merk, 6s 8d. The chaplains were encouraged to take part in the academic life of the college, 'to study in any of the foresaid faculties'.

The cantor, who fulfilled the same role as the precentor at St Machar's, was responsible for the music to be sung and the training of the choristers, for punishing those who were not singing correctly and noting those absent from divine service. The sacrist was second in command and the Second Foundation sets out his duties in detail. He marshalled the processions, looked after the vessels, the candles and books, polished the brasses and cleaned the entire chapel. Like his opposite number at St Machar's he had the 'control and keeping of the clock, for which he is to find olive oil at his own charges'. The sacrist, like the cantor, received twenty merks yearly, with an additional twenty shillings for his cleaning duties. He also received an additional half merk annually for washing the altar cloths, the albes, long white garments with narrow sleeves tied with a girdle, the amices (hoods), and 'other similar raiment', all of them of linen, 'at least four times in the year'. One wonders where he put up his washing line. Both cantor and sacrist received one merk, 13s 4d, above their salaries for outlay on their personal vestments, surplice, furred hood and almuce, which was a cape, either of fur or fur-lined, essential against the cold of the chapel in winter.

Elphinstone had planned that the ringing of bells would mark the opening and closing of the college and the chapel services. In the Second Foundation the strongest choir boy was to help the sacrist ring the bells for an additional two merks annually. The later Foundation was usually more generous than the First but it had increased the number of choristers, 'youths or poor boys' who had promising voices, from four to six, and to balance the books, reduced their bursaries from five merks, £3 6s 8d, to four merks, £2 13s 4d. The extra two merks would have been a useful perk.

Beginning at six o'clock, the chaplains and choristers of the college sang Matins and Lauds. High mass was celebrated, and in the early afternoon Vespers were sung. The day concluded with Compline, evening prayers and the singing of the *Salve Regina* at which the presence of all those in residence was required. Chapel attendance both for masters and students was normally less demanding than that of the choir, allowing long uninterrupted spells for teaching and studying. On major feast days a more elaborate ritual was celebrated, the whole cycle of the *horae canonica* sung and more frequent attendances of the 'full house' were required. This all may seem curious to the modern, non-Catholic reader, but faith was central to medieval society and the Foundation Bull emphasised that the university was founded for the glory of God as well as the advancement of learning. To quote from the Bull:

> that the realm may be adorned with the gifts of science; that the university may produce men eminent for their ripe judgement, crowned with the graces of virtue, and learned in the teachings of the various faculties: and that there may be therein a cool fountain of whose fullness all the faithful in Christ may drink, streaming thither from every quarter in their desire to be adorned with learning and virtue.

One can see in the mind's eye, a fleeting glimpse of medieval life, a procession of choristers, some bearing tapers, chaplains, scholars and masters, moving slowly towards the chapel in their distinctive garb, summoned by the insistent ringing of the bells and the peal of the organ from the rood loft.

After Elphinstone's death in October 1514, his embalmed body was taken from Edinburgh to King's College Chapel, 'and was buried before the chief altar' writes Boece, who was there, 'with a pomp more mournful than magnificent'.

Chapter 6

Gavin Dunbar
The last great medieval Bishop

All that time that he lived Bishop, which was thirteen years, whatsoever profit or commodity he made by the Church, he bestowed it wholly upon the poor and such publick works, without applying a farthing either to his own use or the enriching of any of his kinsmen.

John Spottiswoode, History of the Church of Scotland, 1655.

In theory the chapter of St Machar's Cathedral elected a new bishop; in fact the canons voted for the favoured candidate of the pope and by the fifteenth century, of the crown. Two strong candidates were in contention for the Bishopric of Aberdeen after Elphinstone's death in 1514. One, the civilist, James Ogilvie, at that time on an embassy to Louis XII of France, was the nominee of the Regent of Scotland; the other, James Forman, Dean of Glasgow, had, somewhat precipitately, already been declared bishop by the pope. However, the mighty Alexander Gordon, third Earl of Huntly, who had commanded the left wing at Flodden and survived, arrived unannounced at a meeting of the canons where the matter was being discussed, and foisted an aged and ailing relative, also Alexander Gordon, on the diocese. Huntly's argument was that in these troubled times it was advisable to have someone at the helm who had powerful friends. Few in Scotland were more powerful than the Earl of Huntly. A few years earlier, acting on James IV's behalf, he had defeated the turbulent warlords of the Western Isles and been handsomely rewarded with high office and vast lands in the Highlands and the North East.

Bishop Alexander Gordon, more suited for St Peter's Hospital for infirm brethren in the Spital, had it been functioning as such, than the control of a widespread diocese and a fledgling university at a time of national crisis, promptly went into a terminal decline, and things rapidly fell apart. Three years later, in 1518, Boece wrote with an almost audible sigh of relief, 'at last Bishop Alexander died'. His description of the arrival of the able and progressive Bishop Gavin Dunbar in Old Aberdeen is one of the most memorable passages in *The Lives of the Bishop:*

> The citizens went out to meet him, by way of honour, along with every nobleman who lived in the neighbourhood...Bells were rung, fifes and trumpets played. He was met by a procession of monks, canons and priests arrayed in costly sacred vestments. There followed the Rector of the College with a great procession of learned men. Whenever he entered a church he was greeted with sweet harmony of voice and organ. The walls glowed with rich tapestries, the floors were covered with carpets, clouds of fragrance were shed from censers.

This portrait of Dunbar, in the ownership of Aberdeen University, is an eighteenth century copy of an original that has vanished. W Douglas Simpson has written: 'The quality of the face by no means suggests the keen, high-souled and powerful prelate that we know Dunbar to have been'.

Gavin Dunbar was born around 1455, his father the son of a Dunbar Earl of Moray, his mother a Sutherland of Duffus. Nor was he the only high-ranking cleric in this distinguished family. In 1524 when he was Bishop of Aberdeen, his nephew and namesake pulled ahead, becoming Archbishop of Glasgow and Chancellor of Scotland. Our Dunbar, who graduated Master of Arts from St Andrew's University in 1475, was Dean of Moray by 1487. As a diplomat and statesman, he was almost in the Elphinstone class, and like the late bishop, held his spiritual appointments concurrently with a number of temporal offices and *ad hoc* embassies. In 1498, 'Master Gawan Dunbar, dene of Moray', was sent as commissioner to Philip, Archduke of Austria to query the issuing of letters of marque against Scottish shipping. This has a touch of Shakespeare's 'sea coast of Bohemia' for the Archduke of Austria might not seem the most suitable person to be licensing privateers. However Archduke Philip had inherited the Dukedom of Burgundy and its considerable possessions in the Netherlands and relations between Scotland and the House of Burgundy were at that time at a low ebb. Dunbar was accompanied on this embassy by David Seton, parson of Fettercairn, with Sir Thomas Tod, provost of Edinburgh and Sir John Rutherford, provost of Aberdeen, representing the royal burghs.

In 1501 Dunbar was appointed privy councillor and Lord Clerk of Register, the latter a high ranking and financially rewarding position that provided automatic membership of the King's Council. As Lord Clerk he drafted legislation, ruled on disputes and was involved in negotiating the marriage contract of James IV and Margaret Tudor, daughter of Henry VII, in 1502. Four years later he became Archdeacon of St Andrews, and in 1512, as Master of the Rolls, was involved in the negotiation of a renewal of the Auld Alliance, on this occasion the ill-fated agreement between James IV and Louis XII of France, which ultimately led to the national disaster of Flodden field. A few years later he was one of the Scottish commissioners who concluded a truce with England at Coldingham Priory. Two of the letters that he wrote on state business with England are still extant, one to Henry VIII who succeeded his father Henry VII in 1509, the other to Cardinal Wolsey.

Of Dunbar, the bishop, as opposed to Dunbar, the statesman, John Leslie, Bishop of Ross, wrote in his *History of Scotland:*

> what he gathered of the bishopric, ilk pennie he spendit upon those three, the kirk, the countrie and the poor, and put not one farthing to any private use or to the profit of his own.

Much the same had been written of Elphinstone. That bishop had drafted his Second Foundation, his 'Mark II' constitution for King's College towards the end of his life. It was en route to Rome for authorisation by the pope when Elphinstone died in 1514. The whole process came to a halt, and a new start had to be made by Bishop Dunbar who oversaw its confirmation by King James V and Pope Clement VII. This was a protracted business, but the Second Foundation was eventually published on 18 December 1529.

Bishop Dunbar's seal attached to the instrument confirming, in 1529, Bishop Elphinstone's Second Foundation of King's College. Dunbar's coat of arms with its three cushions is at the lower end.

The choir of King's College Chapel in 1542. Bishop Elphinstone's tomb, the gift of Bishop Dunbar, is placed centrally, at the edge of the sanctuary, with the high altar and its angels beyond. The little corbels which still survive can be made out, on either side, where the curving apse begins. The choir stalls and their canopies are further to the east than they are today. The magnificent ceiling is unchanged. From 'The Chapel and Ancient Buildings of King's College' by Norman Macpherson, 1890.

Immediately on his arrival in Old Aberdeen in 1519 Dunbar had undertaken a tour of inspection of the still unfinished King's College where morale understandably was low. Of Elphinstone he said, 'Wherever I turn my steps, my mind thinks of him, my eyes miss his well known figure'. He visited the bishop's last resting place before the high altar in the chapel, covered with the carpet that was woven with Bishop Elphinstone's arms and the lilies of Old Aberdeen, but which otherwise was bare. Dunbar was 'filled with pity and indignation', says Boece, 'that the remains of so great a man should be neglected, without a name or any monument to celebrate one whose fame extends over a great part of the world'. He later erected a tomb of black marble at the foot of the sanctuary steps, with a jewelled recumbent effigy of Bishop Elphinstone surrounded by thirteen brazen figures and angels bearing candelabra. This sumptuous sepulchre was later vandalised, but the black marble tomb remains.

The condition of the Bishop's Palace was another problem. On his arrival in Old Aberdeen, Dunbar instructed his factor, Alexander Lawson, to make on inventory of everything that had been left there. His predecessor, the decrepit Bishop Alexander Gordon had not taken up residence, and the lodging where Elphinstone had enjoyed good company and fine sweetmeats had gone to rack and ruin. He had bequeathed his furniture to help pay for the completion of King's College, and hopefully some of it had gone towards that purpose for everything that remained was in a dire state. In the wardrobe were five pairs of torn sheets, seven large and small pillows, their ticking torn, two pairs of fustian blankets 'riven by rats', and nine feather beds, either patched, torn or full of holes. Two old arras beds were 'evil riven', though the great four-poster with the king's arms was intact, as were two arras cushions sewn with Elphinstone's arms. A few desks and settles had survived unscathed and some of the woodwork remained sound. But much was broken or missing and in the great chamber desks and chandeliers had been smashed. In the kitchen were many broken pots and pans and the pantry was a sad sight. Two towels of linen bearing Elphinstone's motto, *non confundar*, I will not be confounded, lay torn. Finally, the south-west tower contained 'ane ald rottin standand bed without ane heid'. Lawson's disgust is discernible. Presumably Dunbar would have lost little time in having the palace refurbished .

At his death, Elphinstone according to Boece, had ten thousand pounds in his coffers and many valuable personal effects. In addition to his furniture he had bequeathed his gold and silver for the completion of King's and for his new Bridge of Dee project. Those to whom Elphinstone had entrusted his legacy were reluctant to release any part of it, arguing that the troubled times militated against such action. Dunbar demanded the funds and his call did not fall on deaf ears. The bishop himself gave generously and at King's College he completed the residential quarters which Elphinstone had planned to form the south range of the quadrangle. This, according to Orem if no one else, gave rise to a spat with Boece. To commemorate his personal largesse, Dunbar wished to grace this wing with his own coat of arms, three plump red cushions set within the royal tressure of Scotland of which he appears to have been very proud. Boece would have none of it, maintaining that the credit belonged to Elphinstone alone. Dunbar retaliated or so Orem maintained; these chambers, he 'caused build up roughly without good workmanship or contrivance'. The illustration from Parson Gordon's vignette, (page 66), shows that the windows, looking across the college garden to College Bounds were higgeldy-piggeldy perhaps indicating irregular floor levels. But Dunbar may well have been innocent of such petty behaviour. The problem could have been the same as that which affected the east end of the chapel. A patch of marshland, subsidence and in this instance, no 'great rafters of oake' in place to shore up the building. This south range was the nearest to the Powis Burn and the boggy land around it. But time has resolved all differences. The shields of Dunbar, of Boece and of Elphinstone himself shine forth from the chapel, directly opposite. Of the round towers flanking the residential wing, one or perhaps both were added by Dunbar who capped them with wooden spires. Elphinstone left several projects unfinished, among them the crown tower and at least one of the external manses which Dunbar completed.

There was no doubt about whose coat of arms would appear on the Chaplains' Court. Dunbar, consolidating the reforms made by Elphinstone to improve standards of worship at the cathedral, had increased the number of vicars choral. In the early days they had lodged with the canons for whom they deputised, but around 1519 Dunbar built 'ane fair palice for the lugeing of all the small prebendaris callit the chaplains of the said kirk' at the east end of the Chanonry, near the junction with the Seatongate. The Chaplains' Court, where the vicars shared a common table, was built round a square courtyard with towers and a well in the centre, (see plan page 37 marked 2). A roll-moulded arched pend, the entrance embellished with Dunbar's coat-of-arms, gave cart access to the courtyard and an underground passage led to the Bishop's Palace and thence into the cathedral. The Chanonry's fourth port, the Chaplains' Port, beside the Court, was built by 1540, across the east end of the Chanonry at the junction with the Seatongate.

To St Machar's Cathedral Dunbar gifted the most sumptuous artefacts and vestments, among them a pure gold chalice with diamonds and rubies, a great silver eucharist, a holy water font with a pedestal of silver, a silver crucifix and a manuscript of the evangelists, of which one side was silver gilt. All were engraved with his arms. An inventory of Dunbar's gifts to the cathedral is recorded in the *Epistolare* which Dr W Douglas Simpson described as 'one of the most precious service books in the pre-Reformation Church'. It was written in Antwerp on Dunbar's instructions and completed by 1527. Now one of the treasures of Aberdeen University Library, its vellum leaves are still in their original binding, covered with leather and securely held in bands of brass. We also owe St Machar's best known features, the twin spires and the heraldic ceiling to Bishop Dunbar. He removed Lichtoun's caphouses, replacing them with the familiar rotund spires, which rise from the battlemented parapets of the twin towers. The spires, built of his native Moray sandstone, provided a more suitably ecclesiastical complement to Elphinstone's great tower and spire.

Dunbar's heraldic ceiling is unique. Many years before, Bishop Ingram de Lindsay had inlaid the roof of the nave with fir which must have cried

'One of the most precious books in the pre-Reformation Church'. A page from Dunbar's 'Epistolare', describing Bishop de Lindsay's work at St Machar's: 'he put a stone roof on the cathedral and laid its pavement...' From the Third Spalding Club Miscellany, Volume 1, 1935.

out to Dunbar for embellishment. Painted ceilings at this time were becoming high fashion in Europe, in castles, palaces, cathedrals, churches, in the libraries of early universities and the town houses of rich merchants. Decor varied from Biblical and mythological subjects to monarchs, fabulous beasts and heraldic devices. Though one might guess that Dunbar would chose the latter, two things set the St Machar's ceiling apart. Firstly, while ceiling embellishment was usually one dimensional, painted straight onto the ceiling in tempera, (egg yoke and water), the heraldic shields of St Machar's are carved in low relief, raised a little from their bosses. In Latin this type of work is called *caelatura,* the word which Boece uses. Secondly, most painted ceilings were primarily decorative, with no ulterior motive other than to show off the good taste, wealth and importance of their owners. Dunbar's ceiling on the other hand makes a political statement. The shields march in an array that declares the independence of the King of Scots and the Scottish church.

Work on the ceiling must have started soon after Dunbar was consecrated bishop in 1519. Perhaps Ingram de Lindsay's inlaid ceiling was replaced, though Boece's use of the word *caelatura,* and he was there when work was in progress, suggests that Dunbar was responsible only for the heraldic embellishment. Whatever ceiling was used, new or old, it was divided it into squares by raised mouldings. Within each square are matching mouldings in the shape of the cross of St Andrew, and in the centre of each, decorative cruciform shapes, reminiscent of the ornate, crystal-like spokes crafted by Fendour for the ceiling of King's College Chapel. The shields themselves are fixed at the intersections of the square

Above, an artist's impression of St Machar's Cathedral as it was in Dunbar's time. Elphinstone's central tower and spire, the south transept below and the choir, extreme right, have now all gone. On the left, Dunbar's twin towers, with Lichtoun's west window between them, the nave, south aisle and porch have survived.
Right, all that remains today.

mouldings in three parallel rows, sixteen shields in each. It has been speculated that, apart from Dunbar himself, Canon Alexander Galloway worked on the design, while the demanding task of implementing it fell, according to Orem, to a master carpenter from Angus, James Winter, who may or may not have been John Fendour.

Progress was fast and completion was probably sometime in 1521. One of several clues to the date is that the papal heraldry shown is that of Leo X who died in 1521, though news of his death would have taken time to reach Scotland. Then the arms of the Archbishop of Glasgow are those of James Beaton who was translated to St Andrew's in 1522 so his 'Glaswegian' shield must have been in place before that date. A third clue is found in Boece's *Lives of the Bishops,* where he says that the great part of the ceiling had been completed 'with wonderful skill'. The *Lives* was printed in 1522, but obviously completed some time before that. This ties in with the presentation of a propine or gift by Aberdeen Town Council to Dunbar in 1522 when he arrived in Old Aberdeen to take up his period of residence.

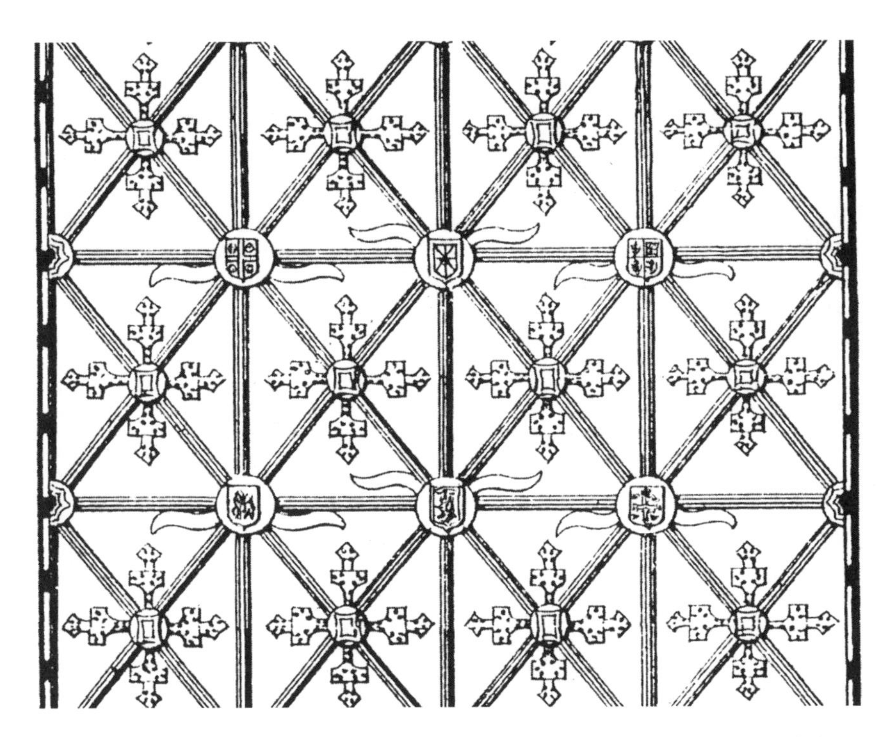

A detail from St Machar's ceiling showing its superb craftsmanship. It was divided into squares by raised mouldings within which were similar mouldings in the shape of a St Andrew's cross. In the centre of each were ornate crosses. The heraldic shields were fixed at the intersections of the square mouldings. Adapted from 'The Heraldic Ceiling of St Machar's' by W D Geddes and Peter Duguid, Spalding Club, 1888.

It consisted of wax (for candles) and 'xii bostis of skorcheatis' (twelve lots of sweetmeats), the latter included 'becaus there is na guyd wynnis now to send to his lordschip'. This gift possibly marked the completion of the ceiling though it seems rather niggardly in comparison with the propine sent by the magistrates to the Bishop's Palace in 1508, probably to mark Bishop Elphinstone's benefactions at St Nicholas Kirk. He was presented with two large casks of wine, delivery charge four shillings, wax crafted into candles and tapers, sweetmeats, one gallon claret, half a gallon Malmsey and half a gallon white wine. Total cost, £16 3s 8d. A visit well-timed for the availability of the 'guyd wynnis'.

But to return to St Machar's, the choice of shields on the ceiling was governed by the heraldic knowledge available to Bishop Dunbar and Canon Galloway at that time and explains a number of errors and eccentricities in the selection, as discussed in *The Message of the Shields,* pages112-113.

Bishop and canon would have been familiar with the arms of the ecclesiastical grandees and the Scottish king and nobility. But what sources could they have used to check on the less familiar escutcheons well over a century before the Public Register of Arms was instigated and before the first printed book on heraldry appeared? I put my query to the Lyon Court, and Ross Herald at Arms has suggested that Sir William Cumming of Inverallochy was likely to have been consulted (as he may have been over the royal arms on the chapel). He was Lord Lyon King of Arms from 1512 until 1519, which includes the very period when the ceiling was under design and construction. The bishop would have known Sir William not only as a North East laird but as a benefactor of King's College, a relation of James Cumming the mediciner, and a relative by marriage of the Blinseile family. There was earlier contact too, for in 1506 Dunbar, as Lord Clerk of Register, had witnessed a charter granted by Cumming who was Marchmont Herald at that time. Moreover, Sir William, as Ross Herald points out, undertook a number of diplomatic missions to the continent on behalf of the sovereign and in common with other heralds of the period, kept an armorial, a heraldic notebook, which he would have made available to Dunbar and Galloway. Heraldic information may also have been provided by Adam Loufoot who some years before had prepared the earliest known Scottish heraldic manuscript. Loufoot might still been an Officer of Arms and available for consultation when the design was being prepared.

The message of the shields proclaims an independent Scotland, but whom did it reach apart from the cathedral's own clergy? The people of Old Aberdeen would have been too busy keeping body and soul together to concern themselves with heraldic riddles and exotic personages. Moreover, the ceiling was high and long and the pattern of the shields did not lend themselves to easy interpretation. Would local people and the scholars of King's had occasion to use the nave at all, given the existence of the Snow Kirk and King's College Chapel? Was the nave even readily accessible during the Dunbar era? The demolition of the caphouses and the construction of the twin spires at its west end, and from 1522, reconstruction work in the south transept, east of the nave, must have turned the area into a building site. But members of the clergy and aristocracy would have known of the ceiling and many who saw it would have appreciated both its message and the skill that had gone into its creation.

Finally, did the ceiling set a fashion in making political statements through interior decor? Perhaps. Around 1581-82, the vaulted ceiling of the hall of Balbegno Castle, near Edzell, was painted with certain armorial bearings which were added to over the years. These can still be made out. Their coded message is thought to mark the approval of the laird, John Wood, for the supremacy of the Stewart junta over the rival Douglases following the execution of the Regent Morton during the minority of James VI. After the affair of the Gowrie Conspiracy when James's life was apparently threatened, the arms of the Earls of Gowrie, earlier supporters of the junta, were painted out. No such eradications, at least not of this type were recorded at St Machar's.

In 1521 Bishop Dunbar granted land in the Chanonry to Alexander Galloway for the annual rent of 12s 4d and the canon, prebendary of Kinkell, was able to start work on his own manse. Kinkell, a small but wealthy parish with seven churches under its belt became a prebend in 1420, but a hundred years later still lacked a manse. The land earmarked, 'beside the common way which goes to the mountain commonly called Dunnydronis Hill', the Mote Hill of Tillydrone, lay at the north-west boundary of the Chanonry and just north-west of Mortlach Manse. It had been gifted by Bishop Henry de Lichtoun to Gilbert de Johnstoun in a charter of 1444, was sold by Alexander de Johnstoun to Canon William Mowat of Lonmay just over forty years later, and thence to Galloway. It was clearly an awkward site which may explain a reluctance to build there on the part of earlier possessors, but a trifling matter to a man of Galloway's skill. Moreover, the situation had a particular appeal. Galloway, official of the diocese, heard cases in the consistorial court which convened in the cathedral. A manse just across the road would prove very convenient. Like its neighbour, Mortlach, Kinkell Manse stood in what became the grounds of the present Tillydrone House, No 12 the Chanonry.

In 1531, almost at the end of his life, Dunbar founded a hospital, an almshouse, for elderly, indigent men, at the north end of the Chanonry just west of the present entrance to Seaton Park, between the manses of Tullynessle and Monymusk and opposite Mortlach. The deed of mortification by Dunbar conveys the sum of £100 Scots of annual rent belonging to him, and paid out of the yearly feuduty due by the burgh of Aberdeen under Robert the Bruce's charter of 1319. The Bishop's deed of gift was confirmed by James V on 24 February 1532. Dunbar made a second donation by conveying twenty pounds Scots annually out of lands in Skene. In the founding charter, Dunbar gives precise details of its size, layout, rules and regulations:

> The house of the hospital shall be a hundred feet long, and about thirty-two feet wide, and that it shall be divided so as to accommodate twelve poor men in separate rooms, by making in both parts of the house six rooms, each fourteen feet long and twelve feet broad.

Twelve as always, reflecting the number of Christ's disciples, and the men's rooms were relatively spacious by the standards of the time. The rest

The Message of the Shields

King James V

King Carlos I
of Aragon

King Louis I
of Bohemia

The shields of St Machar's ceiling present a unique and colourful panoply, but there is nothing casual about their arrangement. They were put in place at a time when rank and order was of the greatest importance. What can they tell us? Taking pride of place at the head of the centre row was the shield of Pope Leo X, followed by archbishops, bishops and the senior prior of the Scottish Church. The message here is that, apart from acknowledging the supremacy of the pope, the Scottish Church is independent. The diocese of Whithorn (Candida Casa) was once subject to the province of York, while the Sodoren or Southern Isles (the Hebrides) and Orkney were subject to Trondheim in Norway, the latter as recently as 1472. Now they march with the other Scottish dioceses. All but one of the ecclesiastical escrolls are impersonal like 'Bishop of Brechin', but Dunbar has personalised his own to read 'Gavin of Aberdeen', indicating that he was the living occupant of the diocese and creator of the heraldic ceiling.

On the south (dexter) side or are the arms of the king, James V, followed by those of St Margaret, wife of Malcolm III (Canmore), and the Scottish nobility, proclaiming the independence of the King of Scots and the nation. St Margaret's shield, her cross floretty between five martlets almost identical with the arms of her great-uncle, Edward the Confessor, is the only one which is not contemporary. She provides the feminine interest in this row for James V was a young lad with no queen, while his widowed mother, Margaret Tudor, was an English princess whose second marriage and interference in affairs of the realm had earned her unpopularity. In 1524, not long after the ceiling was finished, Bishop Dunbar had the distinction of being thrown into prison by Margaret herself, albeit briefly and in the company of Archbishop James Beaton, though for adherence to the cause of the Regent, the Duke of Albany, rather than for omitting her heraldry from the ceiling, or so we are told. Albany's own shield and the twelve Scottish earls follow St Margaret.

On the north, or sinister side, the escutcheons of the Europe rulers present a somewhat eccentric display. Several of them of them belong to Charles V, Holy Roman Emperor. His imperial blazonry heads the line-up, followed here and there by the shields of King Carlos I of Spain (at that time merely the provinces of Leon & Castile), King Carlos I of Aragon and King Carlo of Sicily, all of them Charles V wearing his other crowns. Curiously his Italian and German possessions, and the Netherlands which he inherited from his father, Archduke Philip, do not appear. Pride of place after the Holy Roman Empire is reserved for the fleur-de-lis of France, Scotland's traditional ally. In fourth place comes Henry VIII of England, surprisingly far up the league table so soon after Flodden. Nevertheless he would have been displeased to find himself not only trailing after the arms of the Spanish provinces but also deprived of the fleur-de-lis of France with which the Tudors arrogantly quartered their arms. He is allotted merely the three leopards passant gardant, not used in that form since the time of the early Plantagenets. Was it worse to be insulted like Henry, or omitted altogether like his sister, Margaret Tudor?

Though mistakenly bearing the Norwegian arms, Denmark follows next, a compliment to the young king, grandson of a Danish princess, Margaret of Denmark, Queen of James III, a woman of culture and piety who at one time was considered for canonisation. She brought Orkney and Shetland to Scotland as part of her dowry. Likewise the arms of the Dukes of Gueldres though last in the royal row, was another compliment to King James. The Burgundian princess, Mary of Gueldres, Queen of James II, another lady of great character, was his great-grandmother. Above Gueldres is the escutcheon of the Dukedom of Bourbon. This was yet another compliment, to Charles of Bourbon this time. But plans to betroth James V to a Bourbon princess fell through so that was rather a waste of a shield. Above Bourbon is Bohemia, whose king, Louis I, gets two bites of the cherry also appearing as Louis II of Hungary. Between Sicily and Bohemia is the handsome horse of Poland, while Navarre, honoured because of its French connection, is above Sicily. Cyprus, is above Navarre. Though Cyprus was under Venetian control at that time, the arms displayed are those of the long gone Lusignans. Venice, at the height of its powers, is alas, absent, and we are denied a sight of the splendid winged lion of St Mark's.

The message of the shields then is to stress the independence of the Scottish nation, while acknowledging the supremacy of the pope and the distinctive role of the Holy Roman Emperor. Local heraldry brings up the rear. The arms of King's College is at the end of the centre column, while those of Aberdeen and Old Aberdeen were placed at the rear of the dexter and sinister columns respectively.

Uniquely the creators of the heraldic ceiling have surmounted the arms of Scotland (King James V) top, opposite, with an imperial crown. In later medieval times, this type of enclosed crown, another example of which is shown above, left, signified the imperial status of its wearer. It was more prestigious than the open crown, right, the type given to all the other 'ordinary' monarchs on the ceiling.

of the house was thirty-six feet long and contained a common room on the north side, with a fire, and with storage space for fuel above. There was a common kitchen and meals were to be taken, 'in their own rooms or in the common room if they can manage so to agree among themselves that they can all dine at the same time'. The oratory was on the south side, and the sick were to be placed by a widow nearby so that they could see and hear mass. The hospital, which was dedicated to the Virgin Mary, had a timber steeple with a bell, with twelve little chimneys in the roof, one for each fireplace.

The beadsmen as they were called because 'they used to say their pater noster and their prayers by numbering their beads' had to be aged sixty or over, unmarried and 'of a good conversation'. 'Those troublesome to his

Gavin Dunbar's Hospital, from the drawing by Andrew Gibb.

fellows shall be punished in his person or removed from the hospital', the founding charter decreed. Qualifications for admission included residence in the Bishop's lands, having laboured on St Machar's Cathedral, the Bishop's Palace, the Chanonry manses or the Bridge of Dee. Failing that, 'selection shall be made from other wretched men, the poor the mutilated or those who have served in the King's wars'. No women were admitted. The terms of the mortification allowed the old men ten merks a year issued quarterly, and a merk to buy a white surcoat. Prayers were said in the morning, both in the oratory and the cathedral, while the afternoon was occupied with work in the garden and orchard of the hospital, 'in the cultivation of herbs and fruits for the common use'. At five o'clock more prayers, then supper was at six. The outer gate was opened at early dawn and closed before 8 o'clock. Dunbar's Hospital, completed the year after the bishop's death, bore his own coat-of-arms and those of James V and the following inscription, translated from the Latin: 'The reverend father, Gavin Dunbar, formerly bishop of this gentle seat, ordered this house to be built for twelve poor men in the year from Christ's birth, 1532. Glory to God'.

At St Machar's Cathedral Dunbar did not, as one might have expected, complete Elphinstone's choir. He had his own agenda which included the rebuilding of much of the south transept or aisle under master mason Thomas Franch, Franche, French or Frenssh, his surname surely indicating his ancestry. Franch was one of a family of masons particularly associated with Linlithgow Palace and the neighbouring St Michael's Church. An inscription on the outer wall of the south transept of St Machar's commemorates a family death. It has long been indecipherable but a record survives which reveals Franch's pride in his work : 'Heir lyes Tomas, the Son of Tomas Franch, Master Mason of Brig of Dee and this Isle, 1530'. Bishop

The inscription on the outer wall of the south transept of St Machar's Cathedral is now indecipherable but in the nineteenth century it was recorded as saying: 'Heir lyes Tomas the Son of Tomas Franch, Master Mason of Brig of Dee and this Isle, 1530'.

Dunbar's magnificent tomb in the south transept of St Machar's Cathedral. Note his coat of arms, right, and the battlemented cornice along the top, a tribute by Alexander Galloway. The effigy is not his. From the drawing by John Mitchell, from Logan's Collections, Third Spalding Club, 1941.

Dunbar was buried in the south transept in 1532, but poignantly Franch had buried his own son, also Thomas, first.

Dunbar's ornate arched tomb-recess dominates the transept. It is surmounted by a cornice of a different style and in a different sandstone from the rest of the tomb, bearing the hallmarks of Alexander Galloway's work. It alludes in miniature to the corbelled and battlemented parapet of the twin towers of St Machar's, as does his own sacrament house at Kinkell. A quirky tribute to Dunbar, perhaps an allusion to Galloway's role as architect and certainly a testament of his originality.

The tomb was damaged, though not badly, in the infamous covenanters' raid of 1640, while the bishop's marble effigy was said to have been broken up in 1693. In spite of such vicissitudes, the tomb remains a splendid piece of sculpture though unfortunately the glass canopy thoughtfully provided by the Ancient Monuments Board of the Ministry of Works or its successors, to prevent further weathering, has overtones of the bus shelter.

After Dunbar's death, and in spite of the uncertainty of the times, a new scheme was afoot at last to finish the choir of St Machar's. 'The Reformation coming on', says Orem bluntly, 'put a stop to the plan'.

Dunbar, Galloway and Franch were involved in other architectural projects, outwith Old Aberdeen, the most important of which was the Bridge of Dee. These are noted overleaf.

Dunbar, Galloway and Franch, Architects and Master Masons.

The Bridge of Dee, 'ane nobill and subtantius brig...'

In the 1520s Bishop Dunbar and Canon Galloway were involved in a number of architectural projects in and around Aberdeen, indicating good relations between the cathedral and the royal burgh. The most important of these was a bridge across the Dee, replacing the ford near the Ruthrieston Burn's outflow. It was Bishop Elphinstone who got this long mooted proposal off the ground only to be balked by the Flodden crisis. According to Boece, 'he prepared many stones and wood, and as much cement as appeared to be sufficient...' assembled a term of 'trustworthy labourers' and had the piers built before construction was halted. Dunbar got the scheme underway again, appointing Galloway to design and oversee the work, and Thomas Franch to head the masons. The Bridge of Dee was constructed between 1520 and 1527 and was eventually handed over to the magistrates of Aberdeen in December 1529. They acknowledged that Dunbar, who endowed the Lands of Ardlair for its upkeep, 'on his grit, exorbitant and sumptiuiss expensis had bigit of new ane nobill and subtantius brig'. Justified praise indeed, for it was the finest bridge in Scotland. It was embellished with heraldic shields and inscriptions, the most important of the latter reading in translation: 'Gavin Dunbar, Bishop of Aberdeen, ordered me to be built across the River Dee, AD 1525. Pray for him'. In the original Latin 'Bishop of Aberdeen' is rendered as Po(n)tifex Aberdonen(sis), an apt pun since pontifex can mean bishop or bridge builder. Dunbar went to town on heraldic shields, the final score at completion reading: Dunbar, 8, Elphinstone, 2, Scotland, 2, King James V, 1, the Regent Albany, 1. They are unique and of considerable historic importance.

The Bridge of Dee improved communications with the south immeasurably and gave great impetus to trade though those present at its inauguration would not have forseen that, albeit widened, it would still be coping with traffic entering Aberdeen from the south the best part of five hundred years on. But they would have noticed how well it combined grace with sturdiness, the muscularity of its piers and parapets, and the turrets at either end giving it a fortress-like aspect. So it seemed logical that in July 1529, when the magistrates decided to 'fowse and waw' the burgh, that is to build a ditch and wall around it, they appointed the 'venerable clerk, Maister Alex. Gallaway as principall directour and gydar'. Galloway's scheme for municpal fortifications was duly ratified by the Council, but that was the last that was heard of it.

In the 1520s Dunbar gifted fourteen hundred merks for a new church for the Greyfriars, to be built beside their friary in the Broadgate. Galloway is credited with its design, and Thomas Franch with its construction. Greyfrairs Church survived nearly four hundred years but was demolished at the beginning of the twentieth century amidst great controversy to make way for the Marischal College extension scheme. If it had had a magnificent crown belltower like King's College Chapel its destruction would have been unthinkable. And that thought brings me to the famous Crown Tower whose execution can be attributed to Bishop Dunbar, and in which Galloway and Franch may have had a hand.

Like St Nicholas, Greyfriars Kirk, right, was protected from looting by the townsfolk of Aberdeen at the time of the Reformation. In the late sixteenth century it found itself sharing its terrain with the Earl Marischal's new university though the buildings shown here are of more recent vintage.

King's College Chapel and Crown Tower in the 1840s. Note how the tower has been extended southwards, to the right. The coats-of-arms on the buttresses are from left, those of Margaret Tudor, James IV and his son, the Archbishop of St Andrew's. (The numbering of the buttresses is relevant to Appendix 2, page 266). From R W Billings 'Baronial and Ecclesiastical Antiquities of Scotland', 1845-52.

Chapter 7

The Riddle of the Crown Tower

The steeple hath within it an musical harmonie of costlie and pleasant bells...and a most curious and statlie work of hewn and corned stones, representing to the view of all beholders a brave portrait of the royal diadem.

Appendix to Articles from the University to the King, 1634.

The famous crown tower of King's College Chapel, stoutly buttressed like a miniature version of the west front of St Machar's Cathedral, has dominated Old Aberdeen since the sixteenth century. Its original purpose was not purely ornamental. It was built as a belltower or campanile, its belfry home to the great bells of King's. But while many a campanile is slender and free-standing, the crown tower, at least in its lower courses, is ranged in a solid line with the chapel to the north and the principal's residence to the south, as shown in the vignette in Parson Gordon's Plan, (page 66). Indeed the tower's south buttress gives the impression of sprouting from the eaves of the residence.

To date I have virtually ignored the crown tower, that great icon of Aberdeen University, but with reason. It is inevitably associated with Bishop Elphinstone and James IV, but hopefully it will emerge that this section of the book devoted to Dunbar and his works is the best place to discuss it.

Bishop Elphinstone was frequently in Edinburgh on state business and was bound to have admired the new crown steeple of the burgh kirk of St Giles. He may well have watched its completion when he was official of Lothian in the 1470s. He had an eye for fine architecture and as we know, modelled the central tower and spire of St Machar's on that of St John's, Perth. The St Giles crown steeple may have given him the idea of embellishing the belltower of his new college chapel with an equally splendid crown though he does not make mention of it in either of his Foundations. Dr William Kelly tentatively suggests in his essay 'Scottish Crown Steeples', in

A Tribute to William Kelly, 1949, that Elphinstone's plan for a crowned belltower may have been influenced by the knowledge that his college from its earliest days was informally known as King's or the Royal College rather than St Mary's. (He modestly quashed popular attempts to call it the Bishop's College). Though we cannot be completely certain that the decision to erect a crown tower came from Elphinstone himself, it is one to which he would have given enthusiastic approval, reinforcing the display of loyalty to James IV already expressed by the foundation inscription and the coats of arms on the west and north fronts of the chapel. As Kelly noted 'the crown of great arches represented the imperial crown of the king who was deemed imperial within his own realm'. It would be a symbol of Scotland's independence and a gracious compliment to the king.

The St Giles belltower and its prototype, that of St Nicholas' Cathedral, Newcastle both rose from the crossings of the great parish churches which

The crowns of St Nicholas, Newcastle, left and St Giles, Edinburgh, complete with weathercock, right. Along with that of King's College Chapel, they are the only surviving medieval crown towers in the United Kingdom.

they surmounted. They were designed as square towers and their crowns rise gracefully from their parapets. Kelly's view is that the King's belltower was also originally intended to be a square of 24ft 10ins (7.6m.) But, he argues 'for some unknown reason, after the tower was partly built, it was decided to increase its area'. It was 'stretched' southwards, extended to 28ft 3ins (8.6m) along its east and west sides giving an oblong rather than a square shape. The crown placed over such a base is bulbous in comparison with its elegant predecessors. Why this change in design? Kelly suggests the 'unknown reason' could have been that more room was necessary to accommodate the bells. The Inventory of 1542 lists them; five great bells, Trinitas, Maria, Michael, Gabriel and Raphael, the last three, named after the great archangels; five small bells with iron clappers which marked the half hours and 'two bells for daily use'. At the very beginning of the Inventory, someone in a later style of handwriting has noted down the inscriptions from the great bells. Those on the three 'archangels' state that they were cast by George Waghevens, a member of the renowned dynasty of Flemish bellfounders who also were casting magnificent bells for St John's, Perth. Waghevens, according to the inscriptions, made the 'archangels' in 1519. Obviously, they could not have arrived in Old Aberdeen before that year at the earliest. Were the other, undated, bells in place by then? Probably not according to Dr Jane Geddes in her essay 'The Bells' in *King's College Chapel, Aberdeen, 1500 - 2000*, 2000. She suggests that the small bells may not have arrived in Aberdeen until around 1520 when their bellfounder the Londoner, William Culverden, was at peak production. She argues that the college may have taken delivery of the whole peal at the one time.

Though Elphinstone funded the bells, 'all were the gift of Bishop William', as Boece wrote, and though the Second Foundation, drafted by 1514, has much to say about how they were to be looked after and how their chimes were to mark the passing of the college day, there is nothing to confirm that they were actually *in situ* when it was written. 'The sacrist...shall clean and keep clean the bells and all within the tower', by no means implies that they are there already, or even that the belltower is complete. 'The first of the ringings we wish to last for quarter of an hour' suggests that the ringings had not yet begun. There is reference to the chimes of the 'greater bell' but that appears to have been one of the bells within the chapel which are also mentioned in the 1542 Inventory. The building of the belltower and the hanging of the bells therein was not entirely essential to the running of the college and had been left to the last phase of Elphinstone's building plans. As we know the implementation of this final phase was halted by the disaster of Flodden in 1513 and Elphinstone's death the following year. It comes as a shock to realise that the bishop could never had heard the peal nor seen the great crown tower, nor would James IV ever have been aware of the compliment paid him in the shape of the imperial crown.

After being enthroned as bishop in 1518 Gavin Dunbar rapidly resumed Elphinstone's building programmes. It must have been he who, as chancellor of the university, either ordered the bells or put pressure on those bellfounders already commissioned but who had yet to deliver. It has been suggested that when the five great bells eventually arrived their size was greater than anticipated. Trinitas, probably from the Nottingham foundry, measured 5ft 5ins. (1.65m), according to Orem. Trinitas, and Maria, likely cast at the Exeter foundry, were the two largest bells which according to Parson Gordon 'are of a greater weght, each of them, than any in Scotland besyde'. William Kelly argues that the easiest way of providing more room for the bells was to take down the south wall and extend the east and west walls southwards. This also had the effect of making the west front more imposing, with the crown steeple, on its west and east sides closer in size to that of St Giles. On the other hand, Jane Geddes suggests that the bells might have been brought in through the roof of the belltower and the southern extension undertaken to add stability when the bells were in motion.

In discussing the chapel in his essay on 'King's College Chapel, 1932' in the *Memorial* volume Kelly refers to Parson Gordon's famous comment to the effect that the foundation of the college being built on marshy ground, the whole had to be underlaid with great oak beams at great expense and labour. He points out that the east end of the chapel 'shows signs of the masonry having sunk irregularly; the coursing lines fall towards the east, and the walls lean outwards and are much deformed'. Kelly continues:

> I cannot think that Elphinstone would have chosen a marshy site; but it is possible that a portion is bad, and that some tradition of the difficulty that the masons had with the east end of the Chapel and of the precautions that were taken is preserved in Parson Gordon's account.

This line of thought can be applied to the belltower. Possibly before it was begun it had been noted that the chapel was sinking at its east end and a resolution made that no such subsidence should 'deform' what was to be the great showpiece of the new college, a structure of national importance. With this in mind a further theory has been put forward in a paper by the architectural historian Ian B D Bryce, presented here in Appendix II. Putting forward a number of points including comparison of the thickness of the walls and the positioning of the plinths, Bryce argues that the 'stretching' to the south and the resultant oblong shape, far from being an afterthought or a late adjustment, was part of the original plan, dictated by the marshy terrain. 'There seems no reason to doubt', he states, 'that here we have the reason for the offending oblong shape, the extruded buttress and the asymmetrical façade - extended foundations standing on rafters of oak....The oblong shape was not a choice but a necessity dictated by the particular circumstances of the site'.

The belltower was carried as far south as it could go, 3ft 8 ins (2.24m). The principal's residence, which judging by Boece's comment, 'he covered the College church... and almost all the other buildings with lead' was competed before Elphinstone's death, would have stood in the way of further expansion. This final and most memorable work on the original King's College must have been carried out between 1519 when the arrival of the bells was imminent and late 1521 when the *Lives of the Bishops* was ready to go to Paris for printing for Boece was able to write:

> The church has a belltower of immense height with a stone arch in the shape of an imperial crown, built with wonderful art and raised above the leaden roof. It contains thirteen bells, pleasing the ear with sweet and holy melody.

Who designed the crown and who built it? The Grays have been mentioned as possible masons. John Gray was appointed master mason to St Nicholas Kirk in 1484, the same year that his probable kinsman, Alexander Gray, busy on St Giles, was appointed 'master to the work to the Town' (of Edinburgh). Their dates indicate that one or both could have been involved in the building of the King's College Chapel, but given that they were experienced master masons in the 1480s, they might have been gey long in the tooth for tackling the crown in 1520. It is rather the distinguished architectural team of Dunbar, the instigator, Galloway, the designer and Franch, the master mason that comes to mind. All were currently involved in these capacities on the Bridge of Dee project but that was a stop-go affair which did not entirely preclude other commitments. Canon Alexander Galloway was rector of King's in 1521 and I cannot envisage the crown steeple being built there at that very time without the canon, with his love of emblems and symbols, having some personal input. He had recently completed the design of the heraldic ceiling at St Machar's and would still be in creative flow. Though Elphinstone himself is silent on the crown, he may well have discussed its design with Galloway to whom he was very close in his later years, stressing the prestige of the closed, imperial crowns that he had seen in the courts of kings and emperor during his travels in Europe. It may even be a possibility that the crown tower was solely the product of Galloway's fertile mind. He had already topped the shield of James V, at the head of the dexter row on the St Machar's ceiling, with an arched crown, closed at the apex, the only imperial crown given to an 'ordinary' king on the St Machar's ceiling. Franch, as a mason, would have enjoyed the luxury of constructing a crown of arches by placing flying buttresses, which did not have some vital mass to support, in a dramatic circle.

Though the crown of St Nicholas, Newcastle, terminated in a little spire, and St Giles also had a spirelet and a weathercock as well, there is evidence that the crown steeple of King's terminated in a much smaller decorative crown, a finial in architectural terms. Boece does not mention a top crown. It would have gone up after his *Lives of the Bishops* was written. The great arches, for most people *the* crown of King's, would scarcely have been complete when he went to press, let alone a decorative crown on top. Writing on 'The Medieval Building' in *King's College Chapel, Aberdeen, 1500 - 2000*, Richard Fawcett advances the theory that this top crown may not have been added until sometime during James V's personal rule, from 1528 to 1542, being 'consistent with that monarch's known concern for the heraldic expression of his kingship'. One can speculate that the top crown could have been put in place at King's in 1530, a last triumph for the old team which was still around. Dunbar was still chancellor, Galloway was rector for the third time in 1530 and Franch was still in Aberdeen, for he buried his son that year in the south transept of St Machar's.

Franch must have returned to Linlithgow in 1530 or soon after for according to some sources he was appointed master mason to James V at that time. During the 1530s he worked on the king's massive reorganisation of the palace there. He was also master of the kirk work of the neighbouring Church of St Michael's and referred to as such in a contract of 1533. It was here that his predecessor at Linlithgow, his father John, ('fadder to tomas, master mason of Brig of dee') was buried. In the early 1530s a west tower was added to the original structure of St Michael's terminating in a crown of open stonework, with four arches, just like King's. At 24ft square, (8cm) it was much the size that the crown of King's might have been were it not for the need to extend the belltower southwards.

In Linlithgow Palace itself, an ornate fountain with features similar to the crown steeple of King's, was completed for the inner courtyard by 1538. It was topped by an arched crown in stone incorporating the velvet 'bonnet' of the crown beneath its arches. Since stone is not the best medium to convey the richness of velvet perhaps this was originally achieved by paintwork, essential for heraldic carvings. Today, without the paintwork this crown resembles a Christmas pudding minus the holly. It may be that a crown of a similar style was already in place as the top crown of King's. (But this is not the top crown we see today)!

None of this proves that Franch built the crown steeple at King's College or its finial. All we can say is that he was one of the leading master masons of his day; that he returned to Linlithgow from Old Aberdeen after the crown steeple and possibly its decorative crown finial were in place at King's; and at the time Franch was master mason at the Linlithgow palace and church complex, a mason there showed expertise in building ornamental crowns. Dr Kelly has argued that Franch does not claim any connection with the work at King's on the memorials he incised in memory his father and son. 'I feel certain that he would have done so if he had held a responsible position at that work'. But it is clear from these memorials that Franch considered the Brig of Dee his masterpiece. It is a brilliant piece of structural engineering and design, ahead of its time. He wished to be identified as its mason He could not foresee that the crown of King's would gain such significance as a unique symbol of northern academe. Architecturally he may

The fountain in Linlithgow Palace, topped by a crown finial. The original top crown of King's may have been similar. From MacGibbon and Ross's 'Castellated and Domestic Architecture of Scotland', 1892.

Linlithgow Palace, left and to the right, the crown steeple of St ;Michael's Church. From John Slezer's 'Theatrum Scotiae' of 1693.

have considered it to be what in musical terms Sir Thomas Beecham christened a lollipop; delightful, decorative, charming, but lacking in *gravitas.*

Of the four medieval Scottish crown towers, only two remain, those of King's College, Old Aberdeen with four arches and St Giles, Edinburgh, with eight. The four-arched St Michael's Linlithgow, was taken down around 1821 in a dangerous state. Likewise a fourth crown with eight arches at Haddington Parish Church built perhaps as early as 1450 has failed to survive. The only extant English medieval crown is St Nicholas, Newcastle, with four arches. The crowns at King's, St Giles and St Nicholas have all experienced extensive alterations and repairs down the years.

Chapter 8

End of an Era

Uproar and turmoil
Council Register of Aberdeen, 16 June 1559.

Martin Luther's attack on the sale of indulgences, nailed according to tradition to the church door at Wittenberg in Saxony, the act against Catholic doctrines that set the Reformation in motion, took place in 1517, the year before Bishop Gavin Dunbar made his triumphant entry into Aberdeen. By the end of his life, murmurs of the Reformation were growing ever louder in Scotland. The vision of the heraldic bishops marching proudly down the centre row of St Machar's ceiling under Pope Leo's banner was a fragile one, even when the shields were going up. Before their paint was dry, the 'bukis of the heretik Luthyr' were being brought into the country by the east coast ports, particularly Leith, Dundee and Aberdeen. Parliament took action, passing an Act against Heresy on 7 July 1525, in whose promulgation Dunbar, as a Lord Spiritual, played a major part. It ordered the imprisonment of those importing 'sic filth and vice' and the confiscation of their ships and goods. The month after the Act was passed James V wrote, at Dunbar's request, to the sheriffs of Aberdeen, Sir John Rutherford and Thomas Menzies of Pitfodels, commanding them straightaway to 'tak inquisitione' and confiscate the goods of any Lutherans they might uncover. Whatever its immediate outcome, this anti-heresy Act had no lasting effect. On the continent new doctrines such as Luther's justification by faith were gaining acceptance and old ones, such as transubstantiation where the bread and wine of the eucharist were miraculously converted into Christ's body, and the value of intercession by the Virgin Mary and the saints, were under attack. At St Andrews in 1528 the well-born young Patrick Hamilton, a disciple of Luther's, became Scotland's first Protestant martyr. He was tried for heresy, convicted and burnt at the stake, an act which had the inevitable effect of stimulating interest in the reformed religion.

For centuries the Catholic Church had been undergoing a slow decline. By the early sixteenth century it was gathering pace. During Dunbar's episcopacy it was clear that certain of his own clergy were not carrying out their duties. On 16 March 1524 the Town Council complained 'that thair kirk had stand lang desolet of divyne service'. Apparently there had been had a falling out among the clerics of St Nicholas who had abandoned the kirk. Dunbar was not in residence in Old Aberdeen so the magistrates sent Menzies of Pitfodels with three horsemen to track him down and get him to commission 'sum uther bischop' to effect a reconciliation among the clergy. 'The haly tyme of Pasche' (Easter) was drawing near and the Town Council were determined to have services up and running again in their beloved Mither Kirk. Would such unpriestly behaviour been tolerated by Elphinstone who famously 'reformed the clergy and restored the worship' on first coming to the diocese?

Dunbar was by no means oblivious to the failings of his clerics. In 1529 he purchased lands near Elgin in his native Moray, and from their revenues endowed two chaplainries at Elgin Cathedral where masses were to be said for the souls of his parents. The provisions of his foundation are more detailed than usual regarding the behaviour of the two chaplains, who had to be, in the following order, of good conversation, without concubines or bidies-in *(absque concubinis aut focariis)* and to be expert in Gregorian chant. Charges of concubinage and immorality were frequently laid against the Church as were pluralism (the holding of more than one living), simony (the buying and selling of positions in the Church), and absenteeism. Sir David Lindsay's play, *Ane Satire of the Three Estates.* denounced the Church for its ignorance, self-satisfaction and exploitation of the poor, and that perhaps was the greatest scandal. From the twelfth century onwards revenues of individual parishes were 'appropriated' or allocated to cathedrals, monasteries, collegiate churches and universities, resulting in impoverishment at parish level. By Dunbar's time the funds of 95% of parishes in the diocese of Aberdeen were absorbed in this way, around half of which went to St Machar's. In Scotland as a whole, the revenue of the Church was around £400,000, that of the Crown, £40,000.

Though the port was well-placed to receive both the new writings of the continental reformers and Tynewald's Bible in English, Aberdeen, unlike Angus and the Mearn, Dundee, Fife, Ayrshire and the Lothians, had no underground Protestant cells. Elphinstone had been at pains to appoint well educated priests of good moral standards. Both he and Gavin Dunbar, were generous benefactors of the diocese and men of patent goodness. St

Machar's Cathedral and King's College, the principal recipients of their generosity, were devoutly Catholic as were the leading families of the North East. Chief among these was the House of Gordon at whose head was George, fourth Earl of Huntly, a major player in national affairs.

His grandfather, Alexander, the third Earl had received vast grants of lands throughout the north from James IV for his role in subduing the unruly Highlands and Islands, and was appointed hereditary sheriff of Aberdeen and Inverness and Lieutenant General of the North where he was expected to maintain order. These lands and offices had been inherited by the fourth earl who would also serve as a privy councillor, and as Chancellor of Scotland. Other prominent Catholic families included the Earls of Erroll, the hereditary constables of Scotland and the Menzies dynasty, the leading family of the 'auld blud of the toun', who were virtually the hereditary provosts of Aberdeen, controlling the city from 1423 for two centuries and within that period occupying the provostorial chair for nearly 130 years. As for the average Aberdeen burgess, though he took pride in St Nicholas Kirk, which represented the burgh's wealth and his own largesse, he had apathetic tendencies when it came to religion. Little wonder that when in 1532, the year of Dunbar's death, a Franciscan friar abandoned his habit and started preaching Luther's doctrines in Aberdeen, he was met, if not with hostility, certainly with indifference. He went off to Dundee, where he was made welcome.

This, then was the situation when Bishop William Stewart, a son of Sir Thomas Stewart of Minto, Dean of Glasgow and Lord Treasurer of Scotland succeeded Gavin Dunbar. Like his predecessors, he enjoyed putting on a show, and travelled on an embassy to England soon after his consecration 'weill apparellit', with a train of nine mules 'and hyngand at thame, bells of silver overgilt with gold'. He was, according to the historian John Spottiswood, 'a man given to virtue, charitable to the poor, and ready to perform very good work'. He tied up a number of loose ends in Old Aberdeen and his achievements were on a par with those of the pre-Elphinstone bishops. On a practical level, he attempted to improve the administration of the cathedral, decreeing in 1540 that its statutes be revised and written out anew on parchment. Around this time he built the Chaplains' Port, the fourth and last gate in the Chanonry, at its junction with the Seatongate. He had the two western bays of the north aisle of the nave of St Machar's converted to form a consistory house, perhaps on the suggestion of Alexander Galloway, who as official of the diocese would have appreciated the benefits of a permanent courtroom for the consistorial court. He gifted an ornate oak pulpit to St Machar's with carved panels, perhaps locally crafted though showing continental, perhaps French influence. It can still be seen, extensively rebuilt in King's College Chapel.

The site of Chaplains' Port at the junction of the Chanonry and the Seatongate, now Don Street, in the foreground of this photo. The buildings are the surviving wing of the Chaplains' Chambers.

Bishop Stewart's pulpit, drawn by James Logan around 1820. By this time it had been in storage for years, having been taken out of use in 1793. In 1823 it was thrown out altogether. Twenty years later children playing hide and seek at the back of the cathedral found it on a rubbish heap. It was later rebuilt though the surviving original carved panels were incorporated into the new structure. It was taken to King's College Chapel where it remains. From Logan's Collections, Third Spalding Club 1941.

One of the original carved panels.

At King's Bishop Stewart completed Elphinstone's original scheme for the quadrangle, erecting the building that years earlier had been planned to project from the chapel. Tucked below the clerestorey windows, its ground floor contained the college jewel house or strongroom with a classroom at the east end, identifiable in Gordon's vignette by the large windows which allowed maximum light. The interior had two entrances at ground floor level giving access to the chapel. One at the east end linked the classroom area with the choir, while the other at the west end led into the nave opposite the north doorway. These entrances were later remodelled into the two entrances at the east and west end of the Chapel's south frontage, those most often in use today. The library occupied the upper floor of Bishop Stewart's building, and linked by means of a little door with the rood loft of the chapel.

Books were transferred to the new library from Scorpio, the south-east tower which is still with us. It is described in the 1542 Inventory as the former library, though by then it had become a glory hole. The assorted objects in storage included a brass lamp with the founders' arms, a great fir kist where various items from the Hall were kept, an old window sill, a bit of iron off the clock, an iron chain from the well, 'brokin werk aff the altar that wes taine doun', probably bits of the Hercules altar, as well as the college armoury. This was a ramshackle, rundown collection, but certainly capable of inflicting damage: twelve axes, two iron guns without stocks and five chambers and their stone bullets moulds; two guns with stocks, one of them broken, three hagbuts (hand guns), a halbert (a near relation of the Lochaber axe), two staffs with iron points, and a reasonably full suit of armour, 'baik and for geir, ane sellat, ane knapsack and ane pair of splentis', (back plate, breastplate a helmet, its metal skullcap and metal arm protectors). There were also seven spheres, not spears, the writing of the original is clear, the gift of Master Arthur Boece, Hector's canonist brother. The sphere was studied in the second year as part of the physics course and it is surprising to find such items in the middle of the armoury list. Presumably they were simply stored in Scorpio, though at a pinch could be used for hurling at the enemy. This Inventory, either in an act of thrift, or owing to the scarcity of paper, was written in a notebook that belonged to Master John Watson, a regent at King's. His name and the date, 1541, are on the first page, along with the inscriptions from the great

'Ane sellat'. This type of helmet was one of the items in the armoury.

bells of the chapel. Leaves from the beginning and end presumably containing notes by Watson had been removed and the Inventory complied on the remaining pages.

Moving away from the confines of college and cathedral, Bishop Stewart's era gives us a glimpse of the state of the Donmouth. A feud had developed between the bishop and the whitefishers of Futty over the latter's disturbance of the bishop's salmon fishings at Balgownie. In the Council Register of 23 May 1539, the bishop's servants complained, as they had done 'diverse and syndrie tymes in thair maisteris name', that the Futty men were taking salmon from 'the vatter (water) of Done in the auld vattergang'. This old gang or channel was the old Donmouth near Cunnigarhill, silting up at that time. The volatile Don shifting course, had created a new mouth further north. Salmon, being creatures of instinct, would swim up the old channel expecting to reach their redds only to fall easy prey to the Futty men, much to the annoyance of the bishop's netsmen waiting impatiently at Balgownie. The bailies dispatched their officers to the old watergang, to apprehend and imprison those caught removing fish, until they made reparation for damage caused. Another dispute was resolved two years later. According to the Council Register of 17 June 1541 it was agreed between Henry Mowtray, Bishop Stewart's factor, and the Futty fishermen's leaders that wading 'at the watter mouth of Done' to gather bait, would be carried out under strict control. All would wade 'at ane tyme and mak no tary in the watter moutht'. Wading would cease 'if thair be ony fysche swamand thair' to allow them to 'pass about to the brig' (of Balgownie).

The storm clouds of the Reformation were beginning to darken. There was a distressing incident for Bishop Stewart in 1544. At this time, the anti-English, pro-French policy of Cardinal Beaton, and Mary of Guise, Queen Dowager, was in the ascendancy and the Scots Parliament was induced to break off the betrothal of her daughter, the infant Mary Queen of Scots and Prince Edward, son of Henry VIII, king of a now Protestant England, earlier negotiated by the Regent, James Hamilton, Earl of Arran. The proposed match had reawakened old fears of an English domination of Scotland. In an act of reprisal, Henry VIII sent an army under the Earl of Hertford north by sea in the first of a series of invasions of Scotland, which became known as the Rough Wooing. Leith was captured, Edinburgh burnt and the surrounding country laid waste. Fearing an English attack, Bishop Stewart sent some of St Machar's most prized treasures, chalices, jewels, and vestments to a place of safe-keeping north of the Don. The convoy and its escort of priests crossed the Brig o Balgownie which being built 'blind' made it difficult to attack. Just beyond the Brig, however, James Forbes of Corsindae and his men were lying in wait. For a highway robber, James, third laird of Corsindae, was well born and well married, but much

The Brig o Balgownie was built 'blind', making it impossible to see round corners. Drawn and engraved by William Daniell, 1822.

involved in feuding, eventually dying by the sword. He and his band fell on the precious convoy and made off with the entire treasure.

By a charter of 19 August 1544 drawn up soon after the theft, Corsindae agreed to restore the cathedral's treasures on payment of six hundred merks redemption money, though this was converted into a grant of four ploughgates of land, 416 Scots acres, at Montgarry in Tullynessle parish in perpetual feu. Two lists, part of an inventory of the cathedral's treasures made in 1549 reveal what was stolen. The first itemises a number of chalices of silver or silver gilt which were redeemed, the second, which does not mince its words, condemning the robbers as 'children of Satan' lists treasures that were never disgorged by Corsindae, among them, a great monstrance, ampullas for holy oil, crosses, cruets, vestments, altar hangings and 'ane banqhoir', a seat-covering, of tawny velvet containing six ells of Flemish cloth 'with Bishop Gavin's arms in five places, cost £4.' Perhaps with the Corsindae affair in mind, the magistrates of Aberdeen on 18 April 1550, instructed all the chaplains of St Nicholas Kirk 'to compear afore them the morne' bringing all chalices, vestments and treasures so that an inventory could be made.

If Corsindae's sacrilege was indicative of increasing disrespect for the Church, the offensive behaviour of certain clergymen justified such disdain. In November 1550, John Elphinstone, rector of Invernochty was delated (accused) of the cruel slaughter and murder of Thomas Cult of Auld Aberdeen under silence of night, of wasting and destroying the goods of William Lowson, burgess of Aberdeen for ten years, and lying in adultery with his spouse, Jonet Colestone, and of oppression done to Mr Duncan Burnet rector of Methlick umbesetting (besetting) his way within his lodging in the Chanonry and the cathedral church where he was celebrating Matins and striking him to the ground several times with roungis and battounis, (cudgels and batons). A far cry from one of his predecessors at Invernochty, the devout and eident Simon Dods.

Bishop Stewart never knew of these misdeeds. He had died in April 1545, though his passing was perhaps hastened by Corsindae's impiety. His time as bishop truly marked the end of an era, for during those years, many of the old guard at King's College slipped away. The faithful Hector Boece had died in 1536 and was laid to rest in King's College Chapel near Bishop Elphinstone's tomb. William Hay, his boyhood friend and successor as principal, who had taught theology for thirty years, followed him to the grave in 1542. John Vaus, the grammarian died in 1539 though he had a worthy successor in Theophilus Stewart who taught Greek as well as Latin, and had some knowledge of medicine.

In January 1545, three months before Bishop Stewart's passing, a new provost was elected in Aberdeen. George Gordon, fourth Earl of Huntly was chosen by 'the haill toun', that is the ruling oligarchy, when Thomas Menzies of Pitfodels 'renunciat and ourgaif his office of provestry'. This was only the second short break in his provostorial marathon which endured from 1533 until 1575. Menzies had favoured the English match for the infant Queen Mary, good for trade with England, but now, thanks to the Rough Wooing, it was unpopular. He assumed a suitably low profile, at least for the time being. Huntly lost little time in having his uncle, William Gordon, third son of the third Earl installed as bishop-elect. History was repeating itself, for thirty years earlier the third Earl, had foisted Alexander Gordon, an ailing and ineffectual relative on the diocese.

The provostship of Aberdeen seems a small scalp for someone with Huntly's connections. His mother was an older half-sister of James V, and he had been a favourite of the king with whom he was much of an age and with whom he had been brought up. But he had earlier, and without success, attempted to draw the burgh into an alliance in support of Mary of Guise, his half-aunt by marriage. Aberdeen had gone its own way, sending commissioners to a parliament called by the Earl of Arran in 1544, snubbing Huntly's summons to a rival parliament being held at the same time by Mary of Guise. (Indeed with typical Aberdeen thrawnness four magistrates said they 'wald nocht consent to send ony commissaris to ony of the said parliamentis'). Huntly was also concerned at outbreaks of anti-clerical behaviour, an attack on the Blackfriars by a number of citizens, while two others had cheekily 'hingit' an image of St Francis. Acting in his capacity as Lieutenant General of the North, he had them locked up. They were lucky. In Perth a similar offence was punished by execution.

Now, as provost of Aberdeen, and with his uncle installed at the Bishop's Palace in Old Aberdeen, he was able to reinforce his already considerable power base in the North East. Moreover, the Rough Wooing was in a new phase and those Aberdeen burgesses who were packing their goods with the aim of leaving the city could now draw comfort from the prospect of a warrior of Huntly's calibre at the helm who had the means and the manpower to set the town on a defensive footing. The trouble blew over and by 1546 Thomas Menzies was back at the helm. The North East continued to take little interest in Protestantism in spite of the fact that in the year of Menzies' comeback, George Wishart, an Angus man by birth, had been burnt at the stake in St Andrews for preaching the reformed doctrine of rejecting all beliefs and practices for which authority could not be found in the scriptures.

After his consecration as Bishop of Aberdeen, William Gordon, showed his nephew his appreciation, gifting him the temporalities, that is certain ecclesiastical revenues consisting of lands and their rents and in 1549, following Huntly's release from captivity after the Battle of Pinkie, welcomed him back by creating him hereditary bailie of the bishopric of Aberdeen which committed the Earl to maintain and defend the diocese.

Uncle William was one of those churchman whose scandalous lifestyle was grist to the mill of the reformers. Archbishop Spottiswoode whose *History of the Church of Scotland* was published in 1655 wrote:

> This man brought up in letters at Aberdeen, followed his studies a long time in Paris and returning thence was first parson of Clatt and afterwards promoted to the See. Some hopes he gave at first of a virtuous man, but afterwards turned a very epicure, spending all his time in drinking and whoring; he dilapidated the whole rents by feuing the lands and converting the victual-duties in money, a great part whereof he wasted upon his base children, and the whores, their mothers.

We first met Bishop Gordon and his concubine, Janet Knowles, a daughter and sister of leading Aberdeen burgesses, in *The Spital.* He had three sons and three daughters by her as well as two other sons. This was not unusual in itself. Only lesser clergy were permitted to marry, and by 1550, two out of every seven children legitimised were the bastards of priests. But after the exemplary lives of so many of his predecessors, William Gordon's illicit fecundity brought shame to the diocese and embarrassment as least to some of his colleagues. Of greater concern was the amount of church land that, with the consent of his chapter, Gordon was alienating. He was by no means alone. Bishop Stewart, for at least two years before his death, had, in common with other apprehensive clerics, feued out diocesan land. Though canon law forbade its sale, the issuing of feu charters was not taboo, providing the clergy with an annual income in feuduties to be stashed away for the rainy day of their dispossession.

At the start of his episcopacy Gordon had followed Bishop Stewart's lead in issuing feu charters, but by 1547 he was renting out land instead, often on long lease, which fell short of the permanent alienation of feuing. A typical example was an eighteen year lease to Alex Cruikshank in 1549 for half of the toun and land of New Rayne extending to eight oxingang or 104 Scots acres, and a third of the Mill of Old Rayne. For this Cruickshank paid £5 2s 2d annually along with measures of meal and malt, half a mart (the carcass of a fatted cow or ox), a mouton (a sheep carcass), a third of a fatted swine, sixteen capons, sixteen poultry, a third of a goose, and 'ane boll aittis (oats) with the strae'. With numerous deals of this kind, Gordon was able to feed his large family in Old Aberdeen comfortably down the years. Not only small farmers were involved. In 1549 the barony of Fetternear was leased to his nephew Huntly, and 'ane half of the toun of Boighall' to Provost Thomas Menzies. In a growing crescendo the old church lands of Tillygreig, Mameulah, Kirkton of Rayne, Kirkton of Clatt, Daviot, Montgarry, Towie, Goule, the Hospital of Kintore, were alienated and became so entangled with the secular that after the Reformation it was often impossible for the infant Reformed Church to recover what had once been church lands and to fund itself adequately.

Though Gordon's interests appear secular rather than spiritual he was not totally oblivious to the needs of his diocese. The Church was slowly awakening to the need to reform itself and a provincial council or synod of the Church meeting in Edinburgh in 1547 stressed the need for preaching in the dioceses. This was taken to heart by Gordon and his chapter at St

Mameulah today.

Machar's and Master John Watson of King's College was designated a preaching canon. He was to live in Chanonry but had a roving brief to preach throughout the diocese. The language of deed appointing him is remarkable and he may even have written it himself. It recognised the lack of proper supervision of the diocese and of instruction in the Catholic faith. It spoke of the greatness of the harvest, and the scarcity of labourers, the spread of heresy and heretics, and the necessity of supplying the food of the Word of God, the insufficiency of the bishop to preach in all parishes of his diocese and the necessity of supplying his place with men fit for preaching the Word of God who would hear confessions, enjoin penance, preach to the people once a month, give two lectures a week in theology in the cathedral and once in every year preach in each of the common churches of the diocese.

Thus was much of the spiritual work of the diocese thrown on the shoulders of one man. Watson would certainly have required a new notebook, his old one having purloined to take the Inventory of King's College in 1542. A disciple of the renowned preacher, John Ryaerts, Watson carried out his mission conscientiously, emphasising God in Christ, their offer of hope for mankind, reliance on the Bible. In spite of the size of the St Machar's chapter it seems that other clerics were so sunk in inertia or busy elsewhere that they were unable to assist him. A far cry from the days when Bishop Kininmund I preached round his whole diocese in the course of the year. But it may not have occurred, even to Watson, that preaching was not the whole answer. The people would have opted for relief from the burden of teinds and a decent standard of pastoral care.

A little later, in August 1549, Canon Alexander Galloway ordered a visitation of King's College. He was around seventy by this time and in his fourth and final spell as rector. He had been one of Strachan's assessors at the time of the 1542 Inventory when all seemed well but must have been troubled by reports of the college's decline in the few years since Principal William Hay's death. John Bisset, a former regent in arts had succeeded Hay but was in poor health and things had gone downhill.

Galloway had four assessors, the archdeacon and three canons of the cathedral, one of whom Master Duncan Burnet, rector of Methlick would shortly be assaulted by his murderous colleague, John Elphinstone. In the presence of John Bisset, Alexander Anderson, subprincipal, Robert Gray, mediciner, who had succeeded Cumming in 1523, Theophilus Stewart, plus cantor and sacrist, Rector Galloway and his assessors made a thorough inspection. It was quickly evident that Elphinstone's vision of a haven of piety and scholarship had vanished like snow off a dyke. Galloway duly issued a list of fifty-one instructions on how the college should be reformed. The first item sets the tone. The members of staff present were warned to commence reading, teaching and preaching within nine days, or be penalised. Much more in that vein follows. The 'correction' of the canonist and civilist had to be postponed for they were absent. The law students, usually chaplains with their own altars which provided their income, had, like their mentors vanished. 'They neither make their residences and the houses of their chaplainries are become ruinous by their fault'. The regents were warned to commence their lectures immediately after the ringing of the bells so that the students had no occasion for being idle. Masters and students were to speak in Latin only, as were the arts bursars, not only in college but when 'recreating themselves in the fields on pain of losing their bursaries for a third offence'. Theology students were warned to keep their proper hours, dress correctly, cut their hair and shave their beards. No note had been taken of their names since 1546, these were now to be entered. They were no longer permitted to delay ordination to the priesthood. That was something of a racket which allowed the pursuit of lucrative careers while still enjoying a benefice. Scales of fees according to the social class of the student were set out. Subprincipal Alexander Anderson, who had been Galloway's vicar at Kinkell, was to look after the bursary money and the academic dress.

The college buildings and external manses were in a poor state, and the masters were to account for the funds set apart for their repair, and for the funds for the purchase of oil for the lamp which burned before the Holy Sacrament, within fifteen days. The necessary building repairs were to be carried out within the next nine months. 'A proper economus' (formerly known as the provisor) was to be found who must keep daily accounts while the common procurator, the master elected by his fellows to administer the college, was to provide him with all necessaries, meal, bread, fish, coal, candles. *'Cibus sit recens'* (let the food be new), was one ominous instruction and the principal was told to provide privies as soon as possible. The principal, subprincipal, regents, procurator and economus were to attend to the decent appearance of the college and all its parts, within and without, as good a dictum for all university campuses now as then.

Galloway also supported the calls of the provincial council for greater emphasis on preaching. Chapel services were to resume as in Elphinstone's day. The masters were to preach in Scots to the people at least seven times a year and in their common churches four times, while theology students were to be encouraged to practice preaching in the common churches. This was welcome backup for Canon John Watson out in the diocese. Galloway's 'hit list' was a brave attempt to reinstate the Bishop Elphinstone's original Foundations. Though Bishop William Gordon as the Chancellor of the University, immediately ratified his recommendations it is uncertain if any of them were ever implemented.

In 1553 Theophilus Stewart, perhaps inspired by Galloway's dictum that, 'the grammarian must be virtuous, learned, studious and unwearied in giving instruction', brought out a fourth edition of Vaus's *Rudimenta*, printed in Paris as were its two predecessors. It contained something new, an appendix, 'The Statutes and Laws of the Grammar School', (Latin grammar that is), thought to be written by Stewart himself. The school was housed in the little lodge beside the entrance to King's, shown in Parson Gordon's Plan. It may have been built at the same time as Bishop Stewart's library when masons and building materials were on site. The Grammar School, initially an adjunct of the college, operated as a preparatory school in the main for university hopefuls, though whether the college students themselves were now taught there or at the grammarian's manse is unclear. Some years later, under the contentious New Foundation, the gramarian's salary was reduced below that of the regents, indicating that he was expected to make up the deficit from Grammar School fees. It also indicated the 'privatisation' of the school.

Like Galloway's 'hit list', Stewart 'Statutes and Laws' displays the medieval obsession with rules and regulations some of which were quite likely to be disobeyed. The timetable was gruelling. After prayers, lessons began at seven o'clock. Those who could not remember their declensions were either ticked off or caned by the headmaster, who ended the early morning session with a lecture to the assembled school at eight o'clock. The boys then hurried to breakfast. Further lectures followed, including one from the headmaster on the Latin authors, Terence, Virgil or Cicero. Dinner was at noon. The afternoon session lasted from two till six, then the pupils hastened to evening prayers, probably shared with members of the college in the chapel.

The boys were to speak only in Latin, Greek, Hebrew, French or Gaelic. Pupils from the North and Highlands must have been enrolled, for Gaelic had been dying out in the Aberdeen area since the twelfth century. Though this regime was less strict than at King's itself, there was still a veto on speaking in the vernacular. This was rather rich given that the *Rudimenta* itself was written in Scots. Bartering and gaming seem to have been popular and duly strictly regulated by the authorities. 'There is to be no play with books, money, clothes or food for stakes. Only the elder pupils may play for shoelaces or pins'. Games of chance were forbidden as 'a snare to the poor'. Punishments were laid down for latecomers, dunces and truants, for brawling, talking in class and dawdling en route to the toilet. Privies were clearly in place by 1553, at least at the Grammar School. As at King's, a policy of spare the rod, spoil the child prevailed. Each master was to have his own cane and pupils are ominously referred to as *qui sub nostra ferula militant*, (those who soldier on under our cane).

The school was well staffed with a headmaster, his deputy, and a number of under-masters. New staff also continued to be recruited to King's during those difficult years. In 1557, James Chalmers, a priest and a master of the Grammar School of Aberdeen left his stall in the choir St Nicholas Kirk to become a regent in 'the new college of Ald Aberdeen', though four years later, just after the Reformation he retreated to the continent where he spent the rest of his life. Marischal College was not then in existence so there was a fair amount of traffic from St Nicholas Kirk and Aberdeen Grammar School to King's College. Principal John Bisset had been rector of Aberdeen Grammar before becoming a regent of King's. In March 1545, during Huntly's provostship, the magistrates gave John Kilstairs, Aberdeen's 'servitour and singer' leave to study at 'the College in Auld Abirdene', allowing him to keep his stipend of 40s annually, provided he continued his duties in the choir of St Nicholas Kirk on Sundays and holy days. His musical abilities were clearly appreciated in Aberdeen, but he may have intended to improve his qualifications by studying theology. But given the religious uncertainty, a degree in theology was no longer seen as the passport to a lucrative career as it once had been and there was a drift away from Scottish universities in favour of continental ones.

The reformed faith was continuing to gain ground. Half of Europe had abandoned Catholicism by mid-century. Northern Germany and Scandinavia followed the teaching of Luther while the South German states, parts of Switzerland and of the Low Countries as well as the Huguenots of France, followed the more radical teaching of John Calvin of Geneva who preached of predestination and the salvation of the elect. In England, Henry VIII had carried out his designer Reformation as long ago as the 1530s.

In Scotland Protestant reformers were faced with serious difficulties. In 1554, Mary of Guise, the devoutly Catholic dowager queen, had ousted Arran and taken the reins as Regent, spurning the Protestant Earls and filling high offices with Frenchmen. By December 1557 she was completing negotiations for the marriage of her daughter, Mary Queen of Scots, to the Dauphin Francis, heir to the French throne. The marriage contract included a secret agreement that if Mary died without issue, the crown of Scotland would pass to France, a major Catholic power. In the same month, opposition to the dowager's plans was taking shape. A group of Protestant Lords and one laird, John Erskine of Dun, a King's College graduate, signed a document, the First Band (Bond) of the Protestant Congregation in Scotland, denouncing Catholicism and committing their 'whole power, substance and very lives' to establishing the reformed faith. Their popular name, the Lords of the Congregation, came from this document. This was the prelude to a difficult struggle to sweep away the moribund and corrupt old Church and get rid of the French.

At provincial council and at higher General Council level, within the Catholic Church, efforts continued to be made to reform the lumbering dinosaur of the Scottish Church. Among much else, bishops were instructed to reform their own lives, and no bishop's private life was more in need of reform than that of William Gordon. In late 1558 he sought advice from his dean and chapter, not on morals, however, but on 'staunching of heresies pollutant within the diocese'. They duly obliged, providing him with a remarkable memorandum on 5 January 1559 which went well beyond its brief. It was clear that there had been outbursts of sacrilege and desecration for the memorandum recommended that 'gravators', that is letters of censure, were to be sent to Aberdeen, and the parishes of Banchory Ternan, Echt, Kinnernie, Midmar, Auchindoir and Kearn, admonishing those involved in burning the kirk of Echt or casting down images 'in ony kirkis within the Diosie of Aberdene'. They were to be cursed (excommunicated) solemnly at the market crosses of Aberdeen and Old Aberdeen. Those suspected of heresy were to appear before bishop, dean and chapter.

The Earl of Huntly, as bailie of the bishopric, was to defend and maintain the Catholic faith and he or his deputy was to be present at the Bishop's Palace 'as he beis requirit for assistente'. But the memorandum goes beyond these mild attempts to 'staunch' heresy; it seizes the opportunity to set out a strict programme of reform as required by the provincial council. Preaching is to be carried out throughout the diocese, including the sending of preachers to kirks which have not been preached in Lent so the people are not in danger through the lack of hearing the true Catholic faith. The revenues of churches that will not conform are to be sequestrated. Absentee clergy are to resume residence in the Chanonry and 'reforme their kirkis'.

The most remarkable aspect of the memorandum was its criticism of Bishop Gordon's lifestyle. It begins moderately, not mentioning any names, suggesting that the bishop 'cause the kirkmen within his diocese' to remove their open concubines as directed by the provincial council. His chapter is to do likewise 'in all scharpest manner' and see to it that everyone under their control does the same. By the end of the memorandum, after the other points have been dealt with, the question of immoral conduct is taken up again. The tone has become one of outright anger at Gordon who is asked to show a good example by getting rid of 'the gentillwoman by quhom he is gretlie slanderit', presumably Janet Knowles. Unless that is done, the stubborn will say, 'they can nocht accept counsel and correction of him quhilk will nocht correct himself.' He is advised not to be over familiar with those whose religious beliefs are suspect, and when he goes to the country for relaxation, he should chose company commensurate with his own rank. Finally, reform should begin within his own household.

Among members of the chapter signing the memorandum was John Watson, by now parson of Clatt, and one suspects his hand in its authorship. He had criticised immorality among the clergy in his sermons, but behaviour back at head office must have undermined his cause.

Too late. On 11 May 1559 John Knox, a disciple of Calvin's at Geneva and newly returned to Scotland, preached an inflammatory sermon against idolatry at St John's Church in Perth, whose tower and spire Bishop Elphinstone had used as the model for St Machar's. The Reformation had begun in earnest. Knox's sermon triggered off the looting of churches and friaries in Perth itself, in Scone, Stirling, Linlithgow, Edinburgh and in

St John's Church, Perth, whose tower and spire Elphinstone admired and where John Knox preached his rabble-rousing sermon.

Dundee, long a hotbed of Calvinism. St Andrews, Jedburgh, Fyfe, the Lothians, Angus and the Mearns all went over to the reformed religion. The Lords of Congregation, who had lost their early impetus, kittled themselves up again and drew up a Second Band on 31 May 1559, pledged to defend Protestantism and free the country from 'the bondage and tyranny of strangers'. It was signed by a notable convert to Protestantism, Lord James Stewart a natural son of James V. After Knox's vehement sermon Mary of Guise had ordered Government troops to Perth to deal with preacher and burgesses. The Lords of Congregation and their supporters rose up in arms against her, and war began.

With riots and iconoclasm and now a civil war to contend with, Bishop William Gordon was concentrating not so much on mending his morals as hiding the treasures of St Machar's. In July 1559 he delivered the 'silver worke' of the cathedral including a pax, (a silver tablet kissed by the priest at mass), censers, chalices, a cross, a gold chain, a great ring, two crowns and a silver image of the Virgin Mary weighing seven pounds to the custody of twelve of his canons. In November he delivered even more spectacular treasures, sumptuous vestments in cloth of gold, hangings, altars cloths of velvet, a gold chalice studded with diamonds and rubies, silver chalices, crosses, censers, staffs, a bishop's mitre as well as Gavin Dunbar's personal gifts to St Machar's and more into the care of his nephew Huntly at his stronghold, the Place of Strathbogie, an earlier version of the chateauesque ruin we know today as Huntly Castle. One can imagine the scenes of drama in the cathedral, as the canons and their servants worked hurriedly in candlelight, bundling up the treasures as the horses of Huntly's escort stamped impatiently outside.

Bishop Gordon had dispatched his treasure in the nick of time. Aberdeen alone of all the major towns in Scotland was lagging in acceptance of the Protestant faith and at the end of December 1559, a 'rascal multitude', a phrase John Knox applied to the rowdiest of his followers, conscripted by the Lords of Congregation, marched from Angus to hurry things along, or as Provost Thomas Menzies put it, 'to distroy and cast doune the kirkis and religious places thairof under colour and pretence of godlie reformatioun'. The mob's routine in casting down the kirks and religious places was first to carry off the valuable timber, lead and precious ornaments, then to set the building on fire. St Nicholas Kirk was first on the list, but the cupboard was bare. In June the treasures had been entrusted to members of 'the auld blud' for safe-keeping on advice from their chaplains. Their expectations of loot disappointed, the 'reformers' attempted in frustration to tear down the great steeple. 'The citizens', as one chronicler put it, 'filled with indignation, turned out in force, and drove off the rabble…' If there was less Protestant fervour abroad in Aberdeen than elsewhere, there was certainly determination to safeguard the Mither Kirk and its treasures which were regarded as civic possessions rather than as the apparatus of a discredited faith. The Mearns marauders, now reinforced by a few locals, proceeded to burn the monasteries of the Blackfriars, Carmelites and Trinity Friars. Again the spoils were sparse. Earlier that year, the friars had given over their treasures to the magistrates for safekeeping. Greyfriars Kirk in the Broadgate, was also attacked, the looters starting to strip lead and timber from the roof. Built from monies gifted by Gavin Dunbar only thirty years earlier, Greyfriars Kirk, like St Nicholas, was a source of local pride. The mob was again chased off.

The earliest drawing of the Mother Kirk of St Nicholas.
From 'Scottish Notes and Queries', Vol XII.

Early in the New Year of 1560, the 'reformers' turned their attention to Old Aberdeen, where King's College Chapel and St Machar's would offer rich takings They were foiled at the gate of King's College according to tradition, by the Principal, Alexander Anderson, sword in hand. The scene can be imagined, Anderson in the suit of armour from the armoury and behind him a crowd of masters, students and college servants brandishing the axes, iron guns, hagbuts, halbert, even a few second year scholars ready to hurl their spheres. Such a reception at the walled enclave of King's with its small and easily defensible gate did not appeal to the mob which now headed off to despoil St Machar's Cathedral.

On the way, according to Orem, they vandalised the engravings of the Virgin Mary on the market cross and her effigy on the Chanonry Port. At St Machar's, the cathedral, like St Nicholas Kirk, was bare. Frustrated again, the 'rascal multitude' began to smash everything that came to hand, and burned the cathedral library. This vandalism was halted when the Earl of Huntly, bailie of the diocese, and never more 'requirit for assistente' than at that moment, rode up with the deputy sheriff of Aberdeenshire, John Leslie of Balquhain and their retainers, and put the rabble to flight. Mindful of his duties towards the whole diocese, Huntly sent a 'missive bill' or letter to the Town Council of Aberdeen towards the end of January, charging provost and bailies to be vigilant in their 'menteinans and protectioune' of religious buildings. This was a little late in the day as the mob had presumably gone back to the Mearns.

Provost Thomas Menzies had been conspicuous by his absence from civic affairs after denouncing the approach of the rabble a month earlier. He was disinclined to support the Lords of Congregation as were many of his cronies. A stalemate had arisen in Aberdeen Town Council between those for and against the Congregation whose army was hard pressed in the war against Mary of Guise. She had shipped in as many as 4,000 professional French troops and fortified Leith. At length, early in 1560, after protracted negotiations, the Protestant Elizabeth Tudor, queen of England, who had no wish to be sandwiched between a Catholic power and its satellite, agreed to bring her fleet and army in on the side of the Congregation. The auld enemy of England had become the new friend. There was no rallying against the Lords of Congregation in Aberdeen and the magistrates now knew which side of the fence to opt for. By March 1560 the Council consented to stent (tax) the 'haill communite of the burgh' to the tune of £400 to furnish forty men of war to support the Congregation. Such was Aberdeen's wary acceptance of the Reformation.

In August 1560, the Scottish Parliament accepted a reformed Confession of Faith, abolished papal authority and forbade the celebration of mass. Aberdeen's commissioners brought back with them the burgh's first Protestant minister, Master Adam Heriot, a man of learning, integrity and moderation, a good choice for an area that was still strongly Catholic.

Part Two

Beyond the Bishops

The original gateway to the humanist's manse
in College Bounds

Chapter 9

Dark Days
for Kirk, Queen and College

After the era of the Reformation, the disposition of the people in general seems to have been gloomy and morose.

William Kennedy, The Annals of Aberdeen, 1818.

The plain and inconspicuous Snaw Kirk survived the violence of New Year 1560 unscathed, for the eyes of the 'rascal multitude' were fixed on the crown of King's College across the road. The Snaw had been the parish church of Old Aberdeen for sixty years but some time after 1560 was stood down and replaced by St Machar's Cathedral, which long before had been the parish church of the surrounding area, Kirkton of Seaton. Ever since Bishop Elphinstone had established the Chanonry as an ecclesiastical close the cathedral had been largely out of sight and out of mind for all but its priests and litigants attending the consistorial court held there. Now, as the parish kirk of the extensive parish of Oldmachar it had a new role. The reformed religion, like the old faith, emphasised the pivotal role of the parish church, but preacher and pulpit were centre stage now rather than mass and altar. The spacious nave of St Machar's, with room for hundreds of worshippers, could have been custom-built for the new faith. Stripped of popish trappings, it would have appealed to the most austere reformer and though the heraldic ceiling and some handsome carved woodwork remained, these fixtures were not regarded as idolatrous. Bishop Stewart's pulpit was certainly ornate, but it served to emphasise the importance of the preaching. Nevertheless, the trudge up the Chanonry to endure a lengthy sermon must have seemed to many of the folk of Old Aberdeen a poor substitute for the sumptuous vestments, glorious singing, and evocative smell of the incense of the old faith.

Not that there would have been many lengthy sermons there in the early days. Old Aberdeen was initially part of Master Adam Heriot's remit though he would have had little time to minister there. His hands were full in Aberdeen itself. His flock did not automatically become Protestant overnight and he had to teach the reformed religion. An eloquent preacher, he taught the new faith in the schools, he catechised, that is he taught Protestantism by question and answer, he baptised and generally worked himself into the ground. By 1567 there was some help at St Machar's in the form of an exhorter, John Erskine, an unqualified minister, a 'para-cleric'. The First Book of Discipline of 1561, the 'White Paper' for the reform of the Church, education and poor relief set out by Knox and his colleagues described exhorters and their colleagues, the readers as 'the most apt men that distinctly can read the common prayers and the scriptures to the people...till they grow to a greater perfection', that is until they trained for the ministry. Erskine's job must have been a depressing one. The 'war' damage at St Machar's took years to make good. The choir at the east end, never quite finished and now surplus to Protestant needs was abandoned, pillaged and spirited away by Old Aberdeen's DIY enthusiasts. 'The hands of the townsmen can scarcely be kept off the ruin,' commented Parson Gordon. The rich gifts of the bishops were things of the past, and the continued need for the maintenance, even of this truncated choirless cathedral would become an albatross round the necks of the St Machar's kirk session. Priests continued to live in the Chanonry, unmolested, so there was no shortage of celebrants to carry out the ritual, nor of the apparatus of the old faith, chalices, censers and monstrances. The precious silverware entrusted to the canons in July 1559 would be brought out of hiding for the occasion. At the Snaw Kirk the illicit hearing of mass and secret interments continued over many years.

Worst of all, Bishop Gordon continued to celebrate mass, prohibited though it was on pain of death, behind his palace walls. Unlike Cardinal Beaton and others, Gordon had not found it necessary to go into exile. His powerful nephew, the Earl of Huntly who as Lieutenant of the North oversaw a territory from the extreme north, south to the Mearns and west to the isles was pledged to come to his aid. The civil rights of the Scottish bishops had not been removed and Gordon continued to attend Parliament, though wisely, not the Parliament of 1560, and continued with his policy of alienating Church land, granting a feu charter of land in the North Spital to his mistress Janet Knowles and their three sons and three daughters in 1565.

We left Principal Alexander Anderson in January 1560, sword in hand at the gate of King's College as the mob hesitated, then passed by. In January of the following year, Anderson, along with John Leslie, canonist at King's, and other clerics was summoned to Edinburgh by the Convention of Estates in order to sign the Confession of Faith, and explain why King's College would not adopt the reformed faith. They declined to sign and in the tollbooth of Edinburgh Anderson and Leslie had a ding-dong though inconclusive argument with the Protestant ministers headed by John Knox. Anderson saw no reason to reform the university in the manner laid down by the First Book of Discipline which abolished the teaching of medicine and canon law. There was also a spirited discussion on the mass and the sacraments. There were 'very sharpe and hard disputacions amangst thame', Leslie later wrote in his *Historie of Scotland*. Knox in his *History of the Reformation in Scotland* found Anderson 'more subtil and craftye than learned or godlie', qualities as useful to university principals as much then as now. Though both sides claimed victory, Anderson and Leslie were confined in Edinburgh 'a lang space' or so Leslie wrote and forbidden to preach.

John Leslie (c1527-96) taught canon law at King's College where he had been educated and was official (judge) of the Aberdeen diocese. In 1564 he was appointed a Court of Session judge and two years later was consecrated Bishop of Ross, a personal appointment of Queen Mary. Though his earlier embassy to Mary in France was unsuccessful, he had fallen under her spell, became her secretary, confidential agent, champion and apologist. He wrote a 'Defence of the honour of...Marie Quene of Scotland' which asserted her right to the throne of Elizabeth I of England, a claim which did not endear him to the English Queen.

He was involved in a foolish plot against Elizabeth and was imprisoned for a time. Though he lacked the temperament for a spy or conspirator, he excelled as a historian. His Latin 'Historic of Scotland', was written while in England, as Mary's envoy. It was published in Paris in 1578 and translated into Scots some years later. After Mary's execution, Leslie went into exile in France. He was no stranger to the country. On graduating from King's he had studied at Toulouse, Paris and Poitiers. He became Bishop of Coutances in 1592 and died four years later.

Their incarceration could not have been as long as Leslie would have us believe, for by late March 1561 he was in France as the Earl of Huntly's emissary, attempting to persuade Mary Queen of Scots, widowed by the recent death of her husband, Francis II, king of France, not only to return to Scotland but to land in Aberdeen where Huntly and a force of 20,000 supporters would await her, march to Edinburgh and restore the old faith by force, in her name. Though a devout Catholic, Mary believed that religious toleration was a preferable option to religious wars. She rejected Huntly's wild scheme and instead struck a bargain with her elder half-brother, Lord James Stewart, representing the Scottish parliament. The terms agreed were that she would come back, that she would recognise the Protestant faith, but she would retain her own faith and celebrate mass in private. That summer Mary returned to Scotland, disembarking at Leith in thick fog amidst scenes of celebration and 'fires of joy'.

Principal Anderson had resumed his duties at King's that spring of 1561. The college was vandalised during his absence in Edinburgh, but it is uncertain how much damage was done, or what was spirited away at that time. Parson Gordon reported of Bishop Stewart's jewel house beside the chapel:

> Ther was much pretious stuff layde up ther of old, besyde all this, but long agoe robbed by theeves quho brack in violentlie ther.

The following summer Queen Mary paid her sole, fateful visit to the North East, one of several royal progresses that she made through her kingdom, the sixteenth century version of a royal walkabout, though with serious purpose. Prominent in the royal party was her half-brother Lord James Stewart, to whom she looked increasingly for advice. The entourage arrived in Old Aberdeen that August. Mary held court at the Bishop's Palace and may have celebrated mass privately with Bishop Gordon. She visited King's College whose foundation her grandfather, James IV had so enthusiastically promoted. One of the party, Thomas Randolph, agent in Scotland to Elizabeth I's secretary William Cecil, was not impressed. Though there would have been about nine masters at that time, he noted that the university consisted of 'one college of fifteen or sixteen scollers' small beer even by Scottish standards and diminutive when compared with the wealthy colleges of the Universities of Oxford and Cambridge.

The Earl of Huntly was conspicuous by his absence. Leader of the Catholic peers, he should have been by the queen's side as her blood relative, natural ally and adviser. But for Mary he was a liability. As granddaughter of Margaret Tudor she had laid claim to the throne of England, and her policy of gaining the confidence of English Protestants was likely to be undermined by Huntly's one man Counter-Reformation. Additionally, though her Protestant lords may have first set her against Huntly, she had developed a strong personal antipathy towards him. Nor was the situation improved by the wild behaviour of his third son, Sir John Gordon. But now Lord James Stewart, through his recent marriage to Agnes Keith, daughter of the Earl Marischal, could claim local connections. Dunnottar Castle near Stonehaven had for centuries been the seat of the Keith family. This gave Mary the opportunity to advance her half-brother at Huntly's expense and check the latter's all-pervading influence in the North East. She conferred, secretly at first, the earldoms of Mar and of Moray on Lord James. Both lucrative earldoms were vacant but had been claimed by Huntly within whose geographic sphere of influence they lay and who already administered them. This massive snub brought him into open rebellion against the queen.

Mary Queen of Scots.

It was during the subsequent course of this royal progress that the series of desperate events unfolded which led to the Battle of Corrichie on the Hill o Fare, about four miles north of Banchory. Here the forces of two grandchildren of James IV, Queen Mary and Lord James Stewart, Earl of Moray elect, put to flight the smaller army of a third, the Earl of Huntly. He surrendered on the battlefield, a bitterly disappointed man, then died of a stroke or as Thomas Randolph memorably put it 'he sodenlie fawlethe from his horse starke dedde'. The messy execution of Huntly's son, the impetuous Sir John Gordon, took place five days after the battle, on 2 November 1562 in the Castlegate of Aberdeen, preceded by the hanging of five of his associates, all prominent Gordons. Legend has it that the new Earl of Moray forced his tearful half-sister to watch Sir John's beheading from a window of his father-in-law's house, but on the contrary, if the relatively impartial Thomas Randolph is to be believed, Mary exulted in the fall of the House of Gordon and even found time that day to write to the members of King's

A pageant depicting Mary's visit to Old Aberdeen on 27 August 1562.

College to tell them she had taken the college and its revenues under her protection. She charged her subjects, 'that nane of thame tak apon hand to do molestatioun, harme, greif or inquietatione to the said college...' Corrichie had put an end to any hope of a restoration of Catholicism in the North East at least in the foreseeable future, and the Queen's letter, preserved in the archives at King's College, must have brought a crumb of comfort to the little enclave there. She also exempted the college from the 'Thirds of Benefices' tax which allowed unreformed Catholic clergy to keep two-thirds of their benefices, while the remaining third was used in part to pay the stipends of Protestant clergy. This would have been welcomed by the masters, nearly all of whom were in holy orders and who could now keep their benefices intact. In spite of the dilemmas of her northern progress it would seem that Mary had enjoyed her visit to King's, and privately approved of its staunch Catholicism.

In accordance with tradition, Huntly's corpse had been embalmed, shrouded in sackcloth, and transported to Edinburgh, where in May 1563 the privy council passed the sentence of attainder on it. Huntly's estates were forfeit to the crown which gave the Queen the opportunity to remove from his stronghold, the Place of Strathbogie, the richly embroidered vestments, altar cloths and hangings belonging to St Machar's Cathedral and entrusted by Bishop Gordon to Huntly's care in 1560. This haul was sent to Holyrood and converted to secular uses. When Mary's second husband, Lord Darnley, was convalescing at Kirk o Field after a bout of 'smallpox', his bedchamber was decorated with rich hangings from St Machar's. They also provided the material for a doublet for her third husband, the Earl of Bothwell. Alas, the treasures of gold, silver and precious stones which Bishop Gordon had also entrusted to Huntly vanished without trace.

It may have been soon after the Battle of Corrichie that Principal Anderson sent off the valuables of King's College to some place of safe-keeping. William Kennedy wrote in his *Annals of Aberdeen:*

> Perceiving that the new doctrines were daily gaining ground, and that there was every prospect of a thorough reformation in the university he privately conveyed away all the ancient ornaments and many of the books belonging to the college, alienated some of the revenues, and destroyed several of its ancient charters...

Unfortunately none of these items, including records of the early years of King's were recovered.

In 1563 and again in 1565 the General Assembly ordered the masters of the Scottish colleges to accept the new religion. King's College, unlike St Andrews and Glasgow Universities, would not budge from the old faith. In that latter year, according to John Knox, Queen Mary instructed Bishop Gordon to forbid the Catholic liturgy and the celebration of mass in King's College Chapel. To no avail. The stance of the college was strengthened by the emergence of the fifth Earl of Huntly. Yes, the Gordons were back. Mary had not extirpated all of them. Though he was not involved in the Corrichie affair, Lord George Gordon, the fourth Earl's eldest son, had been sentenced to death. Thanks to the Queen's intervention he escaped execution and was later pardoned. In 1565 he was restored to the Huntly estates and titles, was made Chancellor of Scotland and a Lord of Session. He also received gifts from the Queen, which ironically, are said to have been part of the loot removed from Strathbogie after Corrichie by royal command. In Old Aberdeen, the masters of King's and the Earl's great-uncle William Gordon, still resident in the Bishop's Palace, could breathe more easily if only for a short time. In 1567 Queen Mary's abdication was enforced after her ill-advised marriage to the Earl of Bothwell and subsequent defeat at the Battle of Carberry. Moray was appointed Regent on behalf of the infant King James VI and King's College had lost its protectress. The inevitable showdown between college and Church and State was at last drawing near.

Moderate though he was, Master Adam Heriot's patience with the blatant Catholicism of King's College was at an end. He complained several times to the General Assembly and in 1568 the Regent Moray, anxious to complete the reform of the Scottish universities, appeared on the point of moving against the college. But he had more pressing problems to contend with at that time and their resolution resulted in fresh disasters for St Machar's. Moray, campaigning in the North against supporters of the Queen, led by the fifth Earl of Huntly was desperately short of funds to pay his army. And so the privy council ordered that lead be stripped from the cathedrals of Aberdeen and Elgin and sold to fund the Regent's army. William Birnie, an Edinburgh burgess, was appointed to oversee the removal of lead from St Machar's roof. The voices of Bishop Gordon, Leslie of Balquhain, Provost Thomas Menzies of Pitfodels and others were raised

James Stewart, Earl of Moray (1531-70), the son of James V by Margaret Erskine, was the elder half-brother of Mary Queen of Scots. But for the accident of his birth he would have been king. He converted to Protestantism in 1559 amd joined the Lords of Congregation against the army of Mary of Guise. After he became Regent of Scotland in 1567 his army was continually harassed by the Queen's party lead by the fith Earl of Huntly and his in-laws, the Chatelherault Hamiltons. One gets the impression that Moray had been around for generations, involved in plot and counter-plot, but he was scarcely thirty-nine when he was shot by Hamilton of Bothwellhaugh in Linlithgow in January 1570. Moray had no sons but in 1580 his daughter married James Stewart of Doune who took the title of Earl of Moray. He was slain by the sixth Earl of Huntly in 1592 and is immortalised as the 'Bonnie Earl o Moray' of ballad fame.

in protest, to no avail and the Earl of Huntly, hereditary bailie of the old pre-Reformation diocese, was not in a position to prevent this legalised vandalism. The rapacious Birnie exceeded his instructions, additionally making off with the three bells gifted by Bishop Elphinstone. According to tradition he set sail from Aberdeen to sell them in Holland. The overloaded ship sank off Girdleness and Birnie was thought to have gone to the bottom with the bells, a richly deserved fate. (The location, and hopefully the recovery of the bells should make an interesting project for divers). There were dire

After its fall, Elphinstone's elegant spire at St Machar's Cathedral shown on page 108, was replaced by a curious saddle-back roof, right.

consequences for the cathedral. The removal of lead weakened the steeple above the great central tower, the subject of Elphinstone's meticulous instructions to John Fendour in 1511. 'The violence of a great storm of winde' caused its fall a few years later. Worse was to follow. In the meantime the steeple was replaced by a curious saddle-backed roof, stuck on top of the tower.

Moray, having presumably paid his troops, forced Huntly's submission and settled the area, at last turned his attention to King's College. The reformed Church was dependant on the services of ministers who prior to conversion had been Catholic priests, Knox and Heriot among them, and on exhorters and readers, one of whom, Walter Cullen, minor poet and one of the 'auld blud of the toun', was registrar at St Nicholas Kirk. *The Chronicle of Aberdeen,* his grandly named though scrappy diary is a welcome source of the local and national events of this troubled era. Ordained ministers were as yet thin on the ground and their training was regarded as the principal role of the Scottish universities. The time was long overdue for King's to conform.

In 1569 the General Assembly along with the privy council issued a commission to John Erskine of Dun, now superintendent of Angus and the Mearns, to hold a visitation of his old college and inspect the lives and the doctrines of its members. In short, to reform the college. Principal Anderson, his subprincipal and three regents were summoned to the Kirk of St Nicholas where on 30 June they appeared not only before the Laird of Dun but the Regent Moray himself. Despite pressure from Moray, 'his grace's godly admonitions' as it was politely described, Anderson and his subprincipal refused to sign the Confession of Faith, a document which set out the doctrine of the reformed faith. And so the five masters were thrown out. They were declared 'unmeet and dangerous to have care of the instruction of youth' and ordered 'to remove furth of the said colledge with all diligence'. They were forbidden to teach publicly or privately anywhere in Scotland. Erskine of Dun ordered that the sentence against them be read out in the kirks of both Aberdeens the following Sunday, 3 July. But the purge was not wholesale. The canonist, the civilist, Theophilus Stewart, the grammarian, and Gilbert Skene, the mediciner were not summoned and continued in place, possibly because overnight they had become Protestants. Skene, was something of a celebrity in these dark days for the college. He wrote the first medical text book in Scots, *Ane breve descriptioun of the pest,* which dealt with the cause and cure of the plague. It was printed at Edinburgh in 1568 where he later set up in practice. In 1581 he became mediciner to James VI.

The man given the task of introducing Protestantism to King's College was the thirty-one-year-old Alexander Arbuthnot, appointed principal on

3 July 1569 in succession to Anderson. Born in 1538 he had studied philosophy at St Andrews and civil law at the university of Bourges in France for five years, returning home in 1566 to take up a legal career. But he soon realised that his true vocation lay in the ministry. He turned to the study of theology and two years later became minister of the joint charges of Logie-Buchan and Forvie. Now as principal of King's he had to carry out a revision of the arts and theology curricula, to correspond with the doctrines of the reformed church. The arts course must adopt a new approach to philosophy uncluttered by medieval scholarship, while theology students must study the Bible and the word of God pure and unadulterated from the original Hebrew or Greek. No more reading of Nicholas of Lyra's *Commentary on the Old Testament* at supper time. If Arbuthnot seemed a trifle inexperienced for the job he had great learning and an agreeable personality. Archbishop John Spottiswoode whose *History of the Church of Scotland* was published in 1655 reported that he was 'pleasant and jocund in conversation and in all sciences expert; a good poet, mathematician, philosopher, theologian, lawyer and in medicine skilful'. He counted among his friends the most influential people of that era; John Knox, George Buchanan, described by Dr Johnson as 'the only man of genius his country had ever produced' and the reformer Andrew Melville, presently to return to Scotland from Switzerland and generate a stirring up in religious matters whose effect would be felt for centuries. Arbuthnot also had the advantage of the right pedigree for the times. His cousin, Robert Arbuthnott of that ilk, was head of the Mearns landed family, later ennobled as the Viscounts of Arbuthnott by Charles I. Robert's first wife was a daughter of John Erskine of Dun but she had died childless in 1529. His second wife, Christian Keith, was a sister of George, Earl Marischal, who later founded the Protestant Marischal College. Christian's aunt had married the Regent Moray. It was Moray who had appointed Arbuthnot as principal of King's College and the Laird of Dun as representative of the Church who had admitted him to that office.

Sharing this ceremony of induction was an old friend from his St Andrews days, James Lawson the new subprincipal. Lawson had been private tutor to the sons of the Countess of Crawford in Paris and at Cambridge and subsequently returned to St Andrews to teach Hebrew. He was now summoned to introduce this language, whose teaching was required by the First Book of Discipline, to King's College. The appointment of new Protestant regents followed. That 'obstinat papist', Bishop William Gordon, found himself presiding as Catholic chancellor over a Protestant university, but no matter, with the departure of the canons adherents of Huntly had started to colonise the Chanonry so he had friends around him. The Earl himself was out there fighting to replace Moray's

Protestant regency with a Catholic government in the name of Mary Queen of Scots. A step in the right direction, at least for the Gordon camp, was the murder of the Regent Moray. But by 1573 this particular civil war had ended in defeat for the followers of Mary. Huntly 'decessit suddentlie' three years later, not on the battlefield but 'cumyn fra ye fuitbau'. He was succeeded by his teenage son, George as sixth earl.

Back in Old Aberdeen, Subprincipal Lawson, in addition to his teaching duties at King's, was inducted at St Machar's Cathedral. At last Oldmachar parish had its first full time Protestant minister. In Aberdeen itself, at St Nicholas Kirk, he also gave assistance to Master Heriot whose health was failing. A few years earlier Lawson had impressed John Knox who designated him his successor, putting the noses of certain Edinburgh clergymen out of joint. Knox died in 1572, so just three years after coming to Old Aberdeen, Lawson had to leave college and cathedral and accept the call as parish minister of Edinburgh. What had started out as a promising Protestant repeat of the Boece-Hay partnership was not to be fulfilled.

Principal Arbuthnot took over from Lawson as minister of St Machar's. He had lessened his workload by shedding the charges of Forvie and of Arbuthnot kirk to which he had been appointed on becoming principal, evidence of the great dearth of ordained Protestant ministers in these post-Reformation years. Now, in addition to preaching at the cathedral and catechising throughout the extensive parish of Oldmachar, (the parish was not disjoined and Newmachar parish created until 1609), Arbuthnot had his teaching duties to fulfil at King's, and, most important, his plans for curriculum reform. He also took steps to help secure the financial future of the college. In 1574 a number of royal grants from old church property were made to King's including all income from the subchantery of Aberdeen (that was the Spital), the rectory and vicarage of Forvie, the chaplainries of Westhall and Folayroule (Folla Rule) with their manses and glebes and the properties of the Carmelite Friars of Banff. In 1579 revenues of the deanery of Aberdeen and the rectory and vicarage of the parish church of St Machar were added. In return the principal was to preach in Oldmachar parish. These grants were made 'on account of the insufficiency of the revenues' and were not inconsiderable. (In 1637 the feuduties for the Martinmas term from Westhall, Folla Rule and Banff alone amounted to £124 as opposed to the £181 16s 4d contributed by forty-one other properties of which the college was feudal superior).

Outwith kirk and college, demands and commitments at local and national level crowded in on Arbuthnot. He assisted at St Nicholas Kirk, and the reader Walter Cullen, reports how he inaugurated the new elders and deacons there. He served on the committee to select a new master for the Grammar School of Aberdeen, a lengthy process involving the oral examination of several candidates in St Nicholas Kirk. As Spottiswoode put it, 'the chief men of the north without his advice could do almost nothing which put him in a great fasherie'. His prominent role in the deliberations of the reformed Scottish Church was probably the most time-consuming of all. He regularly attended the General Assembly and was twice moderator.

In 1574 Andrew Melville, scholar, university reformer, presbyterian hard-liner and still only twenty-nine years of age, returned to Scotland from Geneva to become principal of Glasgow University. Born in Montrose and educated at St Andrews, his roots, like those of the Arbuthnots, the Erskines of Dun, the 'heretic' George Wishart and the Keiths were in Angus and the Mearns. He set about introducing a system of university reform, the New Foundation, partly based on the fashionable ideas of the French Huguenot, Petrus Ramus which reduced faculties to two, arts and theology. The teaching of law and medicine was to be abandoned. Arbuthnot was enthusiastic about Melville's proposed reforms and the latter's nephew James, the diarist, gives an idyllic picture of how after a meeting of the General Assembly of 1575 he and his uncle:

> past to Angus in companie with Mr Alexander Arbuthnot, a man of singular gifts of lerning, godliness, and sweitness of nature, then Principall of the College of Aberdein whom with Mr Andro (Melville) communicat anent the haill ordour of his College in doctrine and discipline.

Both men agreed, according to James Melville, on the reformation of the colleges of Glasgow, which Melville had more or less raised from the dead, and King's. But by the late 1570s it was Glasgow and St Andrews that had adopted the New Foundation. Only King's awaited what was grandly called 'reform and establishment', though one imagines (no records are extant for this period) that the arts and theology curricula were in tune with the New Foundation's principles. Like the First Book of Discipline its primary aim was the training of parish ministers. Medicine and canon law had already been thrown out by the First Book, and only civil law was left to be scrapped under the New Foundation. For four years, a philosophy-based Arts course would be taught; Aristotle would be studied, though less slavishly than in days of yore; Greek, Latin, logic, ethics, physiology, mathematics, geography and astronomy would complete the course. Two years of theology followed including the teaching of Hebrew, Chaldee and Syriac, then the young ministers would be off to the parishes. Traditionalists at King's saw it as a betrayal of Elphinstone's Old Foundation (the Foundations of 1505 and 1515), yet there was much that Elphinstone would have agreed with: 'No rich students (shall) be admitted in the place of the poor, and no drones feed from the hive'. He would also have approved of the scale of fees laid down for those who could afford it: sons of princes and the upper nobility, £6; lower rank nobility £4; sons of farmers, ordinary merchants and craftsmen, 40s.

Arbuthnot, a devoted disciple of Melville, was at this time working on a draft of the Second Book of Discipline, the Assembly's new 'White Paper', this time on the structure and organisation of the Scottish Church which was still fluid. Immediately after the Reformation the Church had been run by superintendents such as Erskine of Dun, and commissioners, ministers

John Erskine, fifth Laird of Dun (c1508-1591) rose to great eminence as a church reformer. Was it he who sent the mob from Angus and the Mearns to Aberdeen? As the local laird he had much influence in this his home area, which was strongly Protestant long before the Reformation became a reality. Educated at King's, Erskine had been impressed by Luther's writings which were smuggled into the east coast ports. He was a confidant of George Wishart, had John Knox as a guest at Dun in 1555 and was swayed by his arguments against the mass. Three years later he represented the Scottish Parliament at the marriage of Mary Queen of Scots and the Dauphin Francis in France. He was one of the brave handful of Lords of Congregation who signed the First Band, pledging to work for the establishment of Protestantism. Well thought of by friend and foe alike, Erskine later attempted to mediate between Mary of Guise and the reformers. He represented Montrose at the first General Assembly of December 1560, was superintendent of Angus and the Mearns, and five times Moderator of the General Assembly. He soothed Queen Mary when Knox drove her to tears. She called him 'a mild, sweet-tempered man'. After Erskine purged King's College, ex-Principal Anderson would have seen him in a different light.

His descendant, David Erskine, Lord Dun (1673-1758) built the present House of Dun near Montrose. In 1980, the twentieth and last laird, Mrs Millicent Lovett, bequeathed the property to the National Trust for Scotland.

who combined administration with parish duties. Never very popular, they had, by 1572 been replaced by Protestant bishops, approved of by Knox as a lesser evil. The episcopalian system which raised its bishops above his fellow men was anathema to Melville, now in the forefront of religious as well as educational reform who while abroad had been much impressed by the presbyterian teachings of Theodore Beza. As was only to be expected, the Second Book of Discipline, published in 1578, opted for Melville's (and Beza's) ideas; the replacement of the bishops by a presbyterian system in which the Church would be governed by a series of courts or councils, from ministers and elders convening at kirk session level dealing with their own congregations, to the presbytery, the court which gave this system its name, then the synod and finally to the governing body of the Church of Scotland, the General Assembly. This system was accepted by the Assembly but only after bitter debate.

Enter now the young king, James VI. An advocate of the episcopacy, he saw the bishops as the means of controlling the Church. He and Melville were on the threshold of a lasting feud, particularly counter-productive when it came to the establishment of the New Foundation at King's, now teetering on the brink of implementation. Since 1578, assorted commissions, royal, parliamentary, and church had sought to 'plant' it there, but attempts had come to naught. By 1583, the findings of the most recent commission, in which George Keith, Earl Marischal, and Andrew Melville were both involved, and with which Parliament and the General Assembly concurred, was that 'the King's College of Aberdeen, no small nursery of our commonwealth in the northern parts of our kingdom' (the Foundation was formally written in the king's name) was ready to accept its own New Foundation, after the manner of St Andrews and Glasgow universities. College members at Aberdeen were to be reduced to twenty-two; principal, four regents, a grammarian, twelve bursars, an economus who would take over the administration of the college from the common procurator as well as the work of the provisor, plus a cook and two servants. Only the approval of the king himself was required. The seventeen-year-old James VI was at this time was extricating himself from house arrest at Ruthven Castle where he had been warded by a group of Protestant zealots, determined to preserve him from Catholic influences in the shape of his favourite, Esmé Stewart, a cousin of his father, Lord Darnley. Though not personally involved, it was known that Melville approved of the principles which motivated the Ruthven Raid as it became known. The king in turn was not likely to approve anything that had Melville's blessing.

The canonist, civilist and mediciner, still apparently *in situ* at King's College and unwilling to accept the compulsory redundancy implicit in the acceptance of the New Foundation, now petitioned James VI to retain the Old Foundation. They had chosen their time well, strengthening the king's resolve to move against Melville and Arbuthnot. James VI wrote from Holyrood, referring disparagingly to the New Foundationers; 'We are surelie informed that...it is desyrit by some persones to pervert the order of the Foundation established by our progenitors and the Estates of our realme…' This royal thumbs-down was the last that was heard of the New Foundation for some time. In the meanwhile Arbuthnot had been chosen by the General Assembly to become parish minister of St Andrews. He must have keenly anticipated the challenge of this important charge and the prospect of working in association with Melville who, having reformed St Andrews University, had become its principal. Instead, and in spite of protest by the General Assembly, Arbuthnot was ordered by the king not to go there, but to continue with his duties in Old Aberdeen, under pain of horning, a technical form of outlawry. It is reported that he was so distressed by this royal diktat that he fell into a decline. His death, doubtless hastened by overwork and concern over the blatant Catholicism of Old Aberdeen, was respectfully recorded by Walter Cullen on 17 October 1583.

Old and New Foundationers would split King's into rival factions for the next half century while the Earl Marischal founded his own university in Aberdeen according to the principles of the New Foundation. It was open for business by 1593. As for Andrew Melville he was outfoxed by the king in the politics of religion and imprisoned in the Tower of London after James acceded to the English throne. He died in exile in 1622.

The Recusants and Peter Udney's Tomb

It must have been with a heavy heart that the ardent Protestant, Principal Alexander Arbuthnot, considered the progress of the Reformation on his own doorstep. The Snow Kirk was a notorious haunt of covert Catholics, but worse still, the recusant (unreformed) bishop, William Gordon, was carrying out Catholic-style ceremonies in St Machar's, Arbuthnot's s own parish kirk seventeen years after the Reformation. Gordon had ordained the reader Walter Cullen to the pre-Reformation office of Vicar of Aberdeen in June 1577. Cullen reported in his Chronicle of Aberdeen: 'My Lord of Aberden (Bishop Gordon) geyf the said Walter Cullen collation (presented him to the benefice) by ane ring on his finger'. Thomas Maveris, sacrist at St Machar's, was one of the witnesses .

Then there was the continuing presence of the ex-principal of King's, Alexander Anderson who, declining to accept the Confession of Faith, remained true to the old faith. He was put to the horn, and his moveable goods confiscated. Now he lived on, impoverished but unmolested, in Old Aberdeen.

Arbuthnot must also have felt uneasy about the true religious convictions of the new elders and deacons when he went across to Aberdeen to assist at St Nicholas Kirk. Prominent among the elders were the 'auld blud of the toun'. Even that diehard Catholic, Sir Thomas Menzies of Pitfodels, served as an elder at St Nicholas, doubtless going home to his fine stane hoose in the Castlegate to hear mass in his chapel, celebrated by his private chaplain, Master John Fulsard, formerly Prior of the Carmelites. Disconcerting though those dual religionists were, Arbuthnot, by the end of his life, was probably even more alarmed by the growth of Counter-Reformation and the arrival of Jesuit priests in Scotland to reclaim the Church for Rome, among them Father James Gordon, the Jesuit superior in Scotland who was a nephew of Bishop William Gordon.

Was Arbuthnot ever aware that within King's College itself, Master Peter Udney, humanist (the new title for grammarian) in 1583, the year of Arbuthnot's own death, had the reputation of being a secret priest of the old faith? Udney subsequently became regent, then subprincipal, but clues as to his priestly status were provided by his memorial stone, shown opposite, a sizeable slab of black Belgian marble, one of several old gravestones forming the pavement of the floor on the south side of the Chapel. With three of its five original consecration crosses still visible it was recognised as the table-slab of one of the Chapel's original six altars, the only one known to have survived the Reformation. Lifted and examined when work was carried out on the Chapel floor in 1931, its bevelled edges indicated that it formerly abutted one of the Chapel walls.

Renaissance-style lettering round the edges of the slab state in Latin that 'the most learned Master Peter Udney formerly subprincipal of this renowned College yielded to the fates on 24 April AD 1601' while a heraldic shield shows a pollarded tree with a stag's head on top, with a pair of greyhounds leaping upwards on either side. The stag's head and greyhounds are part of the arms of the Udny family, but not the tree, (the 'wid') a heraldic pun on Udney's name, which would have been pronounced 'Widney' locally. Around the shield are engraved the initials MPUS , (Master Peter Udney, Subprincipal). The Greek lettering below the 'S' reads All Glory to God. The 'S' could also stand for 'sacerdos', priest.

The inscription near the head of the stone translates: 'I lie back and rest, thoroughly weary of the unjust world; and I have both learnt and taught thy wounds, O Christ'. Was this a link with the five consecration crosses which were symbolic of the five wounds of Christ? The table-slab survived the post-Reformation desecration of the Chapel and Udney must have come across it, perhaps face downwards in a corner, and hidden it away hoping that it might serve as his own gravestone. His wish must have been known to other clandestine Catholics.

This fascinating relic of the Elphinstone era can now be found on top of a radiator at the east end of King's College Chapel where the high altar once stood. An alms plate by J Cromar Watt sits on top.

Chapter 10

The Hilton Land Raid
and the Stocket Compromise

Sir Thomas Gordon of Cluny, knight had againe renewit his suit anent the awaytaking of all differences betwixt this toune and the auld towne.

Aberdeen Council Register, 5 September, 1599.

As cathedral and college adjusted painfully to the new regime and religion, the bailies and councillors of Old Aberdeen looked carefully to their position. With the mighty Catholic bishops gone and St Machar's no longer a diocesan headquarters, their great fear was the swamping of the Aulton by its powerful neighbour, the royal burgh of Aberdeen. Fortunately their jurisdiction remained intact. An Act of Annexation of 1587 declared among other things that those burghs of barony, 'holden of prelates' before the Reformation, exercising trade, electing provosts and generally running their own show, would continue as before, though now they were 'holden of the king'. The chief concern was rather that the important consistorial court which sat at St Machar's and whose lawyers and litigants brought trade to the 'auld toune' might be moved to Aberdeen, or abolished altogether. In the event, the court's wide jurisdiction was parcelled out. The kirks assumed responsibility for crimes against the moral law. Sackcloth and the stool of repentance were the favoured instruments of punishment, though fines were also energetically imposed by impoverished kirk sessions. Wills and wives, or more properly testamentary and matrimonial disputes were centralised in a new commissary court in Edinburgh, while minor civil actions were transferred from the consistorial courts to small commissary courts within their old dioceses, known now as commissariats.

The Aberdeen commissariat had its headquarters at the old 'consistorie place', the consistorial courtroom at St Machar's and to some extent replaced it. The judge, known as the commissary, usually lived in the

Chanonry and was a person of some consequence in the Aulton. It seemed absurd to the ruling oligarchy in Aberdeen that the little village of Old Aberdeen should continue to be the seat of a law court and a university, particularly after the foundation of Marischal College in 1593. A move was put afoot to relocate both in the royal burgh, where King's would stand every chance of absorbed by Marischal. The Old Aberdeen magistrates fought back, complaining to Parliament that 'since the alteration of the religion' and the departure of the canons, Old Aberdeen had 'neither resources nor support except by the jurisdiction of the Commissariat and College'. To blame the departure of the canons for a loss of income is understandable, but this was only a temporary eclipse for the Chanonry. Nevertheless the loss of King's College would have been a severe blow to Old Aberdeen. The magistrates' pleas fell on sympathetic ears, and on 21 November 1597, an Act of the Scottish Parliament confirmed that court and college should remain in Old Aberdeen 'in all tymes cuming...without the removing or transportatioun of the same therefra to the newtoun of Abirdene'. The Lords of Council and Session also granted Letters of Horning at the instance of Old Aberdeen's magistrates which allowed them to outlaw anyone who failed to abide by this enactment. The commissary court and King's College remained in Old Aberdeen to the relief of its magistrates.

The first provost of Old Aberdeen of whom we learn anything was Sir Thomas Gordon of Cluny whose family was descended from the second son of Alexander, third Earl of Huntly. The Cluny Gordons, like others of their kin with a good contact in the Bishop's Palace in the sixteenth century, had acquired land in and around the Chanonry. Sir Thomas, the sixth Earl's 'richt trusty cousin', succeeded his father as Laird of Cluny in 1586. In the following century the population of Old Aberdeen would double from over 900 to approaching 2000 and it seems likely that even in Sir Thomas's time, the 'famous city of Old Aberdeen' was thriving in the way that Bishop Elphinstone had hoped for. Inevitably the Aulton needed more pasturage for its cattle, more peat for its fires and more divots to theek its cottages than was available within its own boundaries. Expansion was constrained by marshland and sandy links to the east and more marshland, hills and the Loch of Old Aberdeen to the west.

In the late 1590s, with true Gordon flamboyance, Sir Thomas set about to provide more *lebensraum* for his people. His thoughts turned to Caprastoun, part of today's Hilton. In the twelfth century, Bishop Matthew had endowed St Peter's Hospital in the Spital with lands around this area, but specifically excluded 'the land we gave to our man Caperon', which may have led to a sense of grievance in Old Aberdeen. In 1593 Aberdeen Town Council sold the Lands of Ardlair and with the proceeds bought

Caprastoun from its owner, the burgess Alexander Forbes. As the Council Register of 30 June 1595 stated, 'The said landis of Caprastoun lyis neir this burgh merchand contigue with the fredome thereof', that is, it marched with the Freedom Lands. (March Stones 52 and 53 now designate these boundaries). A charter of Bishop Adam de Tyninghame of 6 April 1388 in favour of Laurence de Leth gives probably the first description of Hilton with its marshlands and wetlands, its cultivated lands, its wildfowling and hunting grounds, its burns and the pools. It sounded a desirable area if a trifle damp, and it had improved by the late sixteenth century, producing corn, oats and bere (barley), and yielding peats and turfs. Aberdeen Town Council wanted it under its control.

The purchase of Caprastoun did not please Cluny and the folk of the

Caprastoun. Part of the Lands of Hilton in modern times.

Aulton who looked to its possession to solve their own problems. On 11 September 1598 Cluny invaded Caprastoun. He led a band of about fifty men, relatives, tenants, followers, servants and neighbours, including his son Alexander, Charles Ross of Tillynaucht, Gordon of Sauchin, Gordon of Tullyfoundy, 'Patrick Gordon sumtyme in Inver' and 'Adam Gordon in the pelt' (a wolfskin perhaps), who sound like two of the 'broken hielandmen quhom the said Sir Thomas hes subject to his command'. Over two dozen 'indewellaris (residents) in the auld toun of Aberdene' took part including James Mylne, Robert Garden, younger of Blairton, son of the commissary, 'Martin Clerk in Auld Abirdene', Andrew Myln, writer and Robert Collie, tailor as well as William Cruikshank and his son John from Cotton. All 'wer bodin in feir of wer', that is in warlike array, with 'jackis, speiris, steilbonattis, hacquebuttis, and pistolettis'. This was a fairly respectable turnout both as regards social class and weaponry. They came 'upoun horsback under cloud and silence of nicht' trampling the corn under hoof or slashing it with swords. They sought out the tenant, John Sanders, 'in the houss and biggings of Caprastoun to have slane him'. The following month they made a second attack, destroyed haystacks and smashed up a plough. The Aberdeen magistrates would not tolerate such outrageous treatment of their land and tenants. Complaints were made to the king. On 19 December 1599 James VI wrote to the Aberdeen Council ordaining that the complainants be left unmolested in future. Cluny was put under a surety of £2000, and the rest of his crew had to guarantee lesser amounts according to status, for good behaviour, under threat of outlawry.

Even though the Caprastoun raid was abortive, Cluny was determined not to abandon his expansionist policy, or to perhaps put it more accurately to find the additional pasturage much needed by the Aulton folk. During 1599 he pressed repeatedly, 'Sir Thomas Gordoun of Cluny, knicht, had agane renewit his suit', as the council mintues of 5 September 1599 put it, for a delegation from the Aberdeen Council 'to meet him upon the ground above the Hiltowne' presumably not 'bodin in feir of wer' this time, but for a civilised discussion of common pasturage. At this parley the Aberdeen delegation was composed of a formidable array of the 'auld blud' including Provost Rutherford, several of the Menzies dynasty and that 'proud ambeeshous man', former provost John Collison. Nothing came of it.

Not easily put down, Cluny now turned his attention to the Forest of the Stocket, gifted to the people of Aberdeen by a charter of King Robert the Bruce of 1319. This time, legal right, not might, was the tactic. The citizens of Old Aberdeen represented by Cluny and Master Peter Blackburn, Bishop of Aberdeen, argued before the delegates from Aberdeen that the Bishop of Aberdeen's tenants of Murthill had a right of pasturage in the Forest of Stocket by virtue of a charter of King Malcolm's in favour of Bishop Matthew. This, they said, extended to the people of Old Aberdeen. After some charter waving, this claim was successfully rebutted by the 'auld blud'. However, 'for peace and quietness' between the 'twa tounsis' and provided acknowledgement was made of Aberdeen's heritable right of property in the Stocket, the Aberdeen bailies allowed the 'auld towne' commonty of a part of the Stocket but 'onlie for pasturage, fewall, faill and devetts', in other words they could graze their cattle, cast peats, take turf for roofing purposes, but no more. This was acceptable.

During these negotiations, the two sides had met at 'the College Kirk'. Owing to a scarcity of suitable venues in Old Aberdeen, King's College Chapel had been pressed into service as a meeting place.

Chapter 11

The Governance of the Burgh

The bill of complaint (was) given by William Maxwell in Auld Abd against Thomas Watson in Murcar for the bluid-drawing of the said William by casting of ane kebbock of cheese at him to the great effusion of his bluid...

Old Aberdeen Council Minutes, 1 July, 1608.

Though we have reached Chapter Eleven there has been scarcely a word about the ordinary people of Old Aberdeen. Only in exceptional circumstances do they feature in the early charters. The situation changed in 1602. Old Aberdeen council minutes are extant from that time and the Oldmachar kirk session minutes from 1621. As with newspaper reports, such records, by their very nature, concentrate on important people and rogues. Fortunately our knowledge is broadened by the findings of a census taken in 1636, admirably complemented by Parson Gordon's Plan, surveyed from the 1640s and John Slezer's 'Old Aberdeen' drawn around 1690. These sources reveal how the old town looked at that time, who the 'inhabitantis' as they are so often called, were, where and how they lived, and as we now discover, how the town was run.

By the barony charter of 1489 James IV granted Bishop Elphinstone and his successors power to chose the burgh's bailies, sergeants and other necessary officers, and also 'that there be burgesses therein'. The provostship, added by the 'relaunch' charter of 1498 was, at least for much of the timespan of this book, a Gordon monopoly. We have already met Sir Thomas Gordon of Cluny. His high-handed attempts to assuage Old Aberdeen's land hunger at the price of the royal burgh set the tone for relations between the 'twa tounsis' for many years to come. He was succeeded by his son, Sir Alexander, in 1606 and he was followed in 1649 by his depute, fellow Gordon laird and Chanonry resident, Alexander Gordon of Birsemoir. The council or 'the haill counsell and communitie of Auld Abd' as it was styled, was a shadowy body, composed of burgesses which chose itself annually in time-honoured fashion. The bailies, three or four was the norm, were elected, usually at the first meeting of the year. This was an office of some importance, at the sharp end of the government of the Aulton. Election took one of several forms; if the provost were available he chose the baillies, though in those troubled times the Gordons were often away fighting. Post-reformation bishops, though very different kettles of fish from their popish predecessors, assumed the right to choose a provost and bailies, and if they were interested and available they did so, sometimes assisted by the principal of King's College. In 1612, Bishop Blackburn and Principal David Rait chose 'bailies for the toun and colledge boundis'. From the early days until the end came in 1891 there were representatives of the college among the bailies.

Often it was the 'counsell' itself that did the honours. In 1603 it chose as bailies, Alexander Mutray and George Mercer, a lawyer, neither of whom appear to have been outstandingly popular. Mutray was later accused of witchcraft while Mercer was 'abussit and molestit' and threatened with a dirk by one of his less enthusiastic constituents. In 1604 Mr Alexander Irving and the Caprastoun land raider, Mr Robert Garden of Blairton, both of them graduates, were elected, along with Alexander Lillie, commissary clerk depute, and Berold Innes, Mercer's predecessor as economus at King's College. All make frequent appearances in the council minutes. The election, doubtless decided in advance, was by simple acclamation. On 11 October 1644, for example the councillors 'with uplifitit handis' promised obedience, respect, reverence 'and all incuradgment' to the three bailies chosen so that they would be able to discharge their office 'with joy and not with greiff'.

'Incuradgment' was perhaps necessary for the bailies, in spite of their apparent 'gude conceit of themselves', did sometimes did come to grief. But their powers of punishment were extensive, with jurisdiction to punish offences by fine, the jouges, the stocks, branding, scourging or banishment. Those who showed lack of respect could expect harsh treatment. A chilling example of such power was evident in February 1610 when Cathren Lyne wife of Thomas Car called Bailie Alex Forbes, 'swetie (sweaty) hat, clipit brecis, (shrunken breeks), blottit hippis' (fat behind) and said to her husband, 'are thew takin af thai bonnet to ane skait (stupid) cretur'? The couple were banished, given twenty-four hours to get out of Old Aberdeen, otherwise they were to be scourged naked, burnt on cheeks, and thereafter banished. Amusing and well-merited though Cathren Lyne's comments may have been at the time, banishment brought with it not only loss of home, but the prospect of destitution. Without a 'testimonial', a character reference from the authorities which the couple were unlikely to be given, resettlement in another parish would be extremely difficult.

Crime and Punishment

'There has been scarcely a word about the ordinary people of Old Aberdeen. Only in exceptional circumstances do they feature in the early records'. One set of exceptional circumstances was noted in the 'Chronicle of Aberdeen'. Walter Cullen reports that: 'John Gordone and his wyfe callit [ ] Ogilvie, with Mareone Lyone, spous of Archbald Douglas dwelland in Ald Aberdein, and Kattrin Stewin was executt; that is to say, the said John Gordyne was hayngitt, quarterit, his heid putt on the Port; the said wemen drunnitt for the pusenyng of ane barne, (the woman were drowned for the poisoning of a bairn) gottin in adultre by the said Archbald Douglas with Marin Arthour in Ald Aberden. This execution was the xxix day June 1586'. John Gordon's head would have been stuck on the Justice Port in Aberdeen, and the three women drowned in the Pottie, a deep pool off the Quayhead, near Shore Brae. These are about the first inhabitants of Old Aberdeen, outwith the cloth and the college, that we come across by name.

A little later, the escapades of the Panton gang reveal both the harsh penal code of the times and show that at least some folk in Old Aberdeen were comfortably off. On 3 October 1606 the Court of the Bishopric of Old Aberdeen convicted Patrick Panton, a 'common cornstealer' of the theft of 'twa stollin scheip under sylence of nicht'. Patrick was banished and was to be hanged if found in the bishopric thereafter. Two years later all three Pantons were indicted after a stealing spree; a ewe from Alex Marschall, twelve threaves (two stooks) of oats from the 'tails' of John Clark, cordiner, two ewes from Patrick Gordon of Gordonsmills, two ewes from the byre at Peterston (the Powis railway bridge area), ten threaves of great oats also from Peterston, and six pecks of bere (barley) from John Torrie, 'which Alexander (Panton) caused Torrie's son to bring to the yard and winnow in time of preaching', a most heinous offence. They stole a ewe and lamb from James Barcar, beadsman in Old Aberdeen, James broke into Mr Alexander Cheyne's brewhouse, and Alexander and Patrick stole three pairs of new blankets, half a boll of white meal, a mart of beef, two stones of butter, a pair of new shoes, two pair of hose 'and certain other gear' from Mr George Seyton's lodging in Old Aberdeen. Seyton was chancellor of the town at that time, so this was unpardonable behaviour. James and Patrick were condemned 'to be hangit on the gallows 'until they be deid' and Alexander to be 'skurgit naked through Old Aberdeen' and then banished perpetually 'never to come in this side of the Water of Forth'. If he did and was apprehended he was to be hanged forthwith.

Another to whom harsh treatment was meted out, without referral for social work reports, was Margaret Strachan, 'ane notorious common thief'. Armed with a great knife, she broke into the house of John Levie, tailor, in the Aulton during the night and stole 'sundrie clothes, pertaining to sundrie peopell'. On 22 September 1652 she was condemned to be scourged by James Anderson, hangman, 'through the haill toune of Old Aberdeen betwixt the church (St Machar's) and the Spital Hill'. If she was found in the town in the future, she was to be 'drunit' without any further hearing.

The argumentative nature of Old Aberdeen folk, not to mention the expansion of the burgh can be traced through the activities of the council. Reports of rows, blaspheming, flytting (quarrelling) and causing injury, pepper the burgh records. On 8 January 1644 it was agreed to impose on those guilty of 'skolding and trubling the town by flytting, quhilk is a common course in Old Abd' a fine of £3 plus an hour in the jougs at the market cross. Thing got so bad that in October 1655 the council agreed to meet every month to resolve 'all the contraversies amongst the Inhabitantis'. By 1661 owing to the amount of business to be got through, it was decided to meet fortnightly and a new system was adopted. This time, the bailies with the usual assent of the 'haill counsell and communitie' nominated a large group of 'qualifeit and abell persones…to be upon the Counsell for ane year'. They were mainly academics and heritors, among them James Gordon of Seaton who was very active both in civic and church affairs, William Johnstone of Middleton, Captain Arthur Forbes, William Douglas, Professor of Divinity at King's, Patrick Sandilands, subprincipal, Dr Andro Muir, the mediciner of King's and about a dozen other Aulton leading lights, with the additional right to co-opt 'ane corume of the tread men', (a quorum of tradesmen). Twenty-five all told were co-opted with the aim of 'the taking away of all debates and animosities within the toun', and doubtless finding a quorum among their own numbers, for the council minutes reveal that non-attendance by councillors was by no means unknown. With such a large group, perhaps not all of them of the inner circle, there were, inevitably, 'leaks'. The following year it was reported that 'the bailies and counsell ar informed that some of their number doth reveall and publish such things as are done in secrett'. Anyone caught 'leaking' was to be 'removed aff of the counsell', and, inevitably, liable to a fine.

The bailies had duties to perform that were far more serious than dealing with petty squabbles. Keeping the burgh solvent was the most important one. Old Aberdeen's income had declined since the Reformation and fiscal policy ran on a hand to mouth basis. Funds came from a number of sources. Feuars and householders paid a modest property tax of scot and lot. Those who failed to fork out the full amount noted on the stent (tax) roll were instructed to pay double within forty-eight hours 'for not scotting and lotting with the toune'. In addition the inhabitants were stented for civic projects and essential maintenance work in the burgh as required. Heritors, the local landowners, were liable for the public burdens of the parish such as maintenance of roads, schools and churches, but naturally complained on occasion when they were not sure how or on what they were being assessed.

The 'customs' were a major source of revenue. We now think of customs duty in terms of a tax payable on certain imported goods or the dreaded VAT. The theory was the same then, but customs was payable on anything that could appropriately be licensed by the local authority. The right to collect these dues or customs was rouped by the Town to the highest bidder who became the 'tacksman' or 'customer'. He hoped to make a profit at it while the council had ready money in its hand and avoided the scutter of making the collection. At the weekly markets all wares were weighed or measured in the weigh-house and customs dues were paid on them. These, the small customs, were rouped to Alexander Shand in October, 1649 with a bid of 40 merks. He pledged to provide all the weights and measures necessary, a further saving for the council. Inflation, or competition brought about by the cheerful prospect of an increasingly busy market caused Alexander Orum to successfully bid more than 53 merks in 1665. The Aulton had its share of artful dodgers and in 1678 the tacksman was complaining that the measuring of meal and the weighing of butter and cheese, brought in by country people was taking place in private persons' houses in the town to his own loss. The baillies, ever vigilant against sharp-dealing stamped out this abuse.

Ale was the staple drink, and entry to the brewing trade was strictly regulated and enthusiastically taxed. Only two brewers were appointed to each quarter of the town. They paid brew customs and could be threatened with removal of licence for any stepping out of line. In 1655 those brewers unable or unwilling to pay their share of the 'souldours taxatione' (a levy on the inhabitants to raise a given number of soldiers) were to be fined, have their brewing vessels broken, and be 'dischargeit from brewing'. Timber stoups, either those of the brewers or their customers, would be 'broken to pieces at the crose' if they lacked 'the toun's stamp', seared on by branding iron, for that indicated non-payment of the tuppence duty on the stoup, an extra small custom. A £10 fine would also be exacted. But when a brewer, Mr John Johnston, was appointed clerk to town and trades in 1675, the bailies were pleased to free him from paying his brew customs while he held office. One suspects this would have been partly in lieu of salary. The bailies also, on occasion, took the enlightened step of cutting off alcohol altogether when it had become a social evil. In 1691 they were concerned about the behaviour of Thomas Rhind, 'his extra ordinar drinking with the souldiers and others, thereby drinking himself drunk and in his drunken fits troubling his own house and striking and abuseing his own wife and familie, and others, his neighbours'. Brewers were forbidden to sell him 'ale, Bear (barley) Brandie, or aquavite' under pain of a £4 fine. The town's officers were to go through their quarters, advising the brewers of the decision, so that they could not plead ignorance.

Revenue was also brought in by the customs on fishings on the Don, by the two great annual fairs and by rouping the Loch of Aberdeen. The highest bidder acquired the fertile land around it for grazing or cultivation or for renting out to others. Before the Reformation it been church property hence its other names, the Bishop's Loch or the Dean's Loch, or Denis Loch as it appears in the old charters. On 1 July 1601 it was granted by James VI to Thomas Garden of Blairton, commissary of Aberdeen and his heirs. Some years later it passed to his son, Mr Robert, who agreed to sell it to the council in 1613 with a view to its becoming community property. 'The haill inhabitantis of Auld Abd, (ie the residents of the High Street), colledge bundis and chanorie' were stented to the tune of twelve score merks, to be paid within fifteen days of the stent roll going out. Clearly those being taxed had not been over-anxious about acquiring the Loch, at least not at a cost, and the grand scheme came to naught. The Loch was later bought by an Aberdeen merchant. Eventually, in 1647 Provost Gordon of Birsemore and the bailies John Forbes, Thomas Mercer and Master John Lundie, the humanist of King's, clubbed together to buy it for 350 merks on behalf of the citizens. It was then rouped annually, usually to a small consortium of locals. In 1662 Bailie James Gordon of Seaton took it on a nineteen year lease at £10 annually, according to Orem, though the burgh accounts show £20. The deal with the council allowed him the services of:

> a man-servant out of every house of the town, to work a day's work upon his own charges, and (he) shall have liberty to stank or ditch it for draining thereof.

Orem reports that Gordon of Seaton duly ditched and drained it, and 'grew plentiful crops of corn upon it'. When his lease was up, the council returned to rouping it annually. In common with other lochs that have been drained, the Loch of Aberdeen has a habit of coming back, as water-logged playing fields around the Tillydrone Roundabout still testify.

Fines or 'unlaws' inevitably 'for the weal of the Town' if they could be got, were a further source of income. On 29 June, 1604, John Guthrie, college porter was fined 40s for calling Thomas Kemp thief and knave and 'drawing of ane sanger to him', though similar assaults on bailies or the town's officers would be punished by a spell in the stocks, if not banishment. Thomas Watson in Murcar mentioned at the head of the chapter was indeed fined for throwing the cheese at William Maxwell, but the space for the amount has been left blank, Sometimes dual payments were required. In 1611 George Chalmer and his wife were involved in what sounds like a family row. They had gone to the wall of Marjory Chalmer and her daughters where they had cast down a tub of water. The magistrates ordered them to pay £10 unlaw, the fine, and £6 assythment, compensation to the injured parties. As a High Street flesher Chalmer probably had the money, but with many folk living barely above subsistence level, one wonders how often fines were paid. On 24 October 1609 Thomas Baverlay was fined 40s 'for troubling the toun and giffing of Janet Lamb ane cuff'. This old nuisance was a poor beadsman from Gavin Dunbar's Hospital who had no money. His cautioner had to pay for him. If a fine was not forthcoming, goods were swiftly poinded, that is seized and sold to cover the debt, and interesting items thus acquired occasionally make their way into the records, a kist, an ambrey, a brewing vat among them.

There were many demands on incoming revenue. Unlike Aberdeen, the Aulton was not a royal burgh and did not have to pay 'cess' or tax to the crown for the privilege of trading overseas, though it was taxed as part of the sheriffdom of Aberdeen. High on the list of financial commitments were defence of the burgh, road repairs and fabric maintenance, though unpaid citizen labour was made mandatory whenever feasible. Every man had to pave the area in front of his dwelling with cassies, under pain of a £10 fine, while in August 1684 the citizens were instructed to look out their spades and shovels and prepare to red (clear up, tidy up) the highway at the Bridge of Don (the Seatongate at the Brig o Balgownie), under a 14s penalty for non-compliance.

A fair number of salaries, full and part-time had to be met. Since the Reformation the parish had to provide a school and pay the master's stipend and accommodation. Though the salary was not generous it was one of the more costly of the regularly recurring items in the budget and though its payment was shared with kirk session, college and heritors, it was met with difficulty. Then there was the dempster who read out the decisions or judgements of the bailies. He appears in the early seventeenth century but the office disappears while that of town clerk emerges. One of the latter, a notary, Alexander Sandison, was sacked in August 1654 by the 'haill toun' for 'som miscarriage of his office of Clerkschip but he was back by 1663. An entry in the burgh accounts reads, 'delivered to Alex Sandison for his clerk fee, £13 6s 8d'. Either that or his fee was grossly in arrears. The town's officers who kept law and order also had to be paid, as had the scourgers and branders. The 1697-99 accounts show that 3s 6d was paid to John Archie 'for naileing and burning of Duff', while the instruments of punishment required repair and renewal from time to time. Mending the stocks in 1684 cost 14s. Five years later 'ane branks to the cross' cost £1 4s. Though a tolbooth was eventually built, its operation, even on an *ad hoc* basis was, unlike fines, a financial drain. The imprisonment of Elspet Muskie for several days in 1666 cost £2 6s 4d in peats, ale and candles and the services of Mettie Fackoner as jailer.

One vital member of the community was the muckster who mucked the town out, clearing away dung and excrement. In the mid-seventeenth century George Volum performed out this task. He was well-liked. On 7

September 1645 Thomas Mercer and Mr John Lundie took up the freewill offering at St Machar's kirk door and collected £11 6s 8d which was 'all deliverit to George Volum to help buy him ane hors'. Muck abounded as in all Scottish towns and the council endeavoured to make the cleanliness of the town the responsibility of all inhabitants. The value of dung as a fertiliser was also appreciated. In August 1636 it was ordained:

> No man shall lay muck in the wyndis of Old Abd or upon such pairtis of the Calsie that may devigour the toun or impede free passage of horse and men. And sick muck as lyes in thoise pairts alreadie, to be removed by the owneris within four and auchtie hours under pain of confiscatioun.

Then there were always incidentals both anticipated as in 'paper and the binding of the council records, 14s', and unexpected: £1 2s 'for a pairt of a coffin to one that was found dead on the sands'. The 1667-68 accounts hint at some crisis in the new council chamber: 6s 'for ane hors hyre for overtaking the post being gone'. This was followed by 3s 'drink to the post to cause him have a care of the letters to deliver them', a *pourboire* likely to have the reverse effect. In 1666-7 'Item £2 8s' was spent in Widow Forbes's at the first meeting of the council that year. Say no more, except that during the era of the Perwinnes Moss turf wars at Scotstown, the Aulton's representatives appear to have had difficulty in passing the tavern at Dubford. Monies spent on royal celebrations were substantial but essential gestures of loyalty. The accounts of 1687-88 show expenditure of £8 14 for the 'solemnizing' of a royal birth, but not too solemn judging by the 'wine and glasses and ane bonfire' that the money was spent on. (The bonfire required the purchase of peats). Glasses regularly feature in these celebratory entries, replacements presumably for those thrown down and smashed at the previous celebration. Either that or the bailies were sneaking them home.

Incoming funds were quickly disbursed. On 29 September 1643 three bailies including Master John Lundie who was something of a financial specialist, reported on how they had spent the £26 recently ingathered from three sources, fines, entrance silver paid by the new burgesses of trade and the breidsellers' licence fees. Seven fines were collected including two, a merk each, from women. The highest was £2. The seven new trade freemen, admitted the week before included three weavers, two cordiners, Alexander Hervie 'labourer of the grund' and John Irving who had been pushing the boat out for he was due both entrance money and a fine. Entrance silver varied between four merks, £2.13. 4d and 13s 4d. In the 1720s Orem wrote that 'when the magistrates made a tradesman freeman of the burgh he pays only ten merks to the town' so the entrance fee had either risen sharply or the 1643 entrants were paying by instalment. Four women licensed to sell

The Drummer

The drummer was a familiar figure in the High Street. In those days before newspapers, when few owned time-pieces, let alone alarm clocks (though there must have been a few crowing cocks in the Aulton), his services, were vital to the community. He started his day's work by drumming a 'travellia' or call to work at five in the morning and a tapton at 8 o'clock at night. The work was part-time but the drummer had to be on call all day. There were a variety of proclamations to 'go through the toun by tuck of drum' as the bailies ordained: that inhabitants mend the cassies to the Brig o Don (Balgownie), that a visitation of the school was due as well as prohibitions about casting peats and the inspecting of expenses at the town house. The edict about destroying the 'hot and jollie' bitches (Chapter 15) went by drum so that 'none pretend ignorance hereof'.

The drummer publicised the great fairs, and attended them, for which he received extra payment, as he did for any duties outwith the usual. In 1736 for example, the drummer got two guineas from the burgh coffers 'for 3 advertizements anent the customes, one anent receipting soldiers, one about a dead child, one to Flit and one for a fast day'.

His uniform was a costly item for the council, but a smart outfit was a good advertisement for the town. In March 1662 the treasurer was ordained to buy the drummer 'ane suitt of clothes with ane pair of shoes'. This is the bill: Four ellne (ells) of grayes...£4. Stitching and thread and making...£1 4s. Shoen...£1. Plus: To Robert Broune for a skin to the drum...6s. Broune was presumably the glover husband of Helen Anderson whose misdemeanour is featured on page 216. Speaking of glovers, in March 1677, Patrick, son of John Rankin, glover, was appointed drummer for a half year at twenty merks and 'a frie litle Chamber for his accomodatione'.

William Walker, was the best known of Aulton drummers. He seems to have been public-spirited for back in 1669 he was 'fee'd to serve for a Reed Coat for the Toune' the fee being £3 5s. In other words he joined the local militia or home guard. He was appointed drummer in 1683, and the treasurer at that time, Patrick Kilgour the clockmaker, was, 'to cause to mack to William Walker ane long coat of ane purpie collour with quhyt lace thereupon with breiches and stockings of that same collour'. Many's the blaeberry that must have gone into dyeing that outfit. The bill came to £10 3s 6d, nearly £4 dearer than Rankin's.

In 1685 Walker was admitted a burgess of Old Aberdeen as 'drummer and militia man', so he must have kept up his military career. Two years later the deacons of the Trades complained of his non-appearance at the appointed hour. Walker had gone on strike. He was not being paid the promised salary. The matter was resolved and it was agreed that each trade could take twelve pennies off his salary for every unjustified non-appearance in the future. We learn from this episode that he was only expected to go through the town, 'the weather being dry'. All went well for a time and in 1689 he was due for another suit, 'ane long meitt coat', this time, nothing fancy, breeches, stockings of the same cloth and a pair of double-soled shoes. The bailies graciously acknowledged that he 'is now and has been a good space bypast in the tounes service beyond ordinar'. Alas, they spoke too soon, for in 1698 he was sacked for 'ilk times neglect of his office'. He successfully petitioned for council reinstatement and in 1703 his duties were augmented. He was to ring the tolbooth bell at six in the morning and eight at night 'before the drum begin'. He was also to ring the bell on the first Saturday of the month, announcing the start of council proceedings. His yearly salary was made up by members of the community and according to Orem, was 'a crown out of the convener's box, and half a crown out of every trade's box, with 4s yearly from householders, being a penny quarterly, as he thinks most convenient'. (I'm not sure about Orem's arithmetic).

Walker had a dreadful scare in 1716 when a group of rioting Jacobite students forced him to drum the length of the Aulton, as far as the humanist's gate, proclaiming that all persons should come and see 'the Duke of Brunswick in effigie' (a drawing of George I) burnt in a bonfire at the college gates. From his deposition given afterwards we learn that he was then sixty-eight and unable to write. Walker survived this unpleasant episode and kept his job for he had been forced to act under duress. He went on drumming until he was about seventy-four.

In 1722, William Rainie, weaver was appointed drummer. Inflation had taken its toll. His outfit, twice the price of Walker's had the weaver trade working overtime. To William Beverlay for 4 ells and 3 quarters of cloth to be a coat for the Drumer ...£9 10s. To James Turreff for 3 and a quarter ells of sairge to be lyning...£2 2s. To Alex Lumsden for deying the same... £1 4s. To Alex Westland for a quarter yard of blew cloth, 3 doz of matle buttens, buckrom wade silk and other furnitor for the sd. coat...£4 4s. To Androw Simpson for makeing the sd. coat... £1 10s. Total cost, £24.10s

'breid', bread, which was oatcakes, paid 13s 4s each. Marjorie Carll, Margrat Boyis and Merioun Nisbet were old hands, noted the 1636 census and Marjorie Carll had been admitted as burgess in 1640, one of fifteen Aulton women admitted during the seventeenth century. The fourth, was a married woman, Thomas Hervie's wife. Of this £6 13. 4d went to the schoolmaster, Alexander Wilguis, as part stipend, a fee of eight merks to William Watt, clerk, a notary who lived in the Chanonry, four merks to the town's officers and the remaining seventeen merks to James Innes, the town's calsier or pavier, for mending the broken cassies from the Doocot Green to the market cross, a stretch where there were no heritors that could be charged; 'quhilk money is in the hands of James Innes'. Salaries of the white collar (cravat?) workers were sometimes three years in arrears, but calsiers were paid as soon as their work was completed.

There was a good example of this policy of 'on the nail' payment for work completed as well as citizen input, in the autumn of 1636 when the magistrates instigated urgently needed road repairs. Both the north entry to the town which ran from the Brig o Balgownie via the Bishop's Port and the Doocot Green, and Cluny's Wynd were 'in winter so difficult that men and horse are both in danger'. Earlier resolutions to repair them had come to naught. Eventually, on 9 August of that year the magistrates ordained that both thoroughfares be laid with cassies before winter. It was agreed 'with the uniforme consent of the haill indwellers of the Spittell, chanrie and middell toun' (the High Street), that those who had horses and presumably carts were each to bring four loads of sand and stones to the places under repair, and those who hadn't should send 'a sufficient servant with barrowis, tulis, skullis (barrows, implements and baskets)...to carrie sand'. 'The calsier sall be sett to work before every man's door'. Each householder had to provide the necessary sand and stones for his section of frontage and the calsier was to be paid the usual price of 40s the rood. Were payment for the completed work not forthcoming by the time the calsier was finished and ready 'to goe from the door' the householder's goods would be poinded. The final 'Compt of the Cassies', presented to the council by the bailies Master John Lundie and Dr William Gordon, the mediciner of King's that December reveals that these repairs had been a major undertaking. David Donald was paid £12 for taking nine score cartfulls of great stones out of Cluny's yard to the Nether Chanonry Port, while Nicol Torrie, a husbandman who lived on the High Street, was paid £5 16s 8d 'for leiding (carting) sand all the time'. Though it wasn't part of the original remit, 27s worth of causeying was carried out at College Bounds, handy for Dr Gordon who lived there.

Balancing the budget, though an essential part of the bailies' responsibilities was by no means the only one. Fixing the prices of goods to prevent profiteering was another and it is interesting to contemplate that some of the desperadoes who rode forth to lay waste the Lands of Hilton, could later be found sitting about St Machar's Cathedral where the council met, discussing the price of oatcakes like douce bodies. In 1603, ten cakes were to be baked to a peck of meal, presumably in large rounds, containing fifteen ounces 'of guid, weill bakin breid'. (Like breid, 'caikis' were oatcakes, as opposed to fancy cakes). Later ten women were fined 6s 8d, half a merk each for selling their 'caikis' dearer than the price laid down by the bailies. The baxters were to bake 16oz of bread (loaves) for 8d. Candles were 4s the pound or twopence 'the haill candle'. Milk was 12d the pint and no ale was to be sold dearer than 16d the pint, nor beer for more than 18d. The magistrates either acted as 'visitors' themselves, inspecting goods and prices, or delegated these tasks. 'Custodians of the ale' went through the town to check that it was not being sold too dear or too weak. If the latter was the case, it was 'confiscate to the poor'.

The maintenance of law and order, was taken very seriously. Among the duties of Archibald Magkie, appointed town's officer in 1605, was the rounding up and delivery to the baillies of 'upsitteris and drinkeris' roaming the streets after ten at night. Since no drink was to be sold after nine at night this gave an hour's drinking-up time. The town was divided into quarters for policing and a variety of other purposes, among them drilling and containing the plague. These quarters varied but the most usual were, south: the Spital and College Bounds to Douglas Wynd and Bailie Baxter's Wynd opposite, about halfway along the High Street: middle: from Douglas and Baxter's Wynds to Robert Forbes's and George Cumming's Wynds. The Cummings' yard marched with Cluny's Wynd at the Chanonry: north quarter, from there to the Bridge of Don (Balgownie).

In 1662 the quartermasters, perhaps akin to police 'specials', were given explicit instructions for the better regulating of the town. There were thirteen items on the list, including apprehending strangers, vagabonds or suspected persons in the night time 'quha cannot give accompt of themselves'; noting all 'loiterers and unprofitable persons' in their own beats; on coming upon 'any fray or sture' to call on the assistance of neighbours to sunder the parties; to look out for those who failed to provide themselves with fire (fuel) kell (kail, vegetables) and other necessaries but who are professional thieves; to note those who keep horse, cattle 'or any uther bestiall', but have insufficient grass in summer and provinder in winter and those who oppose or impede the quartermasters in the discharge of their office; to look out for 'extraordinarie drunkards, and especialle those who keep ale houses after ten a cloake at night', and those who are 'extraordinar cursers and swearers'; those who give short measure, especially below standard candles. All such were to be reported to the council and bailies to be examined and 'punished if neid beis'.

Civic involvement was not popular with eveyone. On 13 August 1659 'the haill Inhabitantis' were asked if 'everyone of them' would do their bit in watching and warding, scotting and lotting and policing their respective quarters. All agreed except eleven tradesmen, who were then named and shamed and had their right as trade freemen taken away 'until such tyme as they and every one of them buy thair freidome and liberty of new againe'.

Parson Gordon gives an idyllic description of Old Aberdeen between the 1640s and 1660, as 'enclosed with little hills, pleasant cornefeilds, very fruitfull, and with pastures mixed amongst the plowghed feilds', but the worry of a failed harvest was never far away. The 1630s was a time of darth, an unpleasant combination of scarcity and high prices and the bailies forbade the hoarding of food. On 13 December 1634 it was decreed that 'no man within the Toune shall buy mair meill nor serves his awin household'. It was also *de rigeur,* as already noted, that all families be provided with fuel and kale for the winter ahead. Old Aberdeen had a problem with beggars, perhaps greater than other towns of similar size. They had been drawn to the town in the palmy pre-Reformation days by the prospect of alms distributed at the cathedral door, and afterwards by the hope of finding open-handed, well-to-do families in the Chanonry. Care of the poor, that is its own poor, was a parish responsibility and with little for themselves Aulton folk did not take kindly to providing for destitute incomers. Compassionate folk who took in stranger beggars were liable for fine. The First Book of Discipline stated:

> We are not patrons for stubborn and idle beggars...but for the widow and fatherless, the aged, impotent or lamed who neither can nor may travail for their sustentation...the stout and strong beggar must be compelled to work, and every person that may not work must be compelled to repair to the place where he or she was born.

This the authorities of Old Aberdeen took to heart. In November 1635 at a meeting of the kirk session, its moderator, Provost Alexander Gordon of Cluny took steps to revise the poor roll and Archibald Bishop, the Cathedral bellman, 'willingly undertook to purge the toun of all stranger and countrie beggars (and) to begin the morne'. He would receive 12s over and above his work as bellman for his 'diligent performing'. By the following spring the crisis had surely intensified for the bailies decided to carry out a thorough purge. On 9 May 1636 the council minutes reported:

> The said day was taken up ane roll of the haill inhabitantis of the Auld toune, chanrie and spittel, thair bairnes and servandis. As also ane roll of all the other poor folkes within the said Toune and parish'.

The purpose was to seek out 'all infamous person and ydleris, (idlers) those that hes no certaine calling to live by, and wer not provided of kaill and fewall (fuel) and other necessaries of good neighbourhood', and to uncover anyone giving refuge to such persons. Of these two rolls, the 'haill inhabitantis' census has survived and contains a mine of information about the people of Old Aberdeen. The 'poor folkes' roll was also drawn up but is no longer extant. A council minute of 16 May 1636 gives the findings of a tribunal of the thirty 'most honest and aged persones of the Toun' who had analysed and pronounced on both censuses. Over twenty-five families or individuals living alone were to be either banished or in a few cases, given the opportunity to go into service. Some of these families were living in the High Street like 'the haill household within the chancellor's close' which must have been rather embarrassing for Bailie Thomas Mercer who was town chancellor at the time. About a dozen of these noted by the 'most honest and aged' do not appear on the 'haill inhabitantis' census, and must have come from the 'poor folkes' roll.

It was the kirk session that decided which of the poor would remain. Tokens were issued at a given time at the door of St Machar's and those who failed to turn up were banished. The Aulton's poor would carry 'ane floure de luce in leid', the fleur-de-lis or lily of Old Aberdeen on their breasts and receive alms 'at the yetis (gates) of honest men' at an appointed time. The poor of Oldmachar parish had their own badge, a star in lead, and had permission to come into Old Aberdeen only on Sundays to hear the preaching. A week day visit would result in their being treated as stranger beggars and 'chaised away by the scurger'.

Above, an Old Aberdeen beggar's badge of 1722, showing, not a single fleur-de-lis, but the pot of lilies, one of the symbols of the Aulton. The 1636 badge would have been similar, for this was 'the toun's mark'. It is a charming little token, in a pale blue-grey lead, derived from galena, with a hole at the top enabling the beggar to thread through a narrow strip of cloth or leather and wear it round his neck.

Becoming a servant was preferable to begging. In 1644, William Drum and his wife appeared before the notary public, Thomas Lillie and undertook to feed clothe and entertain Elspet Gilchrist, so that Elspet would not have to go through the town begging. Jean Mukart, Drum's wife was to teach Elspet to 'wyff shankis' (knit stockings), over a seven

The Plague

Old Aberdeen was visited three times by the plague during the seventeenth century. In 1604, the bailies took steps to exclude strangers but the 'pest' was back in 1606 and the town was divided into quarters for 'allaying the plague.' The inhabitants were instructed to build up the back dykes at the rear of their rigs, though that would scarcely have kept out anyone determined to get in.

In 1647 there was a major outbreak of plague, fortunately the last in the area, but the worst. The burgh was again divided into quarters for visiting the sick and reporting new cases to the bailies. Three 'visitors', William Cumming, William Lin and Thomas Angus, were to keep an eye on High Street and College Bounds while John Farquhar of Noram, an elder of the kirk, was to inspect 'the haill Chanrie and Chaplenes', the latter being the former Chaplains' Court, now 'flatted'. On 3 July, the bailies ordained that there be no public meetings and no buying of wine or ale in taverns except with a licence from themselves. A round-the-clock watch was to be kept by captains and their men, presumably to keep out those fleeing from Aberdeen where the plague was especially virulent. Women and bairns were forbidden to go there under pain of banishment while men required a special warrant from the bailies. Disobedience would be met with a £20 fine, loss of freedom if they were burgesses and banishment. No weavers, tailors or hammermen were to accept cloth or any other work from out of the town and buying and selling at the market cross was prohibited.

On August 15 'sermones in the kirk' were 'given over for the vehemencie of the infectione' but during the next few weeks there were open air readings at the Corsehill, Dilspro (Grandholm), the Carne Gully, Cookstone, Persley and Scotstown. Given the circumstances, reasonable collections were taken up, and on August 22 a bairn was baptised in the kirkyard of St Machar. Huts were built on the outskirts of Aberdeen for plague victims of both towns, and Aulton folk did what they could to ease the few remaining days on earth of friends and family. Kirk session accounts show that in November and December of 1647, 13s 4d was spent on bread and drink to David Watson, his wife and children in Aberdeen's huts (on the Links), 10s on meat and drink to Hendrie Chalmer in the huts at Ferryhill and 8s for aquavite to Hendrie Kellie's wife in a hut at Scotstown.

King's College retreated to Fraserburgh for one session during plague year, perhaps occupying the old buildings of Fraserburgh University which had existed from 1600 until 1605. Marischal College decamped to Peterhead. In Aberdeen itself 1600 citizens died from the epidemic out of a population of 8000, plus 140 in Fitty and Torry. In Oldmachar parish, including Old Aberdeen the total was only twenty. The restrictions of the bailies were to good effect.

year apprenticeship. Thus Elspet's rights were clearly defined. In 1655 decree was given against James Hay, skinner, for non-payment of Margaret Ellis's half year's service fee. He now had to deliver to her four merks of silver, a coat with sleeves, a pair of shoes a and new sark as promised.

Following the major census of 1636, 'privy inquests' took place periodically throughout the rest of the century. In January 1660 the council delegated nine men in groups of three, (saftey in numbers), to go through the 'haill toune and freedom thereof' noting 'ilk householder and what traid they are and what way they may live'. In November 1697 three citizens of standing went through the town, inspecting 'what louse and ydle persons or stranger are within the toun, betwixt the Bridge of Don (Balgownie) and Spittel. Six months later Alexander Taitt was to be paid £10 scots yearly 'for putting way extranean beggars'. Not everyone warmed to this task. Back in 1666 George Lovie had been fined 40s for not carrying a 'crippell wyff' out of the Aulton as commanded by the bailies. Andro Nicoll was to do the job instead, and anyone making trouble for him to be fined ten merks.

With the menace of famine never far away the bailies were quick to punish those who damaged crops. Their destruction could threaten not only livelihood but life as well. A spate of damage occurred in the 1670s, and fines of 30s were levied on those caught making a path through 'other mens cornes, either oates, bear, pease or any uther graine' on foot or horse. Those who kept geese, drakes and fowls were fined 3s 4d for every bird found amongst their neighbour's 'cornes'. One agrarian transgressor caught in the act was George Archibald who was fined ten merks in New Year of 1666. He had been back and forward, cutting and taking away broom belonging to Kettocksmills, (Thomas Gordon of Kettocksmills, a member of the kirk session), and James Gordon of Seaton. Perhaps he was setting up as broomstick-maker but young broom was valued as cattle fodder in hard times and as shelter for rabbit warrens. Archibald was threatened with banishment for a second offence.

Though they would not have recognised the term, the bailies were also environmentally conscious. There are a number of acts against throwing dirty water in the Powis Burn, while in March 1695 they ordained that no one was to 'shear, pluck up, tak away or receive bent (rushes) from the Links or the Bentie Hillocks, the little sandy hills that were a feature of the beach within living memory. The fine was £10. The bents were popular for theeking cottages, but the bailies would have been aware of the damage caused by erosion.

We have touched only on the tip of the iceberg of the work of running the burgh. We have noted next to nothing of its relationship with the college, the kirk, the king, the covenant, the incorporated trades of Old Aberdeen and the royal burgh down the road, but that will come. Enough to say for the moment that in the Old Aberdeen of the seventeenth century, the bailies' labours for the 'weal of the toun' were never done, and sometimes not appreciated; sitting on the bench, making byelaws, stenting and cessing, imposing law and order and retail price maintenance, stimulating the cash flow, carrying out roadworks, resolving quarrels, containing the plague, collecting fines, keeping an eye on students, prentices and other 'disordelie boyes', organising and policing the market and the fairs, maintaining the armoury, billeting soldiers, seeking out lose and idle persons, being subject to abuse and threatened with dirks.

It is little wonder that some declined the honour. In September 1644 John Lundie and Alexander Spalding refused office. Though they had served many times in the past, enough was enough. Lundie pointed out that he was humanist and master of the grammar school and was expressly prohibited by an act of the last General Assembly 'nocht to be burdinit with ony uther charge, moreover, this toun nocht haveing power to chuise the Colledge Magestratis'. Be that as it may, Lundie remained active in local affairs and kept on the important task as collector at St Machar's Cathedral. Spalding, father of the chronicler, John, pleaded that he was 'greivet with the gutt (gout) in his feit, kneis and legis that he may not walk up nor doun stairis nor keip the churche in tyme of devyne service'. A very useful excuse.

Chapter 12

The Great Fairs

The fairs in popish times stood within the chanry and were great ones.
William Orem, A Description of the Chanonry, Cathedral etc, 1751.

The barony charter of 1489 granted Old Aberdeen the right to hold two annual fairs. It was quite specific about the dates. One should take place 'the day before Good Friday commonly called Skyre Thursday' the other on St Luke the Evangelist's Day, which was 18 October. Orem reports: 'These two markets in popish times stood within the chanry and were great ones. But at the beginning of the Reformation of religion they decayed, by reason of the troubles of the times'. The early 1660s which saw the restoration of the monarchy and the reinstatement of the bishops yet again, also marked Old Aberdeen's determination to promote itself as a leading centre of trade in the North East. The two fairs were revived but competition was intense. Apart from being in the shadow of the royal burgh of Aberdeen, between 1650 and 1707 twelve new burghs of barony would be created in Aberdeenshire while twenty-nine other places had the right to hold markets and fairs.

Then as now it was important to advertise. The burgh accounts for 1661-2 show a fee of £3 to Thomas Angus and of £2 1s to Hendrie Adam for 'procleming our Market' at Fyvie and Banchory respectively. William Johnston shared £2 14s with the drummer for proclaiming the fair at Kinkell and at Trewel Fair which was held at Kennethmont. These men were not council 'casuals' but leading citizens. Angus was a bailie, treasurer and deacon of the weavers, Adam, a leading cordiner and Johnston, a burgess. The fair was also advertised in the *Aberdeen Almanac.* The 1664-65 accounts show that John Forbes, printer, received four guineas 'for insertinge of the marcat in the prognousticatione'. A wet autumn of 1690 must have turned Old Aberdeen into a sea of mud and Patrick Fraser, subtacksman of the town's customs, was paid £3 to intimate that the fair was being held 'within a fortnight efter the ordinarie tyme ...by reason of ill weather and great rains'. Sounds familiar.

The Skyre Thursday Fair or Pasch (Easter) mercat, lasted two days and was spread over the entire town. In March 1662 preparations got underway with the bailies instructing the six quartermasters to allot the stands. The sheep and nolt (cattle) market was to be at Hillhead, ('the hill on this syd of the bridge') with the horse market in the same area but nearer the town. Cloth, linen and wool would be sold at the market cross, the traditional place for cloth sales in Scotland, with the timber market in Cluny's Wynd. Chapmen and trimmers were to have their stands 'about the cross', while other tradesmen were located between the cross and King's College on both sides of the road.

The sales area of the St Luke's Fair was, at least on some occasions, more concentrated. Tradesmen's stalls were set up in the High Street, running from Baillie Forbes's gate to King's College on both sides. The horse market was at the Loch side, and the nolt and kye 'upon the minister's manse', which was in the Chanonry. The sheep market was at the back dyke of the manse so rich deposits would have been forthcoming for the minister's glebe. The cloth market and the chapmen were around the cross, and there was a fishmarket at John Baverlay's and Alex Merser's close heads, again in the High Street. The timber market was set up between Cluny's Wynd and Port. Before the stalls could go up the town had to be cleansed and scourged and 'all tack the guiding (manure) aff af the cassies'. 'Everie one that hes middings and muck within the Toun sall tak away the same under pain of £4'.

The fairs, of course, were about making money and not only for the vendors. They were one of the main sources of revenue for the Aulton. The rent of a stall was fixed at 3s 4d and the customs dues in 1668 for example were levied as follows: each cow, calf, horse or ox, 12d: a ewe, lamb or 'old scheip', 4d: an ell of cloth, linen or wool, 1d: a pair of stockings, 1d: a load of timber, 2s: a pair double-soled shoes (except bairns) 4d, single-soled, 2d: a load of leather, 6s 8d: a single hide, 12d: a pack of wool, 6s 8d. Those two prominent citizens Thomas Angus and William Lin kept a check on the weights and measures, seeing to it that the goods were properly looked after 'and the cassies dichtit'.

The collectors of customs were strategically stationed around the town. In 1655 for example Geo Allan was at the Brig of Done (Balgownie) and took in 20 merks 4s 10d: John Hervie at the Mortar Hole (below the Loch), 16 merks 9d: William Wobster at Powis Brig, £2 18s: William Sangster at the Broomhill (west end of Meston Walk), £5 3s 4d: Andro Baird at Tillidronshill (beside the Market Port), 16s 8d: within 'the bodie of the toune', 40s.

Judging by these figures and the location of the collectors, most vendors came from the north rather than from the Aberdeen area. The customs collected from the St Luke's Fair of 1665, according to the burgh accounts was £24, and from the Skyre Thursday Fair the following Easter, £21 12. These bags of money would have been delivered straight to the town treasurer, waiting for them in the new council meeting house behind the cross. Fairs attracted argument, hot tempers, drunks and troublemakers and before the Skyre Thursday Fair of 1662 the bailies announced that they would attend, 'the two days in the counsell house for hearing and deciding all contraverssies that shall occur betwixt any perties quhatsomevir'. It was an annual problem. On another occasion it was 'ordainit that quhatsumever persones sall trubell or molest any persone to the disturbance of the marcat salbe imprisoned, fyned and examplerie punished according as the falt sall deserve'.

Hence the presence at some fairs of thirty-six men 'sufficientlie armed', six each provided by the six quartermasters of the town, or two men, similarly armed, from every trade, though some dodged out. A typical disturbance took place after the St Luke's Fair of October 1682. Alexander Sted was fined £4 for 'uncivil carriage' towards a man and wife from Kettocksmills, 'abusing them in his drunkness upon the mercat night...following them upon the hie streit with many railling and uncivill speiches'. One can picture the drunk stotting about the High Street. He was also to be locked up, 'keiped in firmance', until he paid, 'and langer during the pleasure of the magistrates'.

Fairs increased in popularity as the seventeenth century wore on. 'That pairt about the crose the time of the mercats is thronged', reported a minute of April 1677. Potential customers could not 'frielie pas and repas up and doun the streites', so the cloth market was relocated to Cluny's Wynd. Stands were to be set up in single rows, 'and no double stands to be set over against others'. The customs of St Luke's in 1692 and 'Pasch mercat' of 1693 'and Whitsonday thereafter' amounted to £133 6s 8d.

When the fair was over the helpers were paid, among them the drummer, piper, officers, and guard. They did quite well. In 1663-64, £4 was expended on 'pipes, candle, tobacco and drink to them that roult the marcat' while Gilbert Mackie who put up the stalls was paid 6s 'for waiting on the fair'. And we need not pity the bailies, apparently confined to the council chambers, waiting to deal with troublemakers and all the revelry passing them by. An item of expenditure, £4 18 6, 'In Bailie Baxters with the Provost and Dean of Guild of Aberdeen the day of St Lukes mercat' noted in the council minutes of 1700-01 sounds like a convivial day for the Aulton bailies and their distinguished guests.

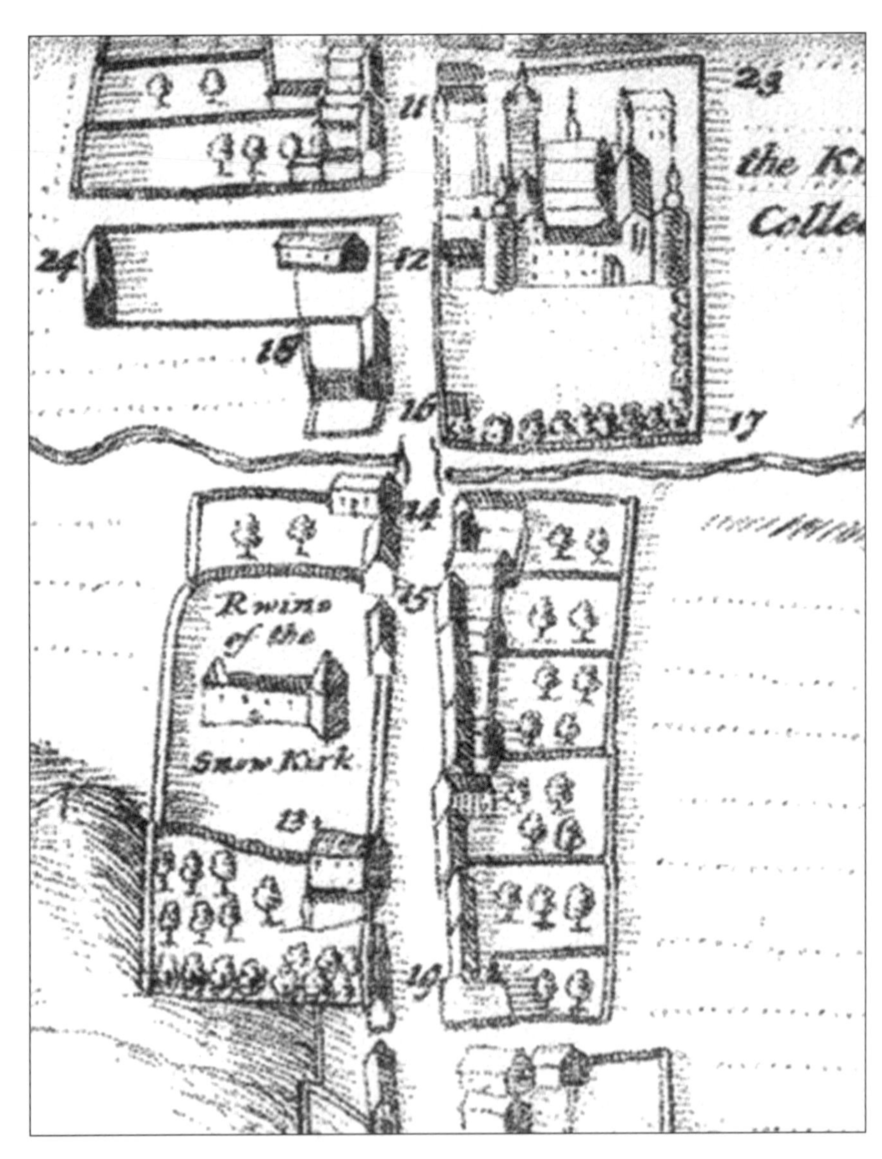

A detail from Parson Gordon's Plan, showing College Bounds as it was in 1661. On the right, between 19 (Ruins of the Civilist's House) and 14 (Powis Brig) is the row once occupied by the Chapel's choir, taken over by the artisans after the Reformation. There is a large house near the centre. The Powis Burn flows past the end of the row, with the King's College garden beyond. On the left hand side the humanist's manse and glebe is at 13. Beyond the Snow Kirk, the canonist's manse is at 14, with the Twelve Roods at 18 and the mediciner's manse beyond to the left of 12.

Chapter 13

College Bounds

About the College, at some distance, are the severall professors houses, some of them ruinous, uthers quyte demolisht, a few of them keept in their first integritie.
Parson Gordon, Description of Bothe Touns of Aberdeen, 1661.

Each of the three major areas of Old Aberdeen, College Bounds, High Street and the Chanonry, developed differently and at different times and the 1636 census, going from south to north acts as a useful vade-mecum for an exploration of the Aulton of the seventeenth century. Long before College Bounds and the High Street acquired their separate names and personalities, the two roads together were referred to in the old charters as the *via regia*, the royal highway. Further north, the Chanonry was ecclesiastical terrain, lined by the manses of the canons with St Machar's Cathedral at its heart. Bishop Elphinstone may well have planned College Bounds as an academic version of the Chanonry. The area was laid out as a university precinct with the manses of the civilist, canonist, grammarian, mediciner and the 'choral row' of the chapel's singers forming an extra-mural campus while King's, a part of the 'colledge boundis', was its focal point. The college was designed as a brilliant showpiece and given the strategic position of the manses at the entrance to the Aulton, it is unlikely that Elphinstone planned for anything other than dwellings of quality and substance, perhaps built of the same stone as the college itself.

One might have expected the Powis Burn to mark the southern border of Old Aberdeen but Elphinstone in his territorial charter of 1498, extended the boundary as far south as he could, to the Spital. And so College Bounds was, and is bisected rather than bounded by the burn, wandering through marshlands in those days, but long since culverted and flowing through the grounds between Johnston and Crombie Halls of Residence, then along the line of University Road. It was the civilist's manse on the east side of the road beyond the burn that marked the southern limits of both college and Aulton. It stood roughly on the site of the present Nos 14-16 College Bounds. In the 1720s the masters of King's noted that 'of a long tyme (the manse) hes been, as is reported, by fyre or some accident ruined and quite demolished'. 'A long tyme' was true for Parson Gordon's Plan reports it as ruinous in 1661.

It was not as if the civilists had gone for good despite the vetoes of the New Foundation in the late sixteenth century. That post, along with those of mediciner and canonist had been re-established after a royal visitation of 1619. The announcement of their reinstatement was off-handedly included in the 'repairs' section of the visitation report, to wit, 'the two turrets on the round towers to be repaired with lead; the offices which were abolished filled up'. But though the post had been resurrected, the civilists themselves, being notorious absentees, saw no cause to have the manse rebuilt. At the time of our current journey of exploration, Mr Roger Mowat, advocate, of Balquholly, a member of an ancient Aberdeenshire family, had been civilist since the 1620s but lived and worked in Edinburgh. He never gave lectures in the civilist's manse on the *Institutes* of Justinian nor wore the gown of Orleans. On the other hand, he never received a stipend. In 1640 he resigned in favour of James Sandilands, younger, canonist of King's. Canon law was not altogether obsolete as one might have thought. The chronicler Spalding, who did not like Sandilands reported in his *Memorialls* that by 1640 he had 'craftily' persuaded the General Assembly to let him teach the canon law relating to wives, wills and teinds, since these topics were still relevant. All the rest 'smellit of poperie' and were discarded. Nevertheless the days of canon law as a subject at King's were numbered, yet again, as Sandilands knew. He neatly transferred his current salary to his new post of civilist. He was also commissary of Aberdeen, so there were murmurings about his two salaries.

Between the civilist's ruins and the Powis Burn was the row where the choral chaplains of King's once lived. The present Nos 18-48 College Bounds, roughly speaking, now occupy this site. Parson Gordon shows about ten houses, either original manses or their successors, some with little outhouses in their yards and all with sizeable 'tails'. The Spital section of the 1636 census, which includes College Bounds, notes eight weavers, four tailors, two wrights, a cordiner and a cooper, a number of whom would have lived in this row after the songsters left or died out. Some College Bounds craftsmen regarded themselves as outwith Old Aberdeen proper therefore not liable for membership of the Old Aberdeen Trades Incorporations whose dues took 'ane considerable pairt' of their members 'sallarie'. The College Bounds men could thus undercut their Old Aberdeen competitors. The magistrates did their best to stamp out this practice. An entry in the council minutes of 6 March 1677 states that 'the haill inhabitants within the colledge bounds' were subject to the jurisdiction of the magistrates, and were to pay their scot and lot. These strictures were carried out with the approval of King's College which still owned the land there. In fact College Bounds men were admitted as Old Aberdeen burgesses of trade from the mid-seventeenth century and probably earlier; others opted for the free-lance option and this altercation grumbled on for years. In May 1689 legitimate souters complained to the magistrates that John Hutcheon of College Bounds brought in new shoes 'several times' to Old Aberdeen (the High Street) where he sold them. His shoes, presumably the unsolds, were duly 'confiscat' to the cordiner trade .

The Powis Burn flowed past the north end of this row, *en route* to the Links. The burn served as the water supply for the southern half of Old Aberdeen and this stretch, now underneath University Road, was the only place where the washing of clothes in the burn itself as it flowed out of the Aultoun, was permitted. The environmentally conscious Old Aberdeen Council regularly issued interdicts against washing days 'at any pairt of Powies burne above the bridge unless they set ther fyres, wash and throw out ther fowll water at some distance from the Burne, where the fowll water may not fall or come thereto'.

Across the burn lay the herb and vegetable of King's College, referred to in Elphinstone's Second Foundation and elaborated on in the New Foundation. Its cultivation was one of the tasks of the college cook. He was to grow vegetables there and supply them for college use. 'And he shall take care to see that the garden and walks shall be kept tidy for the use of the members of the said college; and the remaining produce of the garden he shall be allowed to apply to his own uses'. Beyond lay the college itself. Masters and scholars were not included in the 1636 census for all were known to the bailies of Old Aberdeen responsible for its instigation. Indeed, two of the masters at this time, the Dr John Gordon and Mr John Lundie were bailies themselves. The purpose of the census as we know was not so much to provide a precise headcount, as to seek out idlers and though there may well have been some in the college, this was not the type of idler the baillies were concerned to investigate. At a guess there would have been around thirty masters and students in residence in 1636. Since Alexander Arbuthnot's day there had been three principals, Mr Walter Stuart from 1584 till 1592 when he died at scarcely thirty-six, and Mr David Rait, who served the college successively as regent, subprincipal and principal for some half century. Both supported the New Foundation. The third principal William Leslie, appointed after Rait's death in 1632 was still likely to be occupying Boece's old rooms at the front of the college. A few years later, Leslie and five colleagues would become famous as the 'Aberdeen

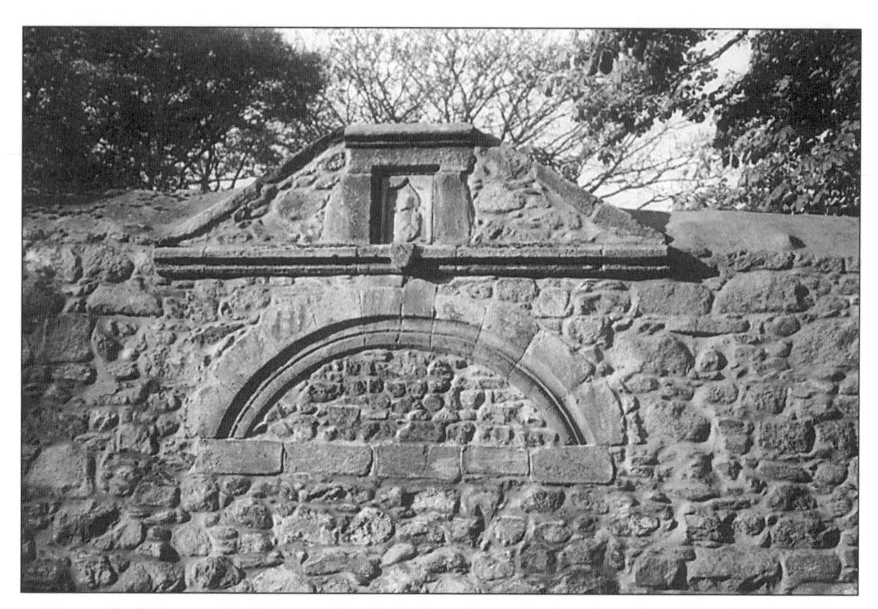

The wall of Humanity Manse, No 19 College Bounds showing the original arch of the humanist's gateway and Elphinstone's shield and mitre.

Doctors' who opposed the National Covenant. Three regents were also in residence at this time, Alexander Middleton, Alexander Garden and Robert Ogilvie living in Hercules, Leo and Cancer respectively, though these quaint Zodiacal names were no longer used for their rooms. Beyond the college lay the High Street.

We cross now to explore the west side of College Bounds to the Snow Kirk and its spacious enclave. In the north-east corner, almost opposite the civilist's ruins, sat the grammarian's manse, or the humanist as he had become, just as the study of Latin was now known as Humanity. Numbered 13 on Gordon's Plan, we can see from his simple sketch that the manse would have been a substantial building of two-storeys with a cross at its gable-end. It survived until the 1860s, though in ruinous state. As noted in Chapter Four, page 71, the arch of the original gateway and the niche with Bishop Elphinstone's shield and mitre, were later built into the wall of Humanity Manse, No 19 College Bounds, which stands on this site. Humanist John Lundie was not resident in his manse at this time, but had gone 'upmarket' to the Chanonry.

A short distance north of the humanist's manse were the 'Ruins of the Snaw Kirk' as Gordon described them. It began to fall into disrepair after the Reformation and a precept of James VI of May 1583 instructed the Snow congregation along with that of the Spital Kirk to 'resort to the said cathedrall of Machar' while the revenues of the 'Snaw and Spittall Kirks', for what they were worth, along with those of St Machar's were granted to King's College whose masters were instructed to:

> dimoleishe and tak doun the ruinous wallis and tymber of the present kirkis of Snaw and Spittall now abusit to superstitioun and idolatrie, and to employ the same for reparation of the said kirk of Machar being utherwyiss a grit and costlie work.

This was a useful way of keeping repair costs at the cathedral in check, but there was more to it than that. 'Abusit to superstitioun and idolatrie' implied that some Aulton folk were still secretly attending mass in its ruins, still looking on it as their true parish church, still feeling a sense of continuity with their forebears. This reluctance to abandon the Snow endured over many years. Secret funerals took place there, combining the comfort of burial in a familiar place with the avoidance of the interment dues charged at St Machar's. On 23 March 1623, the St Machar's kirk session decreed that 'no person tak upon thame to opin the earthe in the Snow Kirk or kirkyeard' except under the official supervision of a reader and a beadle.

The royal injunction of 1583 with regard to demolishing the Snow seems not to have been fully carried out. When Dr William Guild, became principal of King's College in 1640, he quickly turned his attention to the poor state of the college buildings. There was still enough of the Snow left standing for Guild to have its stones recycled for repair work across the road. Immediately on arrival according to Spalding:

> he yokit George Ronald, mason, to the Snaw Kirk, and cast down the walls thereof, such as was standing and caused transport the stones to big up the College yard dykes, and to employ the hewn work to the decayed windows within the college, whereat many Oldtown people murmured, the same being sometime the parish kirk of Old Aberdeen, within the whilk their friends and forefathers were buried.

The royalist Spalding disapproved of Dr Guild, as he did of many others, and may be exaggerating. Parson Gordon's Plan, surveyed from the 1640s, and Slezer's view, published in 1693 show the walls still standing, though the roof in the Slezer drawing looks in a poor condition. Local people continued to visit the kirkyard in spite of Guild's attempts at demolition. In 1649 prayers at the graves of husbands or friends within 'the Snawe Kirkyard as ther wontit custome hes beine', were forbidden by the kirk session of Old Machar on grounds of 'playne superstitione'.

The Snow Kirk retained its popularity though, with the reformed religion well-established, it began to lose its sanctity. Like Douglas Wynd off the High Street, the kirk, hidden from prying eyes, was a favourite spot where 'men and boyes usually playit kits (quoits) in time of sermon', much to the annoyance of the cathedral's 'enforcers' who were detailed to go there the following Sunday to catch the transgressors. It was also a useful meeting place. Co-operation between the two Aberdeens see-sawed from good to bad and back again but was reasonably good in the mid-seventeenth century. The Aulton folk were obliged by their magistrates to meet at the Snow Kirk at five in the morning with spades, barrows, horses and creels, 'to go to the Sand Werk of New Aberdein, a man or woman at least

The Snow Kirk, foreground. Can that be a part of the civilist's manse to the right? Detail from 'Old Aberdeen', from John Slezer's 'Theatrum Scotiae', 1693.

out of every house' to help with the harbour works. This assistance had gone on at least since 1643. By an edict of 7 August of that year everyone who had a horse had to send it 'to Aberdeen to the sand the morne by sevin houris'. The usual fine was levied, in these circumstances 20s per absent horse. Such enforced labour did not appeal to all. In 1655 there had been a frightful row when William Lin, a heritor, active in civic affairs and from time to time elected bailie, tried to force the attendance of George Gibson, cordiner. Margrat Forsyth, Gibson's wife had, according to witnesses, called Lin 'false traitor, land louper's loon, and knave and taking ane chandler (candlestick) in hir hand and swore by the Lord's wundis she suld cleave the said William Lin to the teeth'. It was fortunate that Lin was not serving as a bailie at the time for Margrat was only fined £4.

Burials continued at the Snow. In 1671 the masters of King's hit on the idea of charging interment fees, thus gaining some welcome income for the

The grave-slab of Gilbert Menzies of Pitfodels in the Snow Kirkyard.

college. Burials in the extensive cemetery outside the kirk were charged at 'ane dollar' (£2 13s 4d), and those within the church walls, at 'no les than aucht poundis Scots money.' Mr Patrick Gordon, then humanist at King's, was responsible for collecting this revenue, and was well placed to do so. Beadles sent along from St Machar's were ordered by their kirk session not to open the ground until 'Mr Patrick be payit according to the forsaid raites'. Sir Gilbert Menzies of Pitfodels, one of the 'auld blud', a member of that prominent provostorial Aberdeen family, conveniently died in 1669, enabling his executors to avoid the £8 lair fee. Since those days, kirk and kirkyard have vanished. The original, extensive cemetery was under crop by the early nineteenth century and the original area of the Snaw's interior now forms a graveyard whose residents are Catholics ancient and modern. Menzies' ornate recumbent grave-slab which would originally have been inlaid in a position of prominence on the floor of the kirk, lies open to the skies. The Snow graveyard is now hidden by a row of nineteenth century houses in College Bounds, Nos 21-31, but access can be gained by walking through the Johnston/Crombie Hall gates a few yards south of the pepper-pot Powis gate and turning left along a narrow passage.

Still within the Snow Kirk enclave, we move on from the kirk a little to the north again, to reach the canonist's manse beside the Powis Burn. In 1587, Alexander Cheyne, commissary of Aberdeen and the last canonist, at least pro tem, had died. Canonists and indeed their manses, were superflu-

College Bounds. The Snow Kirkyard lies behind the row of nineteenth century houses, centre.

ous under the New Foundation, and the latter could be translated into revenue for the college. A contract of 1596 mentions one Andrew Gray as resident 'in the Snaw place' and a charter two years later refers to the manse as 'sometime of the Parson of Snow', which the canonist had been before the Reformation, 'but now belonging heritably to Andrew Gray'. On 29 May 1623, some years after Gray's death, Principal David Rait and the masters of King's College gave out a new feu charter in favour of Andrew's son, Laurence Gray at the Mill of Mundurno, a cooper and burgess of Aberdeen, his wife and heirs. It describes 'the Snaw place' as 'the tenement, place and 'hospitium de Snaw' (manse), with its enclosure, garden, marshland etc, lying beyond the Powis Burn. The land in question is further defined, in the conventional style, by reference to the area around it; the cemetery of the church of Snaw and the lands formerly belonging to the town's grammarian, Master Theophilus Stewart then to Master Thomas Lumsden, rector of Kinkell to the south, the Powis Burn to the north, the *via regia*, (College Bounds at this point), to the east and the *mons genistarum*, (the Broomhill) and the 'Lands of Sonysyde' to the west.

This feu charter tells us an assortment of things; that Principal David Rait was quite prepared to alienate university property in College Bounds and make a little money by feuing it out; that Laurence Gray was a man of substance in n his own right; that even since Reformation times, the grammarian Theophilus Stewart was regarded primarily as Old Aberdeen's teacher of Latin grammar rather than the university's; and that Master Thomas Lumsden, rector of Kinkell, was something of a property speculator. Not only had he acquired the grammarian's glebe but by a charter of 10 August 1587 he also acquired the mediciner's manse from Dr Gilbert Skene, with the consent of masters of King's. Skene was long settled in Edinburgh by then and it may have seemed to him, with the New Foundation then in the ascendant, that the college was unlikely to reappoint a mediciner. The mediciners returned however, and lived in their manse at least until the eighteenth century.

Not everyone was happy about the alienation of college property. In 1632 James Sandilands, younger, canonist and future civilist, and like the humanist Lundie a resident of the Chanonry, queried the status of the canonist's manse. He raised an action of removing at Aberdeenshire Sheriff Court to evict Gilbert Sangster and Elizabeth Gray his wife, (a daughter of Laurence?) as 'pretendit tennentes and occupiars of the said canonist of the Kingis College his manss houssis, lyand on the south syd of Powis Brig within the Territories of the said Colledg'. Laurence had evidently stayed out at the Mill of Mundurno. By January 1634 Sandilands had gained an instrument of possession, and that July raised another action to evict Sangster and another resident, John Porter, a wright to trade. Such a large building would have had multiple tenancy. Why such so-called 'unlawful possession' was originally sanctioned is unclear but it was a cause of concern for King's College. In July of that year, Dr William Gordon, the university's mediciner and common procurator or administrator, (he was also Sandilands' brother-in-law), set out for London and the court of Charles I at Whitehall with a list of representations regarding the running of the university. One of these read:

> Some doe unjustly possess and pertinaciously detaine house, lands and rents belonging to this universitie, yea also some of the mansions of the professors within the precinct of the fabric and manses of the universitie.

Whatever the results of Dr Gordon's mission, Sandilands' attempts to evict the pertinacious possessors does not appear to have met with immediate success. The 1636 census notes Elspet Troup and three bairns squatting there, 'in the canonistes hous, extravagantes' and John Porter is still there. Though Parson Gordon indicates merely 'the place wher stood' the canonist's manse, 15 on the Plan, it looks fairly intact. By the time Slezer made his drawing of Old Aberdeen the manse was in a ruinous state, but enough of it remains to indicate that it had been a building of character.

Still keeping to the west side of the road, we now cross the Powis Brig.

Above, detail from Slezer's 'Old Aberdeen'. The ruins of the canonist's manse with the Twelve Roods and the mediciner's manse beyond.

① *The canonist's manse.*
② *The Twelve Roods.*
③ *The mediciner's manse.*

Twelve roods, about three acres of boggy ground lay on the north side between the burn and the mediciner's' manse which was directly opposite King's College. Gordon has incorrectly noted the Twelve Roods as 18, 'Mediciner's House and Præcinct'. But that was further north at 12, correctly noted as 'Mediciner's House et Grammar School opposite'. This was the marshland that defeated Bishop Elphinstone when he was building his extra-mural manses in the early 1500s. Wasteland since time immemorial, these Twelve Roods, for so they were officially designated, were granted by Bishop William Gordon to John Chalmer, servitor to the Rector of Oyne in 1549, doubtless part of the bishop's policy of alienating church lands. The description was not attractive; the Twelve Roods lay between the lands of Mr Robert Gray, mediciner, (he had succeeded the first mediciner, James Cuming in 1523) on the north side, the *via regia* on the east, the 'Broymhill' towards the west and that 'certain piece of land, waste, watery, and almost uninhabitable towards the south'. This was the ground that sloped down to the Powis Burn, and the Latin of the charter sounds particularly grim: *terra vastam aquosam et penitus.*

In 1595 Chalmer's son Robert sold the Twelve Roods to Andrew Gray, our old friend then 'living in the Snaw Place' who was expanding his ownership of property in the area. He rented them to John Porter, wright, who had not yet moved into the canonist's manse. He must have done so by 1631, for in that year, Lawrence Gray, who had also inherited this property from his father, rented the Twelve Roods to John Anderson, deacon of the Tailors' Craft in Old Aberdeen. Anderson bought the place three years later. The 1636 census in whose compilation and analysis Anderson was involved as one of the thirty ' most honest and aged persons of the Town' shows that he had a wife, four bairns and three servants, one female and two male, Andro Duthie and Arthur Anderson who could well have been his apprentices. Being 'honest and aged' did not prevent the tailor from being fined 26s 8d by the St Machar kirk session in January 1647 for being absent from church. His excuse was that some friends had called unexpectedly.

Either John Anderson or his sons had carried out a few improvements at the Twelve Roods. Orem describes the area with 'an house on the west side of the street, almost opposite the college gate with a little yard and some back short rigs at the end thereof. All the rest of the ground was deep sinking mire', doubtless the intractable watery waste referred to in the feu charter of 1595. In 1691, William Anderson, John's eldest son, sold the Twelve Roods to a regent of King's College, Alexander Fraser who had just married Christian Moir, one of the heiresses of Sunnyside. The price was £750. With admirable foresight, Fraser bought land that was not only adjacent to his wife's, but was handily sited for his work across the road.

To remain within the timespan of this book, our exploration of these boggy Twelve Roods must cease here. Enough to say for the moment that if asked to define the Powis estate one would say that it was a council housing scheme lying west of Bedford Road which was planned in the 1930s. That is its recent history. But this was where it all started, in the sixteenth century, at the daunting Twelve Roods nearly opposite King's College. Its story will continue anon. As for College Bounds, there was nowhere in Old Aberdeen quite like it, with its mix of artisans, property developers, and a remarkable anatomist. We have now reached virtually the last house in College Bounds, the mediciner's manse, 12 on Gordon's Plan, where No 53 College Bounds now stands. The 1636 census shows Dr William Gordon and his family resident there.

Chapter 14

William Gordon, Mediciner

A godly, grave, learned man, and singular in common works about the college, and putting up on the steeple thereof most glorious, as you see, a stately crown, previously thrown down by the wind.

Memorialls of the Trubles in Scotland etc, 1624-1645, John Spalding.

Dr William Gordon, his wife, Jean, daughter of James Sandilands, elder, their three bairns and four servants moved into the mediciner's manse in 1632 when Gordon was appointed mediciner at King's. Their neighbour to the south, John Anderson, the tailor, was also new if not to Old Aberdeen at least to College Bounds, for he had moved into the Twelve Roods only the year before. Dr Gordon's house was virtually the last in College Bounds, (though there was one more, at the end of his glebe), and had been the last of the extra-mural college manses to be built. As the Slezer drawing on page 202 shows it was a fine, two-storey stane hoose, standing high among the simple cottages that surrounded it.

There is also a possibility that Dr Gordon's mother lived nearby. The guidwyff of Coclarachie resided in the Chanonry at this very time. The goodwife, a polite form of address for the mistress of the house, and here, for the widow of a laird, was Bessie, whose husband, George Gordon, third of Coclarachie had died in 1633. Coclarachie, a considerable landowner in Aberdeenshire, was a follower of George, sixth Earl of Huntly and first Marquis to be, who had succeeded to the title back in 1576 after his father died 'cumyn fra ye fuitbau'. The sixth earl, true to the traditions of his forebears, had assumed the leadership of the Scottish Catholics. In 1594, Huntly with the Earl of Errol, defeated the royal forces under the Earl of Argyll at the Battle of Glenlivet. Some months before the battle took place, Coclarachie was charged with conspiracy against the true religion and denounced rebel.

Dr William Gordon, mediciner at King's College 1632-40. From the original by George Jamesone.

Coclarachie and his wife had four sons and four daughters. The fourth-born, William Gordon, became a doctor of medicine, perhaps the King's College mediciner. There is no evidence either way though it would be a coincidence if there were two Dr William Gordons going about at a time when mediciners were still thin on the ground. On the other hand, would the son of a notorious Catholic rebel be employed at the protestant King's College? The mystery remains.

Our William Gordon had studied medicine at Padua University, where nearly a century earlier Andreas Vesalius, professor of surgery had pioneered dissection techniques and written his famous textbook *De humani corporis fabrica,* published with its superbly engraved anatomical drawings. After his appointment Gordon lost no time in introducing dissection techniques and presently sought to advance his students' skills. In 1636 he successfully petitioned the privy council for permission to obtain human bodies for study, 'for he had exercised his students sufficiently for the past two years in the dissection of beasts'. In an *Act for the Delyverie of Dead Bodies to the College of Aberdene* the privy council directed authorities in Aberdeen and Banff to deliver annually to him: 'Twa bodies of men being notable malefactors, execute in their bonds, especialie being rebells and outlaws', and failing them:

> the bodies of the poorer sort, dieing in hospitalls, or abortive bairnes, fundlings, or these of no qualitie who hes died of thare diseases, and hes few freinds or acquaintance that can take exception.

After this nothing further is heard of Gordon's work as mediciner, though certainly one of his students, and possibly others did graduate. But he had other things to keep him busy. Soon after his arrival he was appointed common procurator or business manager responsible for the administration of the college. This task was allotted to the economus under the New Foundation but after Berold Innes's day was held by members of the teaching staff as well as by professional economuses. Gordon was much involved in the New and Old Foundation feuding and as mediciner, naturally supported the Old Foundation. Outwith the college he was a conscientious bailie of Old Aberdeen and was one of the hard-working ones, his name often appearing in the council minutes. In 1636 he was actively involved in carrying out, perhaps even the instigator, of that successful council programme for causeying some of the Aulton roads discussed in Chapter 11.

Three years earlier it was as procurator of King's College that Gordon had faced his greatest challenge. On 7 February 1633 'ane gryt storme of snaw with horribill heiche wyndis', according to Spalding, 'threw down the statlie croun, biggit of curius ashlar work af of the steipill of the kingis college of Old Abirdein' and caused considerable damage to adjacent buildings. Spalding's 'statlie croun' is that elusive top crown while the steeple it fell 'af of' were the great arches below. Its fall and that of the adjoining masonry was not surprising for ongoing fabric maintenance was not a priority at King's. Canon Alexander Galloway's devastating visitation of 1549 had instructed its repair while a royal visitation of 1623 ordained that the head of the great steeple should be mended in stone, lead and timber as before. Nothing came of these stipulations, and the stonework deteriorated further. Now it fell to Gordon not only to organise repairs to the upper crown and surrounding masonry, whose jagged ruins faced him from across the road every day, but to raise the funds as well. He quickly contracted with a mason, George Thomson, to rebuild the crown and make good the damage for 10,000 merks according to Orem, £6666 13s 4d Scots, or over £555 sterling. The sum required was large and Gordon worked tirelessly to bring the money in. Three months after the disaster the magistrates of Aberdeen permitted the masters of King's College to invite voluntary contributions from the townsfolk of the royal burgh, and indeed Parson Gordon commented that the mediciner was:

> soliciting everie quher for assistance thereunto, which was contributed considerablie by the noblemen and gentlemen dwelling in the countrey and neerest shyres.

Only five months after the fall of the crown of King's College, Charles I, son of James VI and I was crowned with the crown of Scotland, remodelled at the command of his great-grandfather, James V in 1540. Spalding devotes several pages of his *Memorialls* to the scenes of pomp and ceremony at the Abbey of Holyrood. 'The Marques of Douglas rode immediately befoir the King in his furrit roab, carrying the croun betwixt both his handis'. Yet Dr Gordon was unable to capitalise as fully on the current interest in crowns and coronations as he might have hoped. In spite of his efforts, funds were still inadequate. In July 1634, over a year after the disaster, he set off for the court of Charles I at Whitehall (speed was of the essence and he was there by October), with a list of representations that he was to make on behalf of the university. The 'Appendix' to the list reveals the desperate situation of the damaged crown and contains a novel plea for funding its repairs:

> the universitie...did cairfullie imply both ther purses and ther paines and with some help of the countrie have alreadie imployed thereon about the soume of £200 sterling, viz more than £2000 Scots; and yet the quarter of the work is not perfyted, and we are in danger of that censure of the man quho began to build and left off for laik of expenses.

The man who left off for lack of expenses was Thomson, the mason. The money had run out and he had stopped work. In a counter-productive move the masters had him locked up. The 'Appendix,' understandably, is silent on this development but puts forward the proposition that the king graciously waive 'for some few yeires', the tax, £50 sterling or £600 Scots, paid annually by the Bishop of Aberdeen, Patrick Forbes of Corse, chancellor of King's, and allow him instead to contribute it to the crown repair fund. Judging by the figures quoted in the 'Appendix', inflation was taking its toll. If less than a quarter of the work had been done at a cost of over £2000 Scots as stated, the whole would cost over £8000 Scots, instead of the original £6666, around £1500 Scots over budget. Worse still, the money had run out at around the £2000 mark, £200 sterling, leaving £6000 or £600 sterling to find. It is uncertain whether or not the king granted this remission of tax but if he had, the 'some few yeires' would have amounted to ten to make up the necessary sum from Bishop Forbes' pension. Forbes himself had had a stroke 'sitting in his ain chear in the Oldtoun' in 1632 and died scarcely a year after Dr Gordon's visit to the king. But other contributions did come in. Rather late in the day, in August 1634, Aberdeen Town Council voted a sum of 400 merks, £267 Scots towards the repairs, Thomson was let out of prison and the masters paid him on a daily basis until he had finished his task. Spalding, who would have remembered the original crown declared that its successor was 'biggit up little inferior to the first'. Parson Gordon who would have been not quite twenty at the time of the calamity records that the old crown was 'restored in a better forme and condition'.

The new crown bore a striking resemblance, not to the Scottish crown that Charles I wore at Holyrood, but to the English state crown. Could that have been shown to Dr Gordon during his visit to the king in London in 1634? We know that Gordon, who is credited with designing the crown,

Inspecting George Thomson's work. From 'A Tribute to William Kelly', edited by W D Simpson, 1949.

spoke with William Laud, Archbishop of Canterbury. Did he, channelling his proposal through the Archbishop, flatter the king by craving the honour of having that particular crown sculpted in stone as the upper crown of King. The 'Appendix' had enthused about, indeed had understandably exaggerated, the college's royal connections, stating that it had been 'built at the commandment of the most noble king James the fourth of happie memorie'. Did Gordon with his dextrous, anatomist's fingers make a sketch of the English state crown? We will never know. However, the lantern and the upper crown, as Dr Kelly has pointed out, have a distinctive Caroline 'feel' about them.

In spite of the traumas Thomson experienced during this particular contract (he would not expect to have been both unpaid and incarcerated), he was proud of his work and left his initials and the date 'Anno 1634' on the keystone of the west side of the great arch. Much of his work on the crown tower can easily be viewed today; the top crown topped by an orb and a cross and the 'lantern', the robust octagonal column of blind arcades, that links the great arches with the top crown. He also repaired the copings of the arches extensively, and nearly all the pinnacles. The great arches are still largely original. Thomson came to a sad end, carried off by a stroke by the sound of it. In 1642 Spalding reported that:

> on Setterday the 10th of September George Thomsoune, maister measone, new come from Strathbogie to Abirdene, suddantlie fell over Thomas Thomsone, burgess of the toun his stair, and with the fall became sensles and speichles and depairted this life upone the Thuirsday thaireafter; ane excellent mesoun, of singular devise. He booldit sundry brave booldings; amonges the rest, he re-edifeid the stepill of the college kirk of Old Abirdene.

Two years earlier Spalding had recorded Dr Gordon's own passing:

> Doctor Gordoun medicinar of the colledge of Old Abirdein and common procurator thairof depairtit this lyf upon the tent of Marche in his owne hous in Old Abirdein; a godlie, grave, lerned man, and singular in commoun warkis about the colledge, and putting up on the stepill theirof most glorious, as you sie, ane statlie crowne, throwne doun be the wynd abefoir.

Perhaps we should record that back in 1633, days after the fall of the crown, one Alexander Wright appeared before the Oldmachar kirk session, accused of calling Bailie Alexander Mutray a warlock, for raising the wind that blew down the college crown. Nothing more was heardof this, but in retrospect the fall of the crown could be interpreted not so much as witchcraft as an omen that was fulfilled when Charles I mounted the scaffold in 1649.

No mediciner was appointed during the turmoil of the Civil Wars but in 1649 Gordon was at last succeeded by one of his students, Andrew Muir, one of the earliest medical graduates of King's of whom there is a record. He followed Gordon's footsteps in becoming a bailie of Old Aberdeen. After him, in 1672, came Patrick Urquhart who remained in office for fifty-four years. He died in 1725 at the age of eighty-three. Next door to the mediciner's manse was a common wynd, called, quite naturally, the Doctor's Wynd, though Gordon noted it as the 'Lane which goes to the Broom hill'. It marked the end of College Bounds and the start of the High Street.

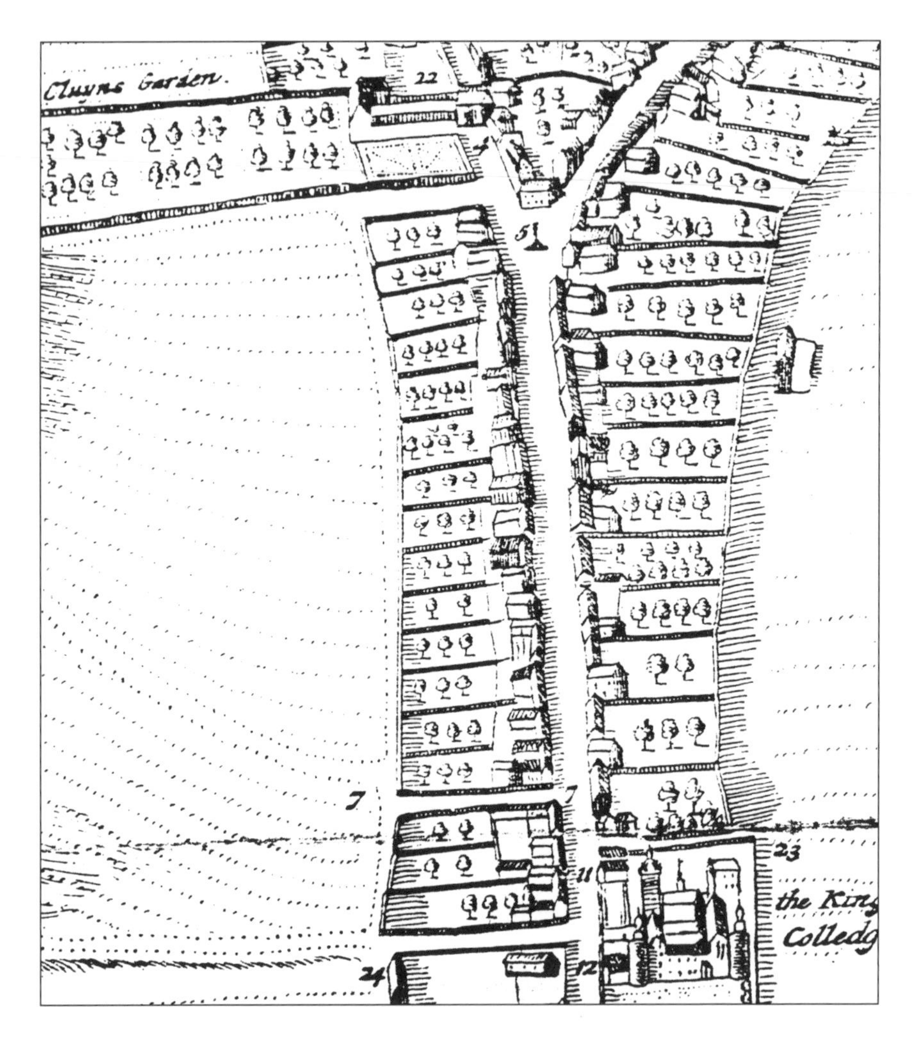

High Street, from Parson Gordon's Plan, 1661. None of the houses shown here are extant, though on the left hand side, Meston Walk lies at the foot of the page, and Douglas Lane is marked 7. Near the top, Cluny's Wynd, now replaced by St Machar Drive, is just below Cluny's Garden. On the right, Berold Innes's Wynd runs between 23 and 11. Wagril's Lane is not shown. The detail on page 202 provides a close-up of the High Street from King's College to the tall houses of the Canonry.

Chapter 15

High Street
In and around the Middle Toun

Old Aberdeen is enclosed with little hills, pleasant cornefeilds, very fruitfull, and with pastures mixed amongst the plowghed feilds.

Parson Gordon, Description of Bothe Touns of Aberdeene, 1661.

And so to the High Street, the old Middle Toun, the heart of Old Aberdeen which in the seventeenth century ran north from the Doctor's Wynd until the 'V' of the Chanonry caused it to divide. Thanks to the 1636 census we can estimate that the High Street then had around 556 residents living in 143 separate households. College Bounds had about seventy residents in fifteen or so households, excluding those at King's College while the Chanonry, the longest of the three roads, had a population of around 149 in thirty-one households not counting the old men of Gavin Dunbar's Hospital and a couple of landed families, all of whom would be well known to the census takers. The High Street, at 338 yds (309m) marginally longer than College Bounds, the last to develop, was the one with the highest density of population. In the burgh records 'Auld Abirdene', the 'Auld Toune' or 'the citie' usually means the High Street alone while 'Spittell' and 'the Colledge boundis', 'Chanrie' and 'Setoun' are described as 'places round about Auld Abirdene'. The High Street *was* Old Aberdeen, just as, centuries before, the Chanonry had been. It assumed that status after Elphinstone hived off the Chanonry to become a dedicated ecclesiastical zone, after King's College became operative, and when craftsmen saw they could make a living by setting up in Elphinstone's 'new town', the lang stracht between the two, encouraged by the presence of the parish kirk of Snaw and possibly even more by the trading inducements offered by the barony charter.

In its early years of development the High Street was known, logically enough for a street that lay between College Bounds and the Chanonry, as the Middle Toun or 'mid streit'. Its growth continued in Bishop Dunbar's day, for there was still land available for feuing out. On 15 November 1531 Dunbar granted a piece of wasteland near King's College to its masters and residents. It lay to the north of the mediciner's manse and was three roods in width and eight roods in length. The college more than likely built a house on this 'wasteland'. Berold Innes, college economus from 1586 had a lane named after him, almost opposite the site of this former 'wasteland'. He likely lived in the house there while Bailie Thomas Mercer, economus from 1631 probably lived in the same house at a later date. According to the 1636 census Mercer's was the first house in what it calls 'Auld Aberdeine', ie the High Street and Chanonry. He had quite a substantial household, his wife, three bairns and five servants, two female and three male, none of whom, given Mercer's occupation were likely to have been artisan apprentices. It had a number of out-dwellings in its yard where the illicit 'haill household within the chancellor's close' would have been encamped at the time of the 1636 census.

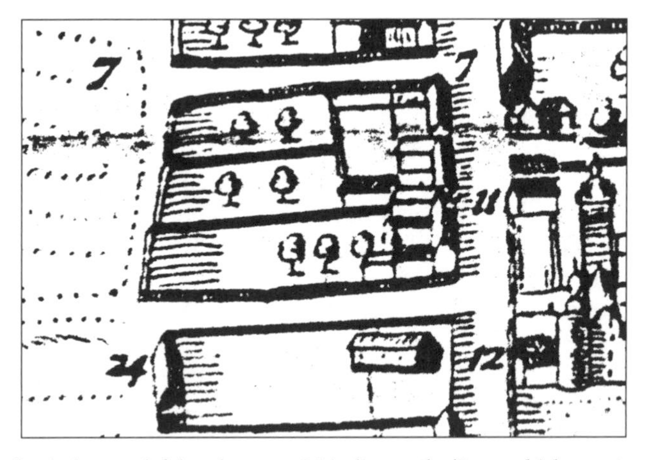

In the bottom left hand corner, 24 indicates the 'Lane which goes to the Broom hill' alias the Doctor's Wynd, now Meston Walk while 7 just beyond is Douglas Wynd or Lane. The economus's house was within this square. Detail from Parson Gordon's Plan, 1661.

Orem notes that it was also occupied by 'the heirs of the deceased George Laing, some time economist (economus) in the King's College'. William Laing, was admitted honorary burgess in 1674 as 'economus of the King's Colledge', while George perhaps a son or a brother was admitted as trade burgess in 1685 under the same designation. The area where the house was sited lay just north of the Doctor's Wynd, 24 on Gordon's Plan, alias 'Lane which goes to the Broom hill', and was bounded by 7 'Dowglasse

The start of the High Street, from Meston Walk. The economus's house was around here.

Wynde or Lane'. By 1800 or thereby, these dwellings were replaced by College Place, No 1 High Street and its neighbours.

Land continued to be given out in the post-Reformation era though by the time Parson Gordon was surveying the area in the 1640s, the High Street was largely built up, with many houses gable-end to the road, a style still much in evidence to this day. Some of the poorer houses would have had mud walls within a framework of timber, plastered and whitewashed, their roofs roped and thatched either with turf, divots, or straw. Some landlords kept a careful eye on such properties. In April 1605 Alexander Schand let a tenement and yard to William Gareoch for the following year and agreed to give him five threaves of straw to make it water tight. The yards and long rigs to the rear of the houses compensated for the narrowness of their frontages. Gordon's Plan shows houses on the longer, curving east side with what looks like workshops for weaving, baking, carpentry or smithying in their yards. Cattle may have been overwintered in the sheds behind the houses. We know from the instructions of 17 September 1662 to the Aulton quartermasters that those who kept 'hors or cattell or any uther bestiall', were expected to have sufficient provender in winter for their needs. Hay would have been plentiful in a good year and neaps were grown in the rigs, though for human rather than bovine consumption. Whatever the make-up of the fodder it seems that by no means all cattle were turned into 'marts', sides of salted beef, for the forthcoming winter. That the High Street was predominantly a rural area is clear from a memorable passage in a burgh statue of 1687. Complaints had reached the bailies that when the local bitches 'ar hot and jollie, they convene a great number of dogs which comes to them'. In their eagerness, the dogs come bounding through 'men's corn and bracks and destroyes the same'. The dogs damage the houses within the town 'and the thacking thereof and…the kale and other herbs within their yards'. The bailies ordain that those keeping bitches in the town are to kill or get rid of them within twenty-four hours, (penalty, £4) which seems most unfair since it was the dogs that were doing the damage.

Still on the east side, several houses near the market cross which was set further south then than now, have what look like substantial residences in their backlands. One of these, the 'Bishop's Lodging' as it came to be called, a two-storey building with attic, was built in 1623 according to the date on its south-west skewputt. Edward Meldrum in *Aberdeen of Old,* 1986 described the

> harled granite walls, interesting fenestration of the street gable and wee dormers in the roof between ridge and eaves. The old double leaf door had simple wrought iron crook and band hinges. The door architraves were dressed of freestone and finely moulded, as were the dressed rybats, stills and lintels at window openings. Inside was a painted timber fireplace panel depicting fishers and their boats at a river mouth.

The skewputt had the initials MJK and MM, and it had been surmised that MJK may have been Master John Keith. He is noted in the Oldmachar

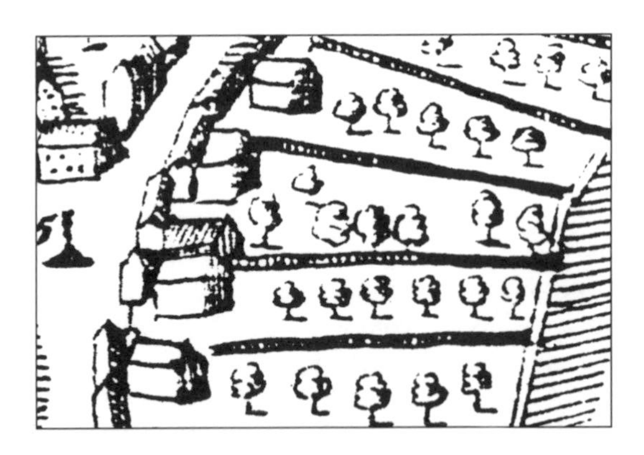

The market cross, 5, left. The 'Bishop's Lodging' is perhaps the house at the foot of this detail from Parson Gordon's Plan, 1661.

session accounts of April 1642 and June 1643, as bursar of divinity at King's College to whom £10 was 'deliverit' on each occasion, probably his bursary. Twenty years earlier he would have been an infant, and unlikely to be building what must have been one of the finest houses in High Street. No likely candidate for residence there emerges in the 1636 census. The 'Bishop's Lodging' survived until 1950, and will be recalled by many. Its later fate will be explored in Volume Two.

Though the High Street we know had not started to develop in the seventeenth century, a handful of superior houses were in existence. According to Orem, 'Peter Aberdein built a house upon the east side of the street, near the cross. This tenement (or landholding) formerly pertained to Mr Alexander Spalding, advocate, and sometime Commissary-Clerk-Depute of Old Aberdeen, where he had a good lodging, well slated, with a timber fore-stair' which would have caused difficulties for Spalding with his gouty feet. The Spalding house which afterwards 'became ruinous and was at last demolished', would have pre-dated Aberdein's house which

The market cross, and to the left, a group of early eighteenth century houses. Alexander Spalding's 'good lodging' stood here.

was built in 1719 though it stood on the same piece of land. A group of eighteenth century houses, handsomely restored, Nos 104-108 High Street stand near the cross on the east side of the street and could well have replaced the earlier Spalding tenement.

But our information on these early houses of quality is scanty. Orem tells a confused tale of Sir Alexander Gordon of Cluny who either purchased a house and yard 'which now lie on the south side of Bailie Baxter's tenement' from Henry Adam, (a prominent member of the cordiner craft), or sold the house to Adam which was more likely. Whichever way, it was 'the first slated house in Old Aberdeen, except those in the Chanonry'. This transaction would have taken place in the first half of the seventeenth century. Bailie Baxter was prominent in civic affairs in the late seventeenth and early eighteenth centuries and a wynd was named after him. It made its appearance too late to be included in Gordon's Plan, but it seems to have been opposite Douglas Lane though a little further north. Gordon does show a handsome two-storey house in this area, and that may have been the one.

Most two-storey houses would have been occupied by a number of tenants and dogged by the usual rows. One such which took place in 1668 was reported in the council minutes. Helen Anderson, wife of the glover Robert Broune was doing a washing and let water seep down to Janet Hunter's apartment below, spoiling her clothes and bedding. Janet remonstrated 'peaceablie', but Helen 'in a furious way fell in scolding Janet, calling hir a drunken jade ...and cruellie did strike hir upon the head divers and sundrie times'. Janet and her husband lodged a complaint and Helen and Robert were fined 40s with a fortnight to pay, otherwise their goods were to be poinded.

Helen Anderson might have argued that she had to wash clothes indoors under unsatisfactory conditions because washing was strictly prohibited in the High Street itself, especially the indecent business of tramping the clothes in public. On 26 March 1689 the council forbade all persons 'to Tramp and wash in Tubs upon any pairt of the high streit from the on end of the toune to the other'. The penalties were 40s to be paid for the use of the town and 12s to the town's officers who were empowered to poind the clothes and washing tubs until payment was made.

Robert Broune, Helen's husband was a glover, but none of his trade are recorded in the 1636 census. That is not to say there weren't any for the census fails to record the occupation of a number of heads of households, and there were at least three in the College Bounds-High Street by the time the *List of Pollable Persons* was drawn up in 1696. The 1636 census does show that the great majority of High Street residents were artisans, victuallers, agricultural workers, and servants, many of them bearers of the distinctive Old Aberdeen surnames, Aberdein, Torrie, Volum, Mercer, Chalmer, Irving, Beverlay, Hervie, Ortoun, Clark, Law, as well as Davidson, Anderson, Cruickshank, and of course, Gordon and all with the usual range of flexible spellings. Of the thirty 'most honest and aged persons of the Town' appointed to supervise the 1636 census, apart from four representatives from the Spital and College Bounds and three from the Chanonry, all were High Street men, weavers, cordiners, tailors, fleshers, husbandmen a skinner, a stabler and a gardener.

The largest group of artisans was formed by the textile workers, headed by the wobsters or weavers. David Abell who lived with his wife and three bairns was 'visitor' or deacon of the weavers' trade at this time. He had nine servants, seven of whom were men, likely his apprentices. Andrew Henderson had with five male servants/apprentices. But these numbers were exceptional. Six weavers worked single-handed and five had only one male servant. All told thirteen master weavers were noted and about seventeen apprentices. There was a cluster of four weavers including Abell and Henderson, perhaps in the middle of the east side of the High Street where there were sheds in the yards, while the others were scattered throughout the Aulton. They were the most open-handed of the Trades, thanks to their sizeable membership. There was one net weaver, Archibald Smythe, a 'wywer', rather than a 'wobster'. Weaving was virtually if not exclusively a male occupation, but of the nine Aulton spinsters or spinners, who provided the raw material for the weavers all but one were on the distaff side. The lone male was William Willox, 'in William Nicoll's land'. Nicoll was a weaver, so had a ready supply of yarn to hand. The weavers would have made plaiding for blankets and cloth for garments. And so next to the tailors. There were six in the Aulton, all male. There were also two women sewsters or sewers. Janet Blake and Margaret Settoun, spinner and sewer shared a house, as did Issobell Fraser, another spinster and Elspet Taylor, the only candlemaker listed in the census. Elspet Torrie who lived with her two bairns and a servant was a shanker, that is she knitted stockings, coverings for the shanks, as did Isobel Kelman's two children.

After the textile workers, the second largest group of artisans was the twelve cordiners or shoemakers. Most worked single-handedly. Only two had male servants. There were tanning pits beside Douglas Wynd almost half way up the High Street, and two cordiners, Robert Orem and John Anderson who lived side-by-side in this area likely used them. John Cruickshank, a heelmaker was a cut above the ordinary shoemaker. His skills were much in demand in Edinburgh and in Aberdeen itself where he became a burgess in 1648, designated as 'heilmaker in the old town, in respect of the few number of craftismen in this trade'. The two skinners or tanners, William Hay and Robert Menzies would have provided the cordiners' raw material. Hay was 'visitor' or deacon of the hammermen craft, and deacon convener or 'vistoure of the haill crafts of the citie' when Bishop Adam Bellenden granted their charter of incorporation in 1637. He lived with his daughter and one male servant and had a bit of property 'William Hayes land' which features on several occasions in the 1636 census. William Forsyth, one of the cordiners lived there with 'his wyff and one bairnie' while of Elspet Gray's 'twa bairnes', one of them was 'ane ydle sone in William Hayes land'. One stabler, Robert Willox, was based about the middle of the High Street, the other, Thomas Cumming, at the Chanonry

The Trades of Old Aberdeen were in existence well before the charter of 1637. Left, the Arms of the Weavers and right, the Fleshers.

end. There was one sadler, Alexander Guthrie, and one cooper, Alexander Wricht. There were three wrights and four blacksmiths.

While the Spital and College Bounds had its own weavers, cordiners and tailors, all providers of eat and drink lived in the High Street. The four fleshers or butchers, George Chalmer, William Buchane, Andro Gray and Robert Blinschell were based there, not in little colonies like some of the weavers and cordiners but well spread out. Chalmer had hopefully mellowed since the time he teemed a tub of water down Marjory Chalmer's wall. They slaughtered their beasts not, as one might have expected, in sheds behind the houses, but in the most primitive of circumstances. As late as 1754 the magistrates prohibited the killing by fleshers of 'swine, oxen, sheep and other cattel upon the street or before the door of their houses' as a cause of 'great inconvenience and danger…to the inhabitants'.

The baxters Alexander Wadie and Alexander Ortoun were located roughly at either end of the High Street, where they would have baked the bread in their bakehouses. While the baxters were male, all seven breid or oatcake sellers were female. Some of them were not above giving short measure and were duly fined by the magistrates if caught. Both Isobell Smythe and Isobel Kelman, mother of the two shankers, sold kale and Elspet Forsyth, the 'dillseller', the dilse or dulse seller would have gone across the links every morning to collect fresh seaweed from the shore. Other women in the food trade included Elspet Gray, puddinwricht and mother of the 'ydle sone in William Hayes land'. She created black puddings rather than fancy deserts. All the brewers in 1636 were women and the census investigated how many were currently serving 'the Aultoun,

Spittell and Chanrie' to wit, Marjorie Simson, Isobel Gavin and Jean Irving. Irving or Irvine would become a famous name in Old Aberdeen brewing. Another Aulton businesswoman, Elspet Leslie was a customer, a collector of customs duty, not the most popular of employments. She lived with her daughter while Agnes Dreden, the comer or midwife, lived alone. Working women headed about thirty-five High Street households and most would have been either widows or single.

There was only one traveller or huckster in the High Street, David Simsone, who lived there with his wife while the male cook, Thomas Spens, had a larger household, wife, mother-in-law three bairns and a servant. Patrick Davidsone sold fish. Alexander Cruikshank, a bookbinder was one of several who served council and college in the seventeenth century. Eight husbandmen or farmers ploughed and tilled the rigs, four gardeners grew the vegetables; peas, neaps, carrots, onions, cabbages, kale. Two laxfishers, Robert Ortoun and George Chalmer would have worked the salmon nets at Balgownie or the Cruives and would have been customers of Archibald Smythe the net weaver. There was only one mason, William Fyffe and one workman, Robert Ross. Harry Kemp, was the solitary keeper and herded cattle for the other residents who, even if not involved in agriculture at first hand kept a beast or two in what was very much a rural society. In 1603 a charge of 8d per cow per week was made. We do not know how good a herd Harry Kemp was, but there were frequently complaints about cattle getting into St Machar's kirkyard. This was by no means unique to Old Aberdeen. Cattle everywhere were anxious to sample the lush grasses of the graveyards, less manicured then than now. Later in the century a law was passed in Scotland making it an offence to allow cattle to graze in any kirkyard.

George Volum, the muckster, whom we have already met also lived the High Street with his wife and sister-in-law. He was not a municipal servant but would have worked for individuals, contracted to clear middens and muck heaps. The scavenger worked in a similar capacity at a later date, though he was a council employee with a wider remit. Later still, scavenger was familiarised to scaffie, and his remit narrowed again. The Volum household was just a few doors along from Bailie Thomas Mercer, two of whose servants were Robert and Alexander Volum. Another Volum, Thomas, was servant to George King, one of the 'most honest and aged persones' who supervised the 1636 census. Of the ninety servants attached to High Street households, thirty-one were male and fifty-nine female. In the largely artisan High Street keeping a servant had little to do with wealth or status. For the master or mistress, a servant meant help at the workbench, in the house or with the children or livestock; for the servant, the job offered food, shelter, and as we have seen in the case of Margaret Ellis, clothing and a bit of money as well.

As already indicated, it is not possible to give entirely accurate numbers of the High Street artisans. The occupations of the heads of thirty-two High Street families are not noted in the census. These are a mix of substantial citizens like George King ,one of the supervisors of the census who would have assumed that everyone knew his occupation, and those of 'of no calling', who were mostly ordered to move on. And given the parallel 'poor folkes' roll', that is no longer extant, it is likewise impossible to be completely accurate about the population of Old Aberdeen at this time, though around 900 seems a reasonable estimate.

There was a small sprinkling of gentlefolk and lawyers who apparently preferred the noise, bustle and smell of the High Street to the charm and seclusion of the Chanonry. Thomas Mercer, lawyer, bailie and economus we have already met. Travelling northwards we come to the home of Mr David Leech, subprincipal of King's College and his wife with 'hir two bairns' suggesting that he had married a widow. They had an unspecified number of servants. Leech was something of an oddball. The son of a Montrose minister, he graduated from King's in 1624 having devoted time during his student days to carving his name in various places on the oak screen in the chapel. He had lived in the chamber at King's once called Cancer and as a New Foundationer was much involved in college politics. He became a regent in 1627, subprincipal five years later, got married around this time and moved into the High Street. Leech produced a fair amount of Latin poetry during his career, some of it while living in the High Street. It including an *Elegy* for Bishop Patrick Forbes of Corse, part of the great volume of elegies which marked the bishop's passing in 1635, and *Philosophy in Tears* in 1637, a lament for the troubled state of King's and expressing hopes that the second Marquis of Huntly would be the saviour of the college. Huntly, appointed to head a visitation of the college at this time is addressed as, 'Scion of Nobility, Great Marquis, Star of the Caledonian region, Thrice hail illustrious hero', with much more in that vein. Leech became parish minister of Ellon in 1638. He declined to take the covenant and as Spalding put it, 'left his church, his charge, his countrie and gone into England'. On his return he had to preach two penitential sermons before being re-admitted to his charge in 1640. Eight years later Leech went with the Scottish army to England and became a chaplain to Charles II. Two years on and he is back in the North East as parish minister of Kemnay. In 1653 received the degree of doctor of divinity from King's College and at the same time was deposed from Kemnay 'for neglecting his charge'. He was said to have 'got a church near London', after that.

Some distance to the north again lived Mr George Clerke. We know nothing of him except that he had a master's degree and is unlikely to have had as turbulent a career as Leech. Next door to Clerke was the guidwyff of Kilstaires, a laird's widow, with five bairns and a servant. A little way further on was John Gordon of Deuchries, a cadet of the Gordons of Haddo, who lived with his wife, two bairns and two servants. He might have been a suitable candidate for the 'Bishop's Lodging', but going by the census he is not placed quite far enough north. One who was in the right area, not far from the Chanonry, was Mr Alexander Garden, Advocate, who lived alone with one male servant, though his was rather a small household for such a large dwelling. Garden had been procurator fiscal of Aberdeenshire and in 1634 was appointed sheriff depute of Aberdeenshire which translates into modern terms, surprising as it may seem, as sheriff principal. Our second High Street poet, he was the author of a collection of sonnets, elegies, epitaphs called *The Grave and Goodly Flowers* and *The Theatre of Scottish Kings,* for which he was paid £66 13s 4d 'for dedicating of his pamphlet to the toune'. He also made a translation into Scots verse of Bishop Elphinstone's life from Boece's *Lives of the Bishops.*

The household of William Fyffe, mason, 'his wyff and thrie bairnes, the eldest 13 yeir' must have been about the last in the High Street, though there is no break in the census. The majority of those who come after him are the lairds, gentlefolk, lawyers, academics and ministers who were known to have lived in the Chanonry in the seventeenth century.

One of the most attractive features of the High Street today are the quaint lanes, or wynds as they used to be called, the courts, and places, the walks and closes which punctuate it, particularly on the west side, leading through to the outfields beyond. A number of these do not make their appearance until the nineteenth century and must wait for Volume Two. But a few are as old as the High Street itself. One we have already come across, 'the common wynd callit the Doctor's Wynd'. Though unnamed in Taylor's Plan of 1773 it is shown linking with the little roads that criss-crossed the district, taking one to the Glebe Hill, (the Manse Hill in Taylor), which survives in part, the site today of the Queen Mother Library, the Meston Building (Soil Science etc) and the Fraser Noble Building (Engineering etc) none of which has yet been overtaken by the biblical fate promised to houses built on sand. It went much further, to the Loch of Old Aberdeen, to Tillydrone and the Cruives, to Inverurie, west to Cotton and Hilton and south to Kittybrewster, Peterstown and Cassie End.

The Doctor's Wynd had been renamed College Wynd by the time Orem was writing in the 1720s and it appears as such in Wood's Map of 1821. The ordnance survey of 1867 shows it as College Lane. After Old Aberdeen amalgamated with Aberdeen in 1891 along with Woodside and Torry, many street names were re-christened more grandly by Aberdeen Town Council. College Lane became College Road and the Post Office Directory

The wynd of seven names. It has been Meston Walk since 1940.

of 1892-93 described its as going, 'from High Street to Hermitage'. Mrs Buchan of Hermitage Cottage, No 2 College Road was the sole resident. The Hermitage itself was the famous summerhouse-cum-observatory which stood within the grounds of the Powis estate which Alexander Fraser had developed from the Twelve Roods of College Bounds. The 'Lane going to the Broom hill' was Parson Gordon's alternative name for the Doctor's Wynd and of course it took one there as well as to the Glebe Hill. The Broomhill was later planted with firs and became the Firhill, then Hermitage Hill in honour of the observatory. The Hermitage was demolished and the hill sold as a sandpit in the mid-1920s. Completely excavated, the former Broomhill, Firhill or Hermitage Hill is now a student carpark in Bedford Road.

Our lane was known as College Road only for a few years. By 1897 it had been absorbed in the recently laid out Bedford Road, which had replaced the old Kittybrewster Road. Bedford Road, the Post Office Directory announced, now ran 'from Powis Terrace to High Street' and Mrs Buchan's address accordingly was now Hermitage Cottage, No 151 Bedford Road. By 1940 Aberdeen Town Council had decided to divert Bedford Road near Firhill Road to connect with Tillydrone Avenue. Aberdeen University Court suggested to the 'Town' that the former College Road/ Lane/Wynd stretch, which would now link High Street and Bedford Road, be renamed Meston Walk. This proposal would honour Lord Meston, the

Chancellor of Aberdeen University who had been appointed in 1928 and who would die, in office, in 1943. 'Baillie Robertson', the Aberdeen Town Council Minutes record, 'dissociated himself from the recommendation'. However, his amendment, to rename this section 'College Walk' did not carry the day, and Meston Walk it duly became and so it remains.

A short distance north of the Doctor's Wynd alias Meston Walk, lay 'Dowglasse Wynde or Lane' as Gordon put it, or the Mid Wynd, one of the most ancient in the Aulton, and a favourite venue for those forbidden games of kits 'in tyme of sermon'. Orem says it was 'so called from one of that name who lived there and had a tenement beside it'. This particular Douglas is a mystery man. My only candidate, Archbald Douglas, is not a very satisfactory one. He was the father of the bairn 'gottin in adultre with Marin Arthur in Ald Aberden'. Like the Doctor's Wynd alias Meston Walk, Douglas Wynd was a thoroughfare rather than a mere passageway out to the common grazing. It skirted the north side of the Glebe Hill, and then, like the future Meston Walk linked up with all the little roads of the district. Both Meston Walk and Douglas Lane, (sadly the term 'wynd' has been done away with), will still take you to the world beyond Old Aberdeen.

Douglas Wynd or Lane, leading west and looking towards the Chemistry Building.

Between Douglas Lane, and the Chanonry there was only one further wynd on the west side in Orem's day, Cluny's or the Loch Wynd, which divided High Street from the Chanonry and led as one might expect along to the Loch of Old Aberdeen. It was of more ancient origin than the other two, predating the High Street and noted in a charter of 1492, as 'the lane between the manse of Invernochty and the land of Master Duncan Shearer, Rector of Clatt'. It was sometimes described as

Cluny's Wynd, looking towards the Town House. The house on the right, Cluny's Port was built around 1770. From the water colour by Alexander Catto.

the vennel from the Chanonry Port to the Loch. When Cluny was laying out his great garden in the 1620s he left the vennel, which lay on his land, for the use of the people. It was at this time it became known as Cluny's Wynd. It vanished in the 1920s, absorbed by the laying out of St Machar Drive, but at time of writing is still remembered by older folk in the area.

On the east side of High Street, only two lanes survive from this era. Berold Innes's Wynd or 'Beroald's Wynde or Lane' as Gordon called it, (23 on his Plan), marked the northern boundary of King's College, the place where College Bounds ended and High Street began, giving access east-wards to these 'pastures mixed amongst the plowghed feilds beyond', or according to Taylor's Plan, to the Oldtown Rigs. Berold Innes, whose forebears came from the Low Countries, became economus of King's College in 1586 and one picks up tantalising scraps of information about him. In a mysterious Aberdeen Council Minute of 20 September 1594, the Dean of Guild is instructed to pay the £16 owing to Issobell Cullen, spouse of David Rutherford, for the banquet given at the time of the reconciliation between certain of the young men of the town and Beroald Innes in Auld Abirdene'. (There are numerous spelling of his Christian name). As a reader at St Machar's Cathedral and as a bailie of Old Aberdeen by 1604, perhaps earlier, he was a person of some importance. A number of small courts sat in the Aulton and Berold, wearing his bailie's bonnet, was there

Berold Innes's Wynd, looking towards the High Street.

on occasion to mete out justice. On 6 June 1605 'Berrold Innes the bailie' attended the college court in company with the principal, subprincipal and masters, while the following year he sat in judgement at the court of Auld Aiberdene 'within the consistorie place'. He was involved in a number of land deals and was still around in 1617 when his name appears on the Old Aberdeen feuars and citizens list of that year.

His wynd, in common with Douglas Lane, was important enough to be laid with cassies. On 11 April 1668 the magistrates instructed the treasurer, Alexander Irving, to organise the causeying and repairing in 'that wynd commonly called Berold Innes Wynd' and the following month finds Irving hiring men and horses to load stones and sand to causey Douglas Wynd.

Taylor's Plan of 1773 shows Berold's Wynd without naming it, while immediately to the north-east is Regent's Walk, a loaning bordered by trees, which goes off through the outfields towards the Links. By 1821, Wood's Plan has lumped Walk and Wynd together, and shows the brewery of Smith Irvine & Co immediately north of the Wynd. In his *Annals* of 1818 Kennedy had already reported on this 'extensive brewery which supplies the citizens and neighbourhood with beer ale and porter'. The ordnance survey of 1867 shows Berold's now named Brewery Lane, dividing the north lawn of King's from the brewery and distinct from Regent Walk, which still goes off through the fields but is now bisected by King Street. The greater part of the

Regent Walk at its junction with Berold Innes's Wynd, beyond, which is undergoing repair.

brewery was swept away for the building of New King's in 1912, though Berold's Wynd/Brewery Lane survives as that anonymous sunken lane below New King's. It is redundant these days and is sealed off on the High Street side by a chest-high wall. Regent Walk is still there, though the granite yards that clustered on its north side during the first half of the twentieth century have been replaced by university buildings.

Wagril's Wynd a short distance north of Berold's is another lane that has survived from the seventeenth century or earlier and originally led into the fields beyond the back dykes. Orem reports that it was cassied in 1666. In his day Baillie Baxter's tenement and Mrs Clarke's lodging were on either side of it, the latter having belonged to the original Wagril. A blacksmith, David Wagrells, was admitted burgess of trade in 1732 and may have been a member of this family. Jean Wagrellis, according to the 1636 census was a servant of the tailor, John Linsie, who lived next door to Bailie Mercer. The first ordnance survey of 1867 shows Wagril's as East Lane, but by the time of the second edition of 1901 it had reverted to being Wagril's though now a Lane. These days it leads to Dunbar Street.

Orem mentions two other wynds on the east side that have vanished. Bevarley's, and Reid's. On 22 March 1642 the Council decided to make a wynd through Gilbert Bevarley's close, 'annent the cross'. This was the easiest way of going about it. Knock down the back dyke at the end of the

Wagril's Lane looking east to Dunbar Street.

close, perhaps do a bit of widening and causeying and, hey presto, a new common wynd was created. The council did not pay Bevarley for this surrender of his land. Market Lane, beside the cross may be the present day version of Bevarley's. Wagril's and Bevarlay's both led through the back dykes. Reid's Wynd was furthest north, in the Seatongate, according to Orem 'so called from a man of that name who lived sometime there'. It was at the 'end of the town as people pass to the Bridge of Don' (Balgownie). From there it became a broad green way to the links 'for the use of the clergy who lived in the chanry and chaplains' chambers'. On 27 March, the council enacted that neither man nor woman on horseback or foot should 'pass doune that Rod or valk called the Reades rod' in prejudice of John Casssie, the heritable proprietor. The penalties for doing were a fine of 6s 8d for those on horseback, 3s 4d for pedestrians. By Orem's time it was more regularly in use for it had been lately repaired. This wynd has vanished altogether.

The High Street rigs on both sides were enclosed by back dykes which added to the walled character of the place. The magistrates insisted that they were kept in a good state of repair though the enemy was probably seen as stranger beggars or those fleeing the plague rather than armed men who would not have been deterred by them. Taylor's Plan of 1773 shows that little roads, the back gates, had developed alongside the dykes and to this day, they allow us to plot the positioning of the back dykes. The East

The East Back Gate, now Dunbar Street.

The West Back Gate, later the Back Road, now Elphinstone Road in its lower reaches.

Back Gate, later the East Back Road ran from the junction of the present Cheyne Road with the Seatongate (Don Street), as far as the Berold's Wynd-Regent Walk junction. The West Back Gate or Road ran from half way along Cluny's Wynd as far south as Meston Walk. The East Back Road was renamed Dunbar Street around 1880, so the West Back Road simply became the Back Road. By 1950 it too was re-christened, as Elphinstone Road. The High Street lies snugly between the arms of the two great bishops.

Chapter 16

The Market Cross

All merchandises salbe presentit at the mercat croce of the burghis.
Edict of William the Lion (1165-1214).

We have reached the end of the High Street and ahead lies the Chanonry. But directly in front of us is that status symbol of the medieval burgh, the market cross, granted to the burgesses of Old Aberdeen by James IV's charter of 1489. Though this was a new privilege for the Aulton, such crosses had dominated the market place for at least three hundred years, not only in Scotland but throughout Europe. Early market crosses, simple stone shafts with a cross finial symbolised the Church in the market place. They were a visible reminder to traders that cheating and short measure would be marked down against them by an all-seeing God, or in practice by His emissaries on earth, the bailies or their officers.

With the exception of their plinths and stone shafts, there were scarcely two market crosses alike in Scotland with local masons interpreting the instructions of the burgesses to the best of their ability. The chroniclers Spalding and Orem provide glimpses of how the original Aulton cross looked, and it was certainly more splendid than the truncated shaft which now sits outside the former Town House. It was topped by a crucifix and according to Orem in his *Description of the Chanonry etc in 1724-25,* 'there was engraven and cut out of stone, at the top of this cross, on the south and north sides thereof, the picture of the blessed Virgin Mary'. This may have been incised on stone, but 'picture' was also used at that time to mean a statue. 'Below are the armorial coats of the Kings of Scotland, Bishop Dunbar, Bishop Stuart and Bishop Gordon yet to be seen', continues Orem. A slightly different commentary on the cross is given in *A Description of Old Aberdeen, 1771,* which is included as a short chapter near the beginning of Orem's book. It is attributed to the topographer Richard Gough who acquired Orem's manuscript when he visited Old Aberdeen in that year.

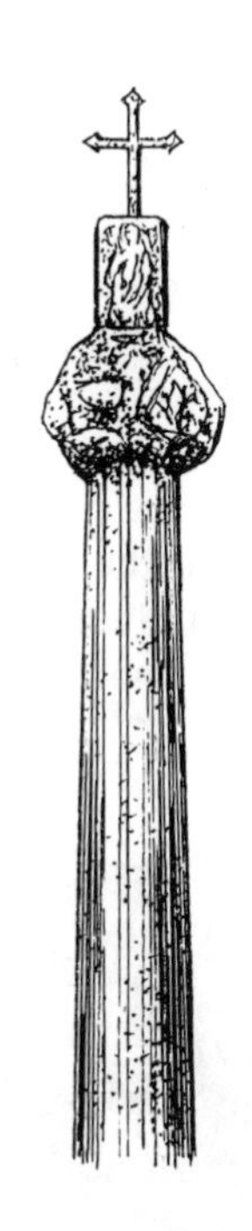
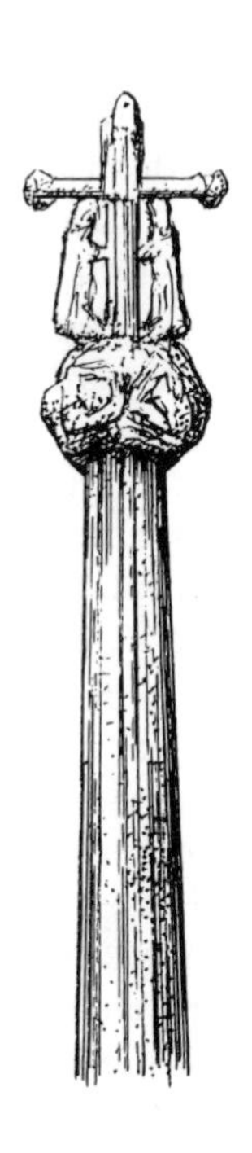

Two different versions of how the Old Aberdeen Market Cross might have looked before the Reformation.

Gough states that the episcopal arms are those of Elphinstone, Dunbar and Stewart. Since these arms were 'yet to be seen' in Orem's day the imperfect heraldic knowledge of either Gough or Orem was unfortunate for they are now indecipherable, though Bishop Dunbar's arms were discernible in the early part of last century.

The age of the cross can be roughly worked out. It dates after 1532 when Bishop Stewart, mentioned by both sources, was enthroned, and at the latest sometime after 1545, when Bishop William Gordon's episcopacy began and prior to 1560 when the reforming mob defaced the 'picture' of the Virgin on the Cross *en route* to their abortive assault on St Machar's. The cross rested from its later travels at the Anthropological Museum at Marischal College whose 1912 catalogue goes for Gough rather than Orem. It provides the bold description: 'Market Cross fragment with coat of arms of Scotland and Bishops Elphinstone, Dunbar and Stewart. Carved in relief in sandstone. Erected in Old Aberdeen circa 1540'. Whatever its exact age a good half century had elapsed between the royal granting of the market cross and its appearance 'in the parting of the streets' where the High Street widened out at its north end.

The cross continued to lose its looks. In August 1640 a posse of covenanting noblemen and academics rode out to 'ding doon' popish emblems in both Aberdeens. 'The crucifix on the Old Town Cross was thrown down', writes Spalding, 'the crucifix on the Newtown closed up, being loath to break the stone'. (Predecessor of the present Castlegate cross, this old 'Newtoun' cross also boasted interior stairs and a roof on which dignitaries could sit when the occasion demanded. The shaft bearing the cross rose through the middle, like a parasol through a garden table).

The fall of the Aulton cross would have taken the defaced 'picture' of the Virgin with it. Its heraldic 'knob' now served as the finial, as it does to this day. The armorial coats of the king and the Catholic bishops, unlike the images of Virgin and crucifix, more martial than Romish in appearance, never came under attack for being religiously incorrect. Thus shorn of its emblems of popery, the cross continued to hold centre stage in the burgh's affairs, a halfway house and meeting place for Chanonry and Seaton residents and those in the High Street, College Bounds and the Spital while the open area around it formed a natural market place.

The woodcut of the heraldic 'knob' of the Market Cross before restoration. The arms shown are those of Bishop Dunbar.

In this, the era before shops came into existence, one of the bailies' most important duties was the upholding of the market. It was an important source of income both from stallage, the dues paid by for the privilege of erecting a stall and from the small customs levied when wares were weighed or measured to ensure that there was no short dealing. The injunction that 'all merchandises salbe presentit at the mercat croce of the burghis' still held good. At the weekly Monday market vendors were under strict orders to come the cross with their goods at six in the morning, staying till twelve noon. Two small markets were set up in 1616, an afternoon market on Fridays for craftsmen's wares, and an early morning flesh market on Saturdays, both lasting an hour. Townsfolk were bidden to go to the cross to buy. Failure to abide by these laws by either by buyer or seller resulted in the usual fine. There were also strict penalties against anyone by-passing the Aulton market in favour of that of Aberdeen. On 17 June 1615, John Croll was found guilty of forestalling, that is buying to sell again at higher prices, and contravening one of the Aulton's acts by taking his fish to Aberdeen 'and not setting thame doun at the cros'. He was also guilty of regrating, in his case, buying meal and selling it dearer on the same day. He was fined £5. On 21 August 1648 the council ordained that no kale or dulse sellers go to Aberdeen 'to sell the same, but only to the Cross of the Old Toune'. The fine for disobedience was again £5. A surreptitious trip to the Aberdeen market, a spot of forestalling or regrating was a tempting option for the profits may well have outweighed the penalties if caught.

The bailies of Old Aberdeen themselves were quite capable of forestalling and regrating, and in a big way. Though the barony charter had laid down that the weekly market be held a Monday, Parliament, in July 1662, permitted a change of market day to Thursdays 'in all time comeing', which had the desired effect, at least as far as the Aulton was concerned, of pre-empting Aberdeen's Friday market. The Aberdeen magistrates quickly undertook a damage limitation exercise, complaining that 'all sorts of merchandice, meall, wheat, oats and all other grane coming to their mercat are forstalled and regrated contraire to the lawes and acts of Parliament'. They made successful supplication to Parliament to have 'the said weekly market in the old toun altered' and only eight weeks passed before the market day was changed again, from Thursday to Tuesday. The Aulton bailies took no notice and a trade war between the two Aberdeens simmered on for years. We must have a closer look at it in Volume Two.

There was a notable exception to the rule that all wares must be sold at the market cross. One of the regulations following Canon Galloway's visitation of King's College in 1549 was that no female brewers or bakers were to enter the college because of 'the great inconveniences arising from such dealings'. They were to be 'received at the gate, or within by a proper servant'. From this stricture it is evident that both male and female sellers of food and drink visited the college to make direct sales, thus saving provisor, economus or cook the inconvenience of having to shop at the cross and contend with the hustle and bustle of the market place.

The cross, was also the burgh's place of punishment. On 18 April 1608 Issobell Jemsone was convicted of stealing William Lyndsay's sark (he could well have been the schoolmaster). It was ordained by Bailie Alexander Mutray, who was chairing the court, that 'she be put to the cross and tirrit (stripped) fra the vest up and scurgit through the Towne, and never to be found within the Bishopric of Aberdeen under pain of death'. On 21 July 1623, Janet Waan an outcast from another parish, confessed to her fall in adultery with Androw Small. Already a convicted vagabond, she 'was to be taken to the Cross, and put in the jo(u)gs' then 'her heid clippit and put out of the toun as ane infamous person'. There is no word of how Androw was treated. The jougs was a hinged iron neck-ring, padlocked at the front and attached to the shaft of the cross by a chain and staple. Those convicted of a crime could also be 'stockit' beside the cross, put in the stocks, which apparently were portable. In 1647 James Moddanes a smith 'dwelling beyond the cassies', perhaps out in Seaton, gave abuse to Bailie Thomas Mercer and drew his dirk to him. That September he was imprisoned and put in the stocks for 'twa nightis and twa dayis', but on out of consideration for the culprit, his wife and bairns, the bailies fined him £20 and sentenced him to sit at the market cross, still in the stocks during Mercer's pleasure, apparently a softer option. He was also banished from the Aulton till the following Easter.

The accounts for 1665-66 show that George Cuming was paid £6 4s for various blacksmithing work, including 'working the yrone work to the crose'. He may have been putting on a new staple to hold the jougs. During 1689-90 new branks, similar to the jougs but more of a scold's bridle, cost the town £1 4s and David Murray was paid 6s for fixing them on. The ironmongery of correction apart, the upkeep of the cross itself was important. The accounts for 1685-86 shows three loads of pinnings and three tubfulls of lime were ordered for it, as well as the transport of three stones 'to hew, to be steps', which would raise it from the ground and enhance its appearance, all at a cost of 17s 6d. James Baverlay, the Sunnyside mason, must have done the hewing. On 8 March 1686 he was admitted a burgess of the Aulton, his entry fee 'in respect of his mason work at the Cross' waived. At the beginning of that year the councillors of Aberdeen had commissioned a splendid new cross, the one which still graces the Castlegate. The Aulton, whose relations with the royal burgh were not then of the warmest, may have felt the need to keep up appearances.

The cross was the focus of commerce and castigation in the burgh and of celebration too. Hard-up though the Aulton was, the bailies, as we know, did not stint burghal expenditure that had the twofold merit of a public display of loyalty to the crown coupled with the opportunity for numerous loyal toasts. On 14 October 1685 according to the burgh accounts, the magistrates bought two dozen glasses at £4 16s, eight pints of wine at £6 8s and £1 10s worth of peats 'to a fire at the Cross to celebrate the King's birthday'.

In 1643 Spalding reported on interesting ceremony there:

> Upon the second of Februar, being Candlemas day, the barnis (bairns) of the Old toun gramar scooll, at six houris, cam up the get (gate, road, in this case the High Street), with candles lichtit in their handis, crying, rejoicing and blyth aneuche. (They) cam thus up to the cross, and round about gois diverse times, climes to the heid thereof and set ane burning torche thairupon. I mervallit at this, being at sic tyme, and quhairof myself had never sene the lyk.

Little wonder Spalding was surprised for candlelit processions had been proscribed since the Reformation as smelling of popery. Worse still, their origins were pagan, dating from Roman times when the citizens went through the streets with torches and candles in honour of Februa, the mother of Mars. The Candlemas schoolchildren's festival had developed out of the custom to present the dominie with money to buy candles for the schoolroom. Now the money was given to the master himself, a topping-up of his salary under the guise of ancient tradition. The pupil presenting the largest sum was proclaimed Candlemas King. Spalding records that the king on this occasion was John Keith the Earl Marischal's brother, though one might have expected to find him attending the Grammar School of Aberdeen near the 'family' university. But there is a chance that he may have been Master John Keith (MJK), bursar of divinity. The children 'convoyed' him (some would have linked fingers under him to form a seat), to his lodging in the Chanonry with lighted candles.

Chapter 17

School and Tolbooth

To build and put up at the cross ane scholl of twa houses hicht with ane wardhous and ane house above the said wardhous to hald the toune and craftis court therin quhen ane occasion sall peroffer.

Old Aberdeen Council Minutes, 17 November, 1641.

The conclusion to Chapter 16 takes us to the threshold of the Chanonry. We are almost there, though not quite. The Candlemas ceremony of 1643 raises several interesting points and illustrates one method of augmenting the schoolmaster's salary. 'The bairns of the Oldtoun grammar school' that Spalding spoke of came from the school in the close outside King's College where the humanist and his assistants taught Latin grammar and prepared the brighter pupils for matriculation at King's. The humanist himself would have taken the arts course studies with the students. In 1635 Master John Lundie grandly styled himself Professor of the *Literae Humaniores*, (the Humanities), when contributing to the funeral elegies for Bishop Patrick Forbes, but when declining a further stint as bailie it was as 'Humanist and maister of the gramer schwill', stressing that he already had two jobs.

While the Grammar was a boys' school there was another school in Old Aberdeen at this time for both boys and girls, its roots in the old sang school of St Machar's Cathedral. In pre-Reformation times, St Machar's, in common with other Scottish cathedrals, ran a sang school and an associated grammar school where the young choristers were taught and trained in the skills of choral music including polyphony. At the Reformation both schools were dispersed. Though the choristers may well have enrolled at the Old Aberdeen Grammar School, centuries of choral tradition, fostered and developed at the sang school, were in grave danger of disappearing without trace. The Reformation was still in its infancy when regret was expressed by many in Scotland over what the Parliament itself described as 'an art almost decayed and shall shortly decay without timeous remedy'. In

1579 a decree was passed that sang schools be restored in all the Scottish burghs. No 'guidelines' were provided as to how they should be run or how the legacy of the old sang schools be preserved, only that the master 'be sufficient and able for instruction of the youth in the science of music'. Despite the best intentions of Parliament, the Protestant alternative, the teaching of psalmody, the singing of a few doleful psalms, in no way compensated for the soaring descants of the Roman Church. But instrumental music was on offer as well, the virginals or the fiddle, and the dominie was expected to be a skilled enough singer to lead the psalm in the parish kirk and to take on the job of session clerk as well. In school he taught the basic subjects as well as music. In time the three Rs prevailed and the sang school evolved into the Scottish elementary or public school and the different names of the sang school of Old Aberdeen over the years, the Music School, the English and Music School and the Common School of the Toun illustrate this evolution.

In the post-Reformation era education was the financial responsibility of the parish. In Old Aberdeen this was shouldered by the burgh, the kirk, the trades, King's College and the heritors, and nowhere is the Aulton's difficulties in scraping together money for essential outlays better illustrated than in the struggle to pay dominie's salary. On 16 July 1607 the council minutes record the request of William Lindsay 'maister of the sangschoil' who also 'begane the salme in the kirk' for three years' back pay. Unfortunately Lindsay's sark appears to have been stolen the following year so his spell as dominie was not without its trials. (It is not recorded if he ever encouraged the sang school bairns to carry out the Candlemas ceremony).

In 1628 Mr Gilbert Ross was appointed schoolmaster as well as reader, chorister and session clerk at St Machar's. The school day was a long one, 6am till 9am, 10am till 12 noon and 2pm till 6pm. Ross also read the prayers at the cathedral at 7am and 5pm in the summer and 8am and 4pm in winter. It was not so much a case of his leaving the class while he nipped along to the cathedral, but rather that the children attended church with him and displayed their prowess at psalmody. In February 1634, towards the end of Bishop Patrick Forbes's chancellorship of King's College, Ross became cantor there, the first since the Reformation, though he served there without stipend. As he put it in the 'Obligation by the cantor to teach music on certain conditions', printed in the Minute Books of King's College 'trew it is that the present rentis of the colledge ar not able to afford me anie stipend atall', and continued:

> I faithfully bind and obleige me to perfome the said office of cantor and scoole maister and...crave no more of the colledge rentis for my office and reiding and

singing in the said kirk than the sowme of thrie score pundis already appoynted and assigned to me by the masteris and members for their part of the maintenance of the said service of reading and singing.

It would appear that the college already made a contribution of £60 towards his reading and singing in the said kirk, St Machar's, and that had to suffice as his King's College salary as well. Ross lived in the Chanonry with his wife and family where a manse was mortified to the use of the master of the music school of Old Aberdeen. He must have given satisfaction as a schoolmaster for in 1636 the weaver craft decided to give ten merks annually towards his stipend. The hammermen, tailors, cordiners, and fleshers agreed to pay five merks annually, and with a contribution from the bailies, that made up the sum of 40 merks. This was topped up by the quarterly school fees. Pupils learning to read paid 6s 8d, reading and writing 13s 4d, reading, writing and singing 20s, reading, writing, singing and playing an instrument, 26s 8d. Unfortunately Ross was 'dischargeit as ane unprofitabill member' from King's College in 1639 through the machinations of Master John Lundie. Though he received his stipend from the council in 1640 at the hands of bailies John Forbes and Dr William Gordon, he vanishes thereafter.

His successor, Alexander Wilguis (Wildgoose), was appointed the following year. The session records of 30 May 1641 set out his duties and they are punishing. On Sundays, the reading of morning prayers was followed by a chapter of the Bible, the singing the psalm, then the catechism, then more reading 'while the Minister cum to the pulpit', then the reading of the marriage banns. Roughly the same procedure was followed in the afternoon with the exception of the catechism and the banns, though there was a psalm and prayers at the end. The same routine prevailed every weekday if 'a sermon is to be preached' and Saturdays apart, prayers were to be read every night beginning 'at the hindmost chap of the bell'. Add to that the secretarial work for the kirk session and the single-handed teaching and the running of the school. It seems that each master had to negotiate his salary from scratch for Wilguis's stipend at that time was made up from 'the casualties of the kirk', that is the casual income from marriage fees at 13s 4d a time, baptisms 4s, and burial fees at 6s 8d in the kirk, 4s in the kirkyard. Add to that the school fees which were as they had been in Ross's day. Wilguis's salary was dependent on a kirk with busy hatch, match and dispatch departments and a well-attended school.

The schoolroom, 'within the town of Old Aberdeen and bounds of the University of King's College', that is in the High Street-College Bounds area, must have suffered from overcrowding. The 1636 census reveals that there were about 290 children between the Spital and the Chanonry, though not all would have been of school age. With the population rising sharply there was talk, soon after Wilguis's appointment, of building a new school, indeed a multi-purpose civic centre. On 17 November 1641 the Incorporated Trades of Old Aberdeen agreed to contribute voluntarily 'to the uttermost of thair power', along with the rest of the town to build a school at the cross two storeys high, with a wardhouse (prison) and a storey above that to contain the Town's and the Trades' meeting place and courts. The council at this time was still convening in the former consistory court house in St Machar's, though sometimes it sat below Reid's loft. The commissary court also sat in 'the old consistorie place' as did the kirk session. In addition, it served as the tax office so careful timetabling was a necessity. For want of a better place, St Machar's was also the Old Aberdeen prison, though given the amount of civic activity not to mention the Sabbath and week day services, it is unclear just where the prisoners were confined. Perhaps they were locked in one of the twin spires, perhaps in Elphinstone's tower which still stood, though the spire had been long since replaced by the saddleback roof.

Where better to erect the proposed new school and other civic buildings than on the most prominent site in town, just north of the cross at the parting of the ways? And where else ? Given the High Street's development during the seventeenth century, this wide area was one of the few remaining central locations suitable for such a major project. At that time Principal William Guild having abandoned the Snow Kirk, was demolishing the Bishop's Palace to secure more building material to repair King's College. Baillies John Forbes and Thomas Mercer decided to take a leaf out of his book for the civic good, at the same time adhering to the Aulton philosophy of re-using old stones. They requested Guild's permission to demolish the bishop's doocot, along with roof and slates from the outhouses of the palace for the building of the new school and council meeting place.

Nothing was heard of this grand scheme for some time and little would have happened during the plague year of 1647. Meanwhile five years into his appointment it was clear that things were not going well for Dominie Wilguis. On May 24 1646, the payment of the 'casualties' was withdrawn, the reason, the kirk's 'gryte burding of debt' and the massive amount of maintenance that needed to be done, a priority on which the 'casualties' would have to be spent. But the kirk was always in debt and there was always maintenance to be done and Wilguis was sacked a few days later. The real reason for dismissal was his 'natural inabilities and bodily weakness', his inability to cope. Discipline was neglected, and Wilguis who 'being often admonished did shun amendment' had to go. The kirk session 'being loth to dismiss him emptie' gave him £100 contributed to jointly by kirk, college and town council. Though this may not be pertinent in

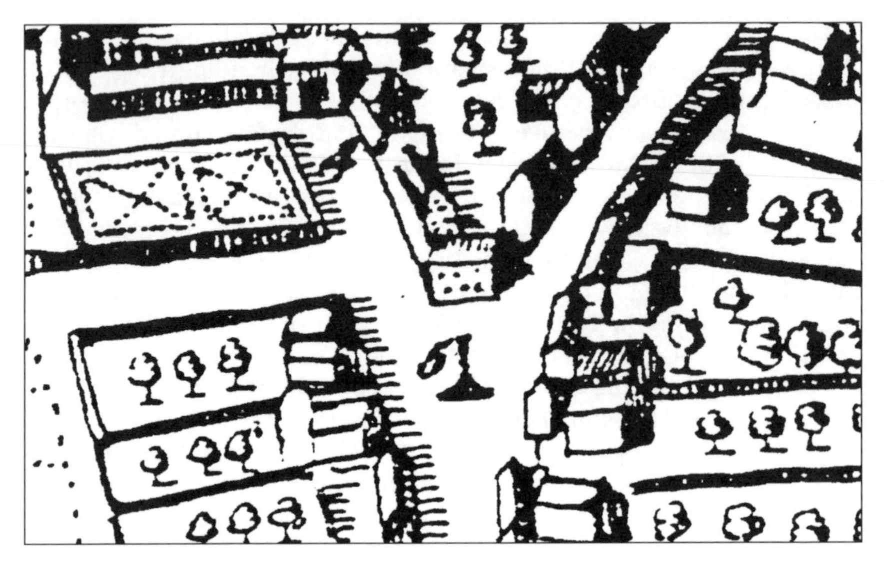

The multi-purpose building housing the school and much else is shown above the market cross, marked 5. There is a separate entrance to the right. Detail from Parson Gordon's Plan, 1661.

Wilguis's case, some of the difficulties about unsuitable teachers stemmed from the fact that King's and Marischal Colleges were now producing substantial numbers of ministers every year. The famine had become a feast. The pick of the graduands went to the parishes which left the less promising 'stickit ministers' waiting for a call to a charge. Teaching was often the only option as an alternative career but it was not so prestigious as the ministry and not all reluctant recruits to the profession had the aptitude for it.

Wilguis was succeeded almost immediately by William Logan, formerly schoolmaster and session clerk at Ellon who negotiated a salary of 200 merks, to which college contributed £40, the kirk session 100 merks the town 40 merks. Arithmetic was now added to subjects taught. The new school apparently had not yet made its appearance for the appointing committee of Principal William Guild and other masters from King's, two bailies, the minister, elders and four heritors promised 'to mail (rent) a schoolhous... together with a chalmer to the Master'. However the funding for the new premises was slowly being ingathered. On 20 May 1649, 'the college and the kirk' agreed to make a contribution to the erecting of 'ane new school hous at the cross' commensurate with their contributions to the annual rent of the former schoolhouse. On 19 December 1649 the kirk session ordained that there was to be a visitation of 'the Musick and Inglishe

Scooles', 'the parents of the bairns (were to be) lykwayes present to see what the chyldren hes profited this bygone quarter'. Parent's evenings are not an innovation and fortunately on this occasion the bairns were found to be 'profiting in learning'. The following year, when presenting his accounts on 30 August, Thomas Angus, city treasurer at that time, reported on the 'unlays(fines), customs silver and borrowit muneys quhilk he reservit for putting up of the skoole'. This amounted to £21 7s 5d. Logan took his leave sometime before 1655, and there was a hiatus before the next dominie took over. Eventually on 19 November 1655 it was intimated from the pulpit of St Machar's :

> that all put ther children to the musick and englisch schooll upon Monday next where they shall find a Master diligentlie to attend them.

The diligent master was William Hay and by the time of his arrival the new school was in the final stages of completion. Its loft was in place by 1656 and the following year, Gilbert Beverlay, William Cumming and James Barnet who had leased the Loch for a year agreed to 'leid' or cart over mortar from the Mortar Hole below the Loch, 'to the use of the new scholl and meitting hous for the toune'. Hay, on arrival, had agreed to take the 'casualties' in lieu of 100 merks of his salary, and was something of a businessman. In March 1659 the Loch of Aberdeen was rouped to him for a twelvemonth which allowed him to let it out for grazing to the highest bidder. He was also given the right to levy 6s 8d 'for ilk beast that falles in the Loch' indicating that it was not yet fully drained.

A Hay dynasty now emerged and lasted into the 1670s for William was succeeded by his son, also William, who became minister of Perth and later, Bishop of Moray. He in turn was succeeded by his brother, Mr George Hay. The accounts for 1671-73 record that £20 was paid in stipend to 'Masters William and George Hay, schoolmasters for the Years of God 1671, 1672 and 1673'. This does not mean that the school had acquired a duo of dominies, rather that the council was back to its triennial system of paying salaries. Stipend for the latter year would belong to George, for William was ordained by then. Visitations continued, four times annually, with the usual representatives of kirk, council and college in attendance. They were an important part of the school year and the master was instructed by the bailies 'to have his schollars readelie prepared to give a specimen of ther knowledge and proficiencie in ther musick and art'. It may have been a nerve-wracking experience for the scholars, but had its compensations. The burgh accounts of 1667-68 show that the bailies spent 8s on '4 pounds of plumdemus (damsons or prunes) to the bairnes'. The 1695 records show that £1 was spent on confections for the visitation.

In 1681 Alexander Cooper who had become dominie in succession to the Hays, complained that his salary had diminished considerably when compared with that of his predecessors 'not withstanding his pains is now greater'. Moreover he couldn't find a tenant for his house, which was surplus to his requirements, perhaps owing to his tenancy of the music master's house in the Chanonry. He was given an additional £20 'out of the kirk's seat rents for his better encouragement' which showed that his employers still had to cast around for money. This brought his salary from the kirk session to £40. The following year he complained again to the session, this time that people in town and parish were not sending their children to school. Years earlier, in 1665 five persons were reported to the kirk session for teaching in the Aulton without the permission of the session or bailies. Master George Hay had complained in 1673 that 'the flourishing of the public school was much impaired by the tolleratioun of severall privat schooles'. This, down the years became the bane of the Aulton dominies for one fee paid to the private school was a fee less for the official schoolmaster. The bailies banned these establishments, apart from sewing schools, or licensed them to teach only 'catechising and the proverbs' and levied 'sic fines as the magistrats sal please to inflict' on those who sent their children there, apparently to little effect.

In 1684 Cooper again sought 'suitable encouragement whereby he might make a livelihood', in other words he was after another rise, otherwise he would go off to a similar post in Montrose. Again we find him having to cadge around for money. The bishop and the heritors were favourable to allowing him an increment and Cooper now looked to the kirk session and the college to follow suit. King's College told him that their accounts were with their procurator, but he should go ahead and secure the contributions of 'the heritors and the trades,' by which time their financial position would be clear. The kirk session was favourable and promised to speak to the college 'seeing it mostly lay at their door'. Cooper must have succeeded for in 1690 he was still there. Soon after he did well for himself, becoming master of music of Aberdeen.

After Cooper's departure it was proposed in 1691 that no master succeeding him should keep 'ane common change', that is a small public house, within the town, on the face of it a curious if perfectly acceptable proviso. However a row had broken out over the appointment of Cooper's successor that caused dissension in Old Aberdeen for years. William Cumming had been chosen in the face of strong opposition. Another candidate, William Smith, formerly schoolmaster at Belhelvie claimed that he had been legally elected while James Gordon of Seaton and Bailie Baxter protested that Cumming's appointment was invalid for a number of reasons. They had a point. He had been sent for to Morayshire, and his supporters on the council and kirk session 'caused examine him privatlie in ane alehouse and by ane arbitrarie and despotick power established him schoolmaster in the Oldtoune'. Cumming survived this controversial initiation and stayed for five years before receiving a call to his birthplace, Elgin.

In July 1696 a large examining panel of the great and the good gathered to appoint his successor, among them those for and against the earlier candidate, William Smith. All agreed that 'to avoid dissention there should be a public competition and the best qualified should carry it'. Smith's name was on the short leet but he was known to be 'disaffected to the government'. He was a Jacobite and since he had settled in Old Aberdeen had rows with his neighbours on political matters calling them 'rogues, loons and cheats' and was felt by his enemies not to be good schoolmaster material, particularly as he kept a public inn. The embargo of 1691 against keepers of change houses now makes sense. It had been put in place to rule Smith out of the previous contest. However Smith, to the dismay of his supporters, cocked a snook by declining to turn up. Another candidate was not up to the mark and eventually Mr William Christie, 'against who there was nothing to object', initially damned by faint praise, was appointed schoolmaster, proved his competence, and was still in office when Orem was writing in 1725.

A council house, that is a meeting place and courtroom for the councillors and trades had originally been planned at the same time as the school, to form part of the same building. While the school was completed around 1650, the council house, with weigh and meal houses below was not finished until almost twenty years later. The availability of money rather than labour would have been the drawback. In 1659 a meeting of the 'haill inhabitantis' was held 'in ther ordinar place of meeting within the new Schooll house' which sounds as though they were making do with a schoolroom rather than the actual council meeting place. In 1666-67 the council accounts record work on the council meeting house to the tune of £22 including timber work, sylling (putting up the ceiling) of the house, 'with the deask and seats round' which looks as though the council house was almost finished.

The building, at length completed, was economic in concept and surprising in dimension. Orem wrote :

> The said school, council, and weigh-house are all under the one roof. This house is lofted, two rooms whereof are appointed for the music school, one laigh, another high; the former for accommodating children who were only taught to read, write and learn arithmetic; and the latter for those who were taught vocal and instrumental music; and upon the same flat is a room towards the east, pretty large

called the Council-House, where there is a bench for magistrates, and a table below it of equal length, with fixed forms round about the same; and a bar that people might not rudely encroach into that particular part of the room where the bench is fixed; whereon the magistrates sit and determine in matters that shall come before them. Above the said bench are the king's arms and below the council-house are the weigh and meal-houses.

According to the burgh accounts for 1667-68, William Ker was paid £6 for painting the King's arms and Alex Christal £2 12s for backing and mulering (framing) them. These must have been the arms for the council meeting house.

By 1692 the music school and council house were in need of repair. A tax of 400 merks was levied on the inhabitants and the convener of the trades offered 100 marks 'as being all they could spare'. George Laing, the college economus, and two members of the trades were instructed 'to buy sufficient trees (timber) and other materials' to carry out the work. It is unclear whether these repairs were completed by 1702 when a new tolbooth and prison house was mooted, to be built on the south side of the school, or whether the repairs and the new work were undertaken together. A prison or wardhouse as part of the complex at the cross had been spoken of back in 1641 but did not materialise and the building of school and council house had made demands on the 'haill inhabitantis' for years. The lack of a custom-built prison had substantial drawbacks. In 1677, for example, the bailies ordained that pupils of the Grammar School or the Music School, and 'such boys as are servants and tradesmens prentices' who were found breaking into yards and taking away carrots, syboues (onions) neips and pease were to be imprisoned in the lime house for want of a better place.

The revived plan for a prison was well received. On 27 September 1702, three bailies, Alexander Fraser of Powis, William Baxter and James Knight asked the inhabitants of Old Aberdeen for contributions and 'none had declined'. Dominie William Christie gave a donation of £12 while the minister and kirk session of St Machar's were so delighted that they agreed that £20 be paid out from their 'penalties', the fines levied by the church. They were particularly anxious for the erection of a prison, since those guilty of thieving, scolding, cursing, swearing, Sabbath breaking and the like were, as we know, 'always secured in the church till they had given satisfaction'.

The new tolbooth, went ahead on the south side of the school facing the cross, was completed during 1703. The 3000 merks which it cost was raised from voluntary contributions. Bailie Fraser of Powis, Bailie Baxter and Bailie John Robertson were among those contributing £30 each though Robertson, one of the local heritors, may have regretted his donation. The

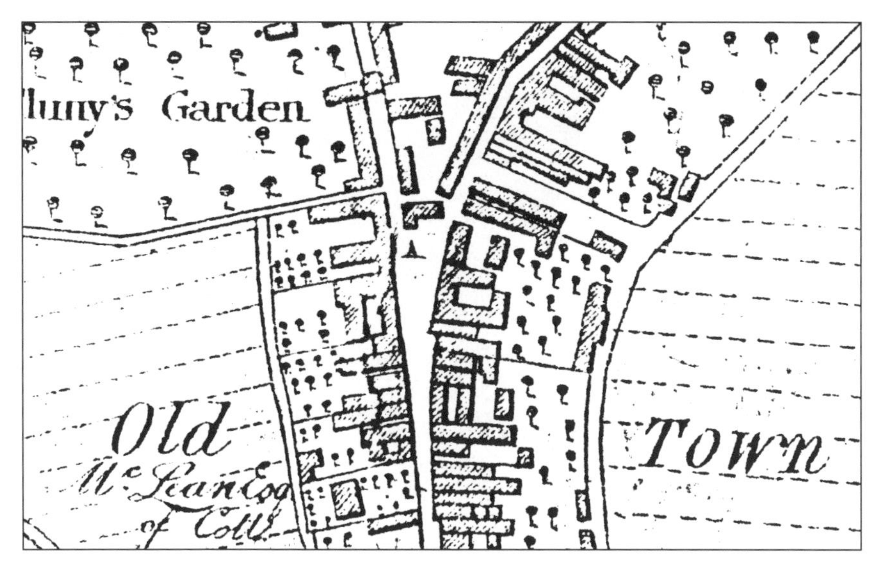

This detail from Taylor's Plan 1773, shows the expansion of the school and council building, just behind the Market Cross, centre. The new wing containing tolbooth and fleshmarket is to the left. This entire complex was taken down in 1788.

building stood near the peat yard which had belonged to Sir Alexander Gordon of Cluny in his lifetime. Here Borrow Shand, Cluny's peatman, had 'built a little house on the west side of the yard' according to Orem. In spite of his generosity, Bailie Robertson claimed that 'music school, council and weigh houses and the new tolbooth stood all on his ground', his wife, Helen Shand being a near relation of Borrow from whom the ground was inherited. The case went to the Court of Session, and, says Orem, dropping a dark hint, 'the magistrates of the town so managed it so that Mr John Robertson and his wife lost the action'. The Robertsons were ordered to pay the town of Old Aberdeen 400 merks expenses, which in Orem's time still remained unpaid.

On 1 January 1704 the accounts relating to building the tolbooth and repairing the council house were open to public inspection to defray any future complaints or 'for stoping all mens mouthes' as the council robustly put it. Those failing to attend at the time set aside for inspection of accounts 'shall not be heard to hereafter'. The bailies knew their inhabitantis. The completed tolbooth had three rooms, the lowest for thieves, the next for prisoners and the third for the bell and clock. The bell, paid for by voluntary contributions, was the work of Albert Gelly a French bellfounder who had set up in Old Aberdeen around 1700. In February 1712 he agreed to cast a bell for the tolbooth for £70 Scots but that was only an approximation of the

The freestone panel above the entrance to the former Town House bears the Old Aberdeen coat-of-arms of three lilies in a pot, three salmons in 'fret', the motto 'Concordia res parvae crescunt', By harmony small things increase', and the date, 1721. It is thought to have come from an earlier building, but which? No new building appeared in that year, though the flesh market at this site was completed in 1723.

Above, the arms of the kings of Scots, with imperial crown, on the east wall of the former Town House. They may date from the reign of James V (1512-42) or earlier, and could have graced the gate of King's College or Kirkton of Seaton Manse.

cost. If the bell went over the weight agreed on, Gelly would have 20s Scots for every pound over, if below the weight, 20s less per pound. It was in place the following year with the motto: *Ad sacra et concilia vocamus*. (We call you to holy things and concilation) *Albertus Gellie fecit anno 1713.* It was rung at six in the morning, nine at night and at public rejoicings. Alexander Hendrie the tolbooth bellringer was paid six pennies quarterly from every family within the town and freedom which he had to collect himself.

The clock 'made by John Mowat, klockmaker' was in place by 1719 at a cost of £37 14. It had a painted dialboard, with 'a globe for the moon's age' and the town's arms. By 1726

Mowat was in hot water for neglecting 'the tounes clock which he undertook to keep right'. Mowat's riposte was that 'his sallary for his pains was so little that it was not worth pains'. However he relented and for the next year he agreed to keep it right for £6 Scots either with the sun, or against the clock that he had made for the Old Aberdeen merchant, Alexander Annand when the sun was not shining. He continued maintenance on the clock for some years.

The schoolhouse complex continued to expand. In September 1706 it was proposed 'how useful it would be to the toun to have the convenience of ane flesh mercat', a sign of a breakaway from the traditional market stall. It took time to make its appearance but according to Orem, a tile-covered flesh market was built at the town's expense on the south side of the council and weighhouse by 1723. By 1788 this whole complex at the cross was taken down and the market cross itself removed (though it eventually returned) to make way for George Jaffrey's masterpiece, the elegant Town House we see today. Its story belongs to Volume Two.

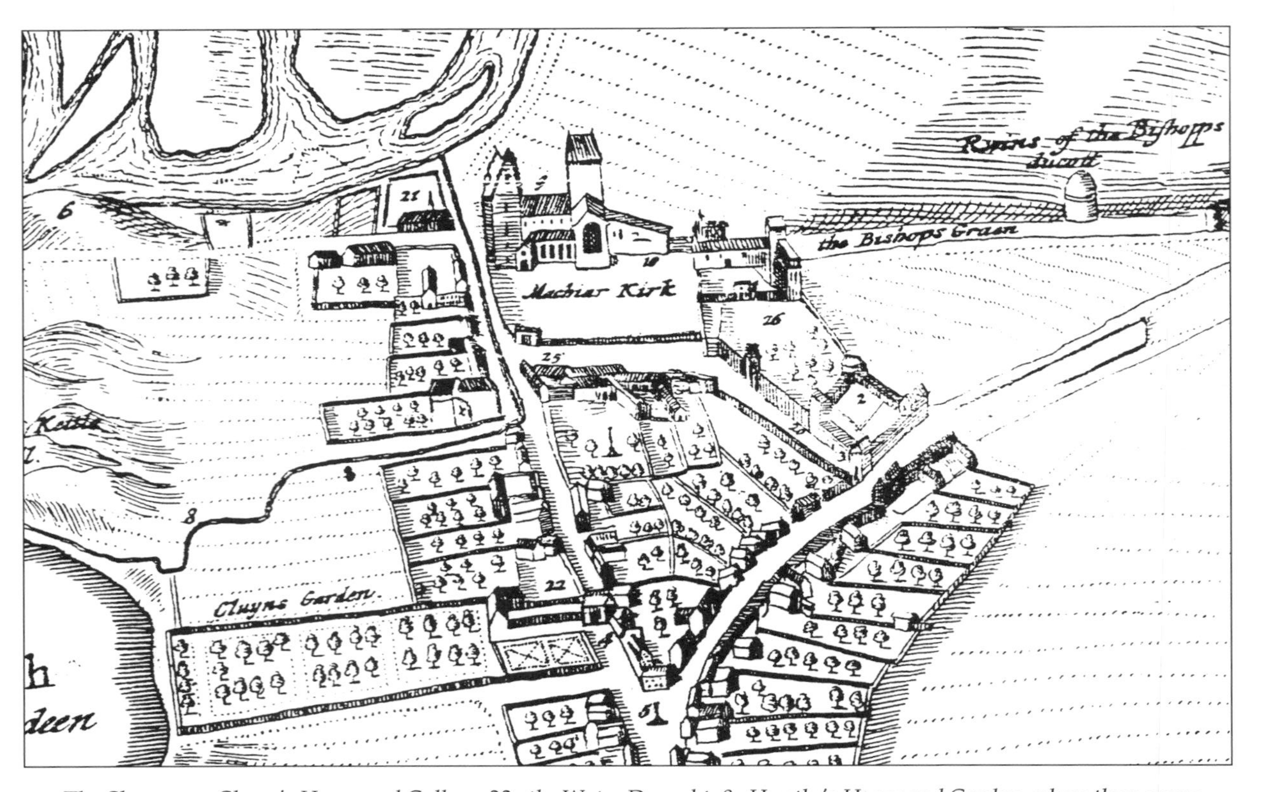

The Chanonry. Cluny's House and Gallery, 22; the Water Draught, 8; Huntly's House and Garden, where there seems to be a larger version of the market cross, 25; Dunbar's Hospital, 21; the Bishop's Garden below the Palace, 26; Chaplain's Chambers, 2; Chaplain's Port, 3. Detail from Parson Gordon's Plan, 1661.

Chapter 18

The final Flowering of the old Chanonry

All (lodgings) are possest by privat men, since the canons (as smelling too much of poperie) wer casheired.

Parson Gordon, Description of Bothe Touns of Aberdeen, 1661.

We leave the multi-purpose building behind the market cross to enter the Chanonry, moving northwards towards Seaton. The wheel is almost come full circle and we are back near where we started. Though the Chanonry lost its exclusive ecclesiastical status at the time of the Reformation, the canons of St Machar's were allowed by the Lords in Council to retain their manses during their lives and for several years they retained two-thirds of their benefices as well. A number of canons stayed on after 1560. They enjoyed the protection of the Earl of Huntly and life must have been pleasant enough. New residents, genteel folk, gradually moved in and in 1573 Walter Cullen recorded the death of Alexander Leslie, Laird of Wardes in 'Ald Aberden' in his *Chronicle.* Where would a laird live but in the Chanonry?

Many of the Chanonry houses shown in Parson Gordon's Plan must be these very pre-Reformation manses for Orem reveals that only a little new building had taken place. From the 1636 census one can estimate about thirty households there, gentry, academics, clergy, church officers and a smattering of ordinary folk in the cottages at the end of the glebes. Twenty-five households had thirty-seven servants among them while nineteen families had bairns or oys (grandchildren) who would have enjoyed the spacious gardens. The Chanonry had become socially if not geographically, the 'west end' of the Auld Toun.

One early transaction, in 1581, was the purchase of Invernochty Manse, the first in the Chanonry on the west side, though even then described as ruinous, by George Barclay, burgess of Aberdeen, and Marjorie Cheyne his spouse. The seller was the murderous rector, Mr John Elphinstone. Sir Alexander Gordon of Cluny, provost of Old Aberdeen, bought the property from a later proprietor, Robert Josse, and having acquired the two neighbouring properties, Turriff and Methlick, enclosed them in 1623 into a magnificent garden which he extended westwards to the shores of the Loch. It would have covered a part of the north side of St Machar's Drive, between the Chanonry and the Tillydrone Roundabout, the area now occupied by Aberdeen University's Auris Ltd and a part of the Cruickshank Botanic Gardens. Cluny had five daughters and a son and the garden must have given them much joy. Orem tells us that he had a pleasure-boat for rowing back and forward to his island summerhouse, possibly a crannog in the middle of the Loch. Folk were now calling the Chanonry Port, Cluny's Port, and Sir Alexander put up his own inscription there.

The port contained a little room or chamber, 'which seems to have belonged to one of the prebends', says Orem, perhaps originally built for Simon Dods's priest of the Altar of the Haly Blude. Here Cluny built a 'brave gallerie', hung it with pictures and joined it to the port chamber. Gordon's Plan shows a sizeable house forming a courtyard with the port and chamber on the east side. The ancient vennel giving access to the Loch from the north-west end of the High Street was in danger of being absorbed when Cluny built his yard dyke, but he allowed the inhabitants of Old Aberdeen 'as much ground as would be a wynd for their passing and repassing'. And so the old vennel reappeared as Cluny's or the Loch Wynd. It was a community responsibility and in 1636 as part of the road improvements programme, was causewayed as far as George Cumming's yard, the last one on the High Street

The creation of Cluny's Garden was one of the most spectacular developments in Old Aberdeen since the building of King's College. However Cluny was not to have it all his own way. In August 1638 the kirk session granted his petition that he share the common dask (pew) betwixt hammermen's seat and the pulpit with his cousin, Alexander Gordon of Birsemoir and their families 'during the time of my lord the Marquis of Huntlie's residences within the Citie of old Abd'. Yes, the Cocks of the North were back. George, second Marquis had succeeded to the title. His father the sixth Earl had been pardoned after his plots against the Crown and returned to Aberdeen to a great welcome. He had accepted the Protestant faith, been made a privy councillor, Lieutenant and Justiciar of the North, not to mention being elevated to marquis. He died in 1636 and his son George now arrived from France to take over the family estates. As provost, Cluny's pew would have been the most prestigious one in the cathedral. He had to relinquish it when his kinsman, the new marquis was in the Aulton. And not to be outdone by Cluny's garden, the marquis acquired two of the canon's lodgings opposite the cathedral, Belhelvie and the treasurer's manse of Daviot, as well as Forbes, and enclosed their yards and glebes to create a garden which would have delighted his ten children. The family lived in Belhelvie Manse which became the Marquis of Huntly's House. If he 'beis requirit for assistente', Huntly could not have been nearer the cathedral. It was his grandson, fourth Marquis of Huntly and first Duke of Gordon who according to Orem:

> built the west dike of the said garden all of stone and high, anno 1715; and after caused build the rest of stone and brick ; and the whole expense of building them amounts to 3100 merks Scots. The bricks in the inner side of the said dike are 47,500, every thousand cost 12s stg. and now it is the best garden in town, or about it.

The Belhelvie and Daviot manse sites are now occupied by the late eighteenth century Chanonry Lodge, the residence of the Principal of Aberdeen University. Their glebes and those of Forbes Manse form the garden as they did in Huntly's day. It is a great sweep of landscaped parkland with a sizeable market garden tucked at the bottom. The bricks in the massive wall can still be counted.

On 14 June 1638, the Marchioness of Huntly, a daughter of the seventh Earl of Argyll, died in Cluny's lodging where she was staying while the Marquis was away from home. He arrived a few days later and Lady Huntly's funeral was a great affair. With a tolling of bells 'out of the haill steeples of Abirdein' and shooting of ordnance, the cortège left Cluny's lodging for King's College Chapel 'with sum company and torche light' where it rested until 26 June. The cortège then processed from the chapel to St Ninian's Chapel on the Castlehill of Aberdeen. After resting there, the remains borne on a coach with horses in deep mourning flanked by six barons and escorted by multitudes of people, returned to the Chanonry. The interment was in St Machar's. Huntly abandoned the old burial place of his forebears in Elgin Cathedral in favour of Lichtoun's aisle, the north transept of the cathedral which he bought from Alexander Scroggie, the parish minister, for 300 merks. This was a silver lining for the kirk session. In addition to having money in hand for urgent repairs, they would also have a restored north transept at no cost to themselves, for Huntly had promised to rebuild it.

Sir Thomas Gordon of Cluny had been buried at St Machar's, but it is uncertain if Sir Alexander was. His own final years were far removed from the halcyon days of his great garden. In 1641 he married Dame Elizabeth Gordon, widow of Sir John Leslie of Wardes. 'Ther wes sum suspicioun betixt them of familiarity', according to Spalding, before Leslie's death. Then the couple fled to Durham at the height of the covenanting troubles,

The Precentor's Manse, also known as the Bishop's House at Elgin Cathedral. The finer houses in the Chanonry would have been in this style.

their trunks following them says Spalding, in a homely touch. Things fell apart after that. Dame Elizabeth died of breast cancer in Durham some eighteen months later, of which Spalding gives a brief but harrowing account. Gordon of Birsemoir deputised for Cluny as provost during his absence but he returned to his house in Old Aberdeen in February 1643, heavily in debt. For a time he had been warded in the tolbooth of Edinburgh. He then, sadly, drops out of the picture.

Though Turriff Manse was part of Cluny's Garden it was, according to Orem, acquired by the Trades of Old Aberdeen who built a hospital for ten poor widows of tradesmen there in 1711. They had 100 merks mortified to them by the late Alexander Mitchell, formerly clerk of the trades of New Aberdeen. (This foundation should not be confused with Mitchell's Hospital, which came into being nearly a century later and further along the road). There were eight women in residence by Orem's time, whose allowance was 20s quarterly from the Old Aberdeen Trades, 'who likewise appointed little kail-yards for them within the close'.

Apart from Cluny and Huntly, who else resided in the Chanonry at the time of the 1636 census? In the long avenue leading to St Machar's Cathedral there were about ten households on both sides of the road. The houses are there on Gordon's Plan. George Middleton Esq, not to be confused with Principal George Middleton of King's College who was a little younger, was a bailie and a prominent elder of St Machar's who had the responsible task of collecting the burial silver and the 'penalties', the church fines. He probably lived near Cluny's Garden with his substantial ménage of wife, seven bairns and six servants. William Burnet is next on the census list, a pillar of society, with wife, three bairns and a servant. He was a writer or solicitor, a feuar on the list of 1617 and among the thirty 'most honest and aged citizens' who deliberated on the 1636 census. In 1643 he was one of those leading citizens appointed 'to go throch the toun upon ane privy Inquest and to gif in ane perfyt list of vagabundis and wyckatt neichbouris'.

Next door to Burnet was the college humanist, Master John Lundie with his wife, two bairns and two servants. Lundie was 'collector to the Sunday collectione' at St Machar's and one of the keeper of the keys of the Aulton charter chest. He also took in the collection at the 'college kirk' on occasion, so the chapel must have been in use from time to time. 'The Commissar' himself, the judge of the commissary court, at this time Thomas Davidson, was in the next house, and his household was a large one; wife, three sons, a son-in-law, two daughters, three male and three female servants. Next came Janet Gordon, her daughter and two female servants, while her neighbour was the goodwife of Coclarachie, possibly mother to Mediciner Gordon. She also had two female servants. Next, Johne Ritchie, bronduster, 'his wyff and twa young bairnes'. Ritchie's employment seems rather curious for a bronduster was an embroider. Then William Watt, notary public and lawyer, who was employed as town clerk. Perhaps he took the council minutes during his era, so helpful to any study of Old Aberdeen. After him, John Garioch with wife, child and two servants and just beyond, the goodwife of Auchrydie and her grandson. The Chanonry, with all these children required a good water supply, and the 'Water Draught' shown by Gordon, was a channel which brought water in from Cotton, flowing between Ellon and Banchory-Devenick Manses, then turning north to disappear down the side of Gavin Dunbar's Hospital. Needless to say, washing in the 'Chanel' was strictly forbidden.

We have now almost reached the cathedral. Can we guess which manses those ten households would have occupied? Here the plan on page 21 comes in handy. Philorth on the east side, and on the west, beyond Cluny's Garden the 'great lodging' of Kincardine o Neil with its oratory were possibilities, the latter surely home to someone important, such as the commissary. Kincardine was acquired by Subprincipal Alexander Fraser who sometime after 1690 demolished it, though not the oratory, and used the stones to build a malt barn near the Powis Burn in College Bounds. This was part of his development of his marshy Twelve Roods now 'called Powies'. In 1712 Fraser sold the oratory and the glebe along with the adjoining lodgings of Deer and Cruden to George Connon, who like Lewis Gordon of Kinmundy, who later acquired part of Cluny's territory, was one of the Chanonry's early property speculators. Deer and Cruden Manses were both demolished during Orem's time, but were also possible as residences for the families of the 1630s. So was Ellon Manse, still there in Orem's time and owned by Thomas Forest, merchant in Aberdeen. Banchory-Devenick Manse, that 'great lodging' between Ellon and Oyne Manses still stood. The resident canon had stayed on at the Reformation, granting it to a relative in 1580. The manse was demolished in 1720 at which time it belonged to the heirs of James Gordon of Seaton. In 1801, David Mitchell, a native of Old Aberdeen and by then resident in Essex, established a hospital to maintain five widows and five unmarried daughters of Old Aberdeen burgesses on that site. More about Mitchell's Hospital in Volume Two.

Oyne Manse was taken down, though only in Orem's time, and leaving the entry gate which must have been rather fine. Oyne was habitable in the 1630s as was its neighbour, Rayne, the archdeacon's old manse. It had been acquired by John Erskine of Balhaggartie as early as 1569 and extended in 1591. It was demolished in 1722 while in the possession of Patrick Walker of Torreleith, another Chanonry entrepreneur. The Manse of Clatt was not available for residence. As early as 1588, Alexander Gordon of Strathavin, a member of a powerful branch of the Gordon family and his wife, Lady Agnes Sinclair, widow of the eight Earl of Erroll were granted a charter of confirmation of that lodging. The charter described it as a ruined manse, yard, garden and tails though part of it must have been habitable. Servants were present when, in July 1591, Harry Gordon of Haddo acting under the instructions of George, sixth Earl of Huntly 'violently put forth their servants' goods ...and took and kept possession of the property'. A complaint was made to the privy council by Strathavin and Lady Agnes. There must be a tale of private feuding behind this outrageous action by the head of the family against a fellow Gordon. Like his forebears, Huntly was leader of the Roman Catholic party in Scotland and was involved with his co-religionist, the ninth Earl of Errol, none other than Lady Agnes's step-son, in plots against James VI. He and Errol defeated royalist forces under the Earl of Argyll at the Battle of Glenlivet in 1594.

Clatt Manse earned a bad reputation and it continued. 'It was called Tam Framper's house because it was haunted', Orem reports without explaining why this should be so. Framper was not an Old Aberdeen name. 'It was demolished because it was haunted by evil spirits'. Around 1655 George Cruickshank of Berriehill, Dean of Guild, who owned the place at that time, recycled the stones like a native-born Old Aberdonian to build a fine L-plan two-storey house at Balgownie 'for accommodating him at the

George Cruickshank's House at the Brig o Balgownie, built from the stones of Clatt Manse.

time of his fishing.' It is still there, so the stones of Clatt can at least be inspected. George Cruickshank's House used to be known, erroneously, as the Chapter House, even though chapter houses belonged to the pre-Reformation period and the cathedral's chapter, who lived in the Chanonry when at home, met within St Machar's Cathedral. They had no reason to journey to the wilds of Balgownie to discuss Church business. During Cromwell's Protectorate (1649-1660) detachments of General Monk's army were quartered in both Aberdeens and some of the remaining stones of Clatt were used by these English troops to build a considerable fort on the Castlehill on the site of the legendary castle there.

We have reached Mortlach Manse, just before the Chanonry starts to curve round to 'little' Tillydrone Road. It is possibly that long house, with accompanying buildings, just opposite the legend 'Machiar Kirk' on Gordon's Plan. As early as 1575 it was in the possession of Thomas Garden of Blairton, the commissary, whom we have met before, conveyed to him by the parson of Mortlach, Mr George Leslie. 'The laird of Banchorie', Alexander Garden, one of many Gardens, is noted in the 1636 census as living around there with his wife and servant, possibly in this very manse. 'This manse and yard are ruined and made corn-ground', wrote Orem in the 1720s.

Next to 'the Laird of Banchorie' in the census comes 'Birsmoir, his wyff, ane young bairne, his two sisters' and three servants. 'Birsmoir' is Alexan-

The garden of Tillydrone House where the manses of Mortlach and Kinkell once stood.

der Gordon of Birsemoir, cousin to Cluny and his successor as provost. We learn from Orem that he lived in Kinkell, Canon Galloway's old manse, 'a large one'. It is to the left of Mortlach on Parson Gordon's Plan, with a smaller house beside it. Like so many others, Birsemoir suffered the early deaths of his children. His wife Elspet Garden was buried in St Machar's in 1642 'with ane deid borne bairne'. In 1645 and 1647, two of Birsemoir's older children followed them to the grave. Afterwards Kinkell belonged to Adam Gordon of Inverebrie. In the 1720s Mr William Smith the minister of the second charge at St Machar's acquired the manse and from its ruins and those of Monymusk Manse across the road built a manse for himself, unusually high at three storeys, on the site of Kinkell.

We leave the genteel folk for a while. Beside St Machar's Cathedral were the homes of its beadles and bellman. First, the solitary household of Archbald Bishop, bellman whom we have already encountered as Old Aberdeen's enthusiastic strong-arm man employed to purge the town of all stranger and countrie beggars, in addition to ringing the bells. Bishop's duties also included keeping the kirk clean, the dogs out of the kirk and goods from the kirkyard. In 1636 he was appointed scourger and the town was to be stented 8s weekly to pay for this service.

Bishop's neighbours at Tulynessle Manse 'on the churchyard dyke with its yard and glebe' (not visible in Gordon), were the Kilgour family who served the cathedral for three generations. The 1636 census shows two families there, John Kilgour elder, possibly retired by then, and James and Harry, presumably his sons, and his grandchild. Next door was John Kilgour, younger his wife and 'twa bairnes'. John Jnr, kirk officer, sometimes assisted by Harry, carried out numerous services between the late 1620s and the 1660s which included bellringing and 'ruling' or regulating the knock or clock. In 1646 complaints were made that 'he hed holden back the knock' and, in one of these counter-productive penalties, he was excluded from his church duties for twenty-five days. He soon apologised, saying that he had been unable to see the sun, which was not gracing Old Aberdeen with its presence at that time. If he had he 'might have observit the time better'. Discipline was a problem during those lengthy services at St Machar's. In 1629 John was instructed to bring back all those that he caught slipping out before the blessing ended. If they returned 'not willingly' he had to report them to the kirk session for punishment. He was not entirely guiltless himeself. In 1638 he was punished for going out of the kirk 'in tyme of sermon'.

He was surprisingly versatile and the tasks he carried out included buying nails for repair work, taking in the burial money when the official collector was absent, taking in the collection in time of plague, buying paper and binding an old session book, buying a winding sheet for a poor woman. Some of these tasks earned him the occasional perk. He was paid 4s for washing the kirk's linen and 12s when he went through the parish to find straw and corn for horses. Brother Harry was more of a casual labourer, mixing lime for the masons, redding and clearing the slates from the kirk in 1645 when there must have been a fall from the roof. In 1649 Harry's daughter Jean caused embarrassment when she 'perturbed the worship...in puling one ane seat out under Margaret Troup' and for cursing and bawling and for disobedience to her parents'. She was ordered 'to mak her repentance'. In September 1666 the kirk session decreed that John Kilgour was to be given all collections taken up at marriage and baptisms for ringing the church bell at nine every evening. He was nearing the end of his career by then, and two years later comes the last reference in the session records. There were complaints about 'the perturbance of the kirk by boys'. The Kilgours and Patrick Stewart were to take turns to 'to wait about the dasks' or patrol the kirk and report the delinquents to the session.

By the 1650s and 1660s two new Kilgours, George and Patrick have made their appearance. We could speculate that they were John Jnr's twa bairns, but there is no proof. Patrick Kilgour was something of a petty criminal in his youth. In June 1664 he confessed to the St Machar's session 'that he went up to the steeple sundrie times with ane chisel and ane mell (mallet) but pretendit it was to dresse (repair) the knock'. He was all the time removing lead from the roof but was spotted coming down with 'ane pairt of the Kirk Lead in his hand'. This he sold to John Robson at Gordon's Mill. In his defence said he had seen students of the college doing the same. The case was serious enough to be remitted to the Sheriff Court. However, Kilgour had skill with clocks and came good in the end. In 1675 he entered into a contract with the kirk session agreeing to maintain the clock until his death. Four years later 'Patrick Kilgour, watchmaker' was elected a member of the kirk session in the August and in the November, admitted treasurer of the town for three years.

His new and exemplary career continued. In 1685 he became a guild burgess of Aberdeen though his work was limited to 'make or mend watches or cast bells as he may have occasion'. No one in the royal burgh, it seems, had these skills. In 1689 he agreed with the Master of Kirkwork of Aberdeen for casting 'the bell that was laitlie riven'. Three years later, on 9 November 1692 he entered into a major contract 'anent the ruling of the kirk clock' of St Nicholas, clearly in a bad way, to 'translate the said clock into a ane pendulum work, conforme to the newest fashione and inventions done at London for regulating the motion of the said clock, and causing her to go'. A fascinating list of the improvements that Patrick was to undertake follows, including causing the clock to 'strick the hours swifter, that the people may not wearie in telling of them'. At a time when few people had the means of telling the time, bells and clocks took on a human dimension. Bells were endowed with cheerful and high-minded inscriptions; clocks were always 'she'.

Virtually contemporary with Patrick was the rather curious George Kilgour. In 1657 George, a writer or lawyer in Old Aberdeen, was admitted burgess there. In 1678 a George Kilgour, sacrist and church officer who had 'fallen in fornication' is now 'scandaled a second time'. He is removed fom his position for 'bad reports are going abroad upon him'. There seems to be two Georges, born out by the fact that in 1686 George Kilgour appears in the burgh records as a notary public while five years later someone of the same name is noted as a beadle, presumably the fallen fornicator re-instated to his old charge. Then in the *List of pollable persons* of 1696 we read of 'George Killgourre, church beddall ther, he being a pentioner in the said church and Bessie Innes his spouse, the said George being a nottar (notary), his poll and wyfes is...£4 12s', one of the highest polls in the Aulton. A lawyer-beadle was a curious combination, but presumably the beadle's post had an element of the hereditary. There is no doubt that he lived in Tullynessle Manse for in 1703 George Patton was paid £1 10s for redding up the churchyard dyke 'betwixt Seatouns styll and George Kilgours house'. This would have been in the north-west corner of the kirkyard, whence James Gordon, the laird of Seaton would arrive to attend church. According to Orem, Tullynessle manse, yard and glebe was the heritable property of

George Kilgour, 'sometime beadle of this church'. His heirs sold the property to Colonel Middleton of Seaton in 1723. At this time, Middleton was expanding the estate of his late father-in-law, Gordon of Seaton, southwards towards the Chanonry.

Immediately west of Tullynessle lay Bishop Dunbar's Hospital which continued its good work after the Reformation. Burgh records provide occasional glimpses of the beadsmen's activities. On 24 October 1609, it will be recalled, Thomas Baverlay was fined 40s 'for troubling the toun and giffing of Janet Lamb ane cuff'. But by no means all of the old men were troublemakers. Some must have been fond of reading for in 1641 John Lundie reported to the kirk session that Master Alexander Gordon had left his books to the Hospital. The master, and later the managers of Dunbar's were men of standing in the community and income was derived from the rents of various Old Aberdeen properties.

Parson Gordon shows the rigs of Monymusk and Westhall to the west of Dunbar's Hospital but their manses have gone. The fate of Westhall is unclear, but the stones of Monymusk Manse were recycled by the Rev William Smith for his three-storey manse across the way, while the Monymusk yard and glebe which stood immediately adjacent to the Hospital were bought by the heritors of the Cruives and Nether Don, and gifted to Bishop Dunbar's, giving the old men more land for their gardens and orchards. Some had their own livestock; beadsman James Barcar had a ewe and a lamb stolen from him by the Pantons, it may be recalled, while a council report of May 1679 reveals that the beadsmen farmed quite extensively and cultivated the ground sloping down to the present Seaton Park. The old men had complained of an outbreak of vandalism. Persons from 'within the toune, chanrie or about the kirke or Tillydronis Hill' had demolished their dykes, trampled and destroyed their corn, bere, oats and kale, made roads through them and broken through the slopes. Fines were to be levied on the culprits. Later Colonel Middleton acquired Gavin Dunbar's Hospital to incorporate in his estate, as well as the nearby Ellon glebe in the Bogforth, which was separated from its Chanonry manse. The story of the Seaton estate, however, must wait for Volume Two.

We are nearly at the end of the 1636 census and about a dozen families remain. Some would have lived in the crofter houses in the glebes, among them perhaps Janet Woode, widow and Agnes Meeke, poor. But only four of these households were without servants, and it may be that some lived in the great manses opposite the cathedral, or in a handful of new houses there. Huntly, as we know, had acquired the former Belhelvie manse as his town house, but Daviot may have stood for a time. Next door Kirkton of Seaton was still extant in Orem's time and he wrote of, 'houses lately built' in one of the yards. Neighbouring Auchterless was ruinous by 1581 when the precentor, Archibald Bethone, whose manse it was, granted a charter in favour of Thomas Garden of Blairton and his spouse, Elizabeth Stewart. Orem reports that the 'lodging, yard and glebe (was) now turned into a croft' and that there were crofter houses at the south end of the glebe. Gordon shows a conglomeration of buildings opposite the cathedral.

Birse, the chancellor's manse was the last in the row, and after the Reformation, the chancellor, Alexander Seton, son of the Laird of Meldrum, passed it to his brother, George, in 1598. A number of distinguished owners followed; the Earl of Dunfermline; Mr John Scougal, son of Bishop Patrick Scougal and commissary of Aberdeen who conveyed it to his brother, Lord Whitehill, a Court of Session judge. Whitehill was one of the small group of speculators who attempted to develop the Chanonry at this time, feuing four stances for building houses at the end of the glebe. He conveyed the manse to the Buchans of Cairnbulg who extended it in the eighteenth century. It then passed to the Buchans of Auchmacoy during whose ownership it was rated at £20 per annum, the highest rated house in Old Aberdeen. After Miss Nicola Buchan's death in 1887, it was acquired by Mr Leslie of Fetternear, a descendant of the Leslies of Balquhain. 'Unmindful of what he owed to the Cathedral', wrote Mrs Katherine Trail angrily in her memoirs of Old Aberdeen, 'he pulled down this very interesting old house'.

The chancellor's manse of Birse. Its demolition began in the late nineteenth century.

Master Alexander Scroggie, minister of St Machar's from 1621-40, would have lived in one of these fine houses opposite the cathedral with his wife, five bairns and two servants. He was the first minister of St Machar's who was not at the same time principal of King's College, (though he was rector in 1636). He was a keen gardener and Spalding speaks of his dwelling house in Old Aberdeen, and 'yairds pleasantlie plantit for the most pairt by himself', indicating a sizeable glebe.

At Birse we turn the corner and walk down the third and final section of the Chanonry which leads to the Seatongate. Beyond the cathedral, the Bishop's Palace, glimpsed just as the corner was turned, was still extant in 1636. Bishop Patrick Forbes of Corse died in 1635 and his successor Bishop Adam Bellenden was driven out by covenanters who looted the palace in 1639. Thereafter it was dismantled by Dr William Guild, principal of King's College, ever on the outlook for materials with which to restore the crumbling college. Guild, although he already had a house in Aberdeen, had been given the palace by Parliament to use as a manse. That was not his aim. 'He took the stones down to the college', says Spalding, 'for such vain uses as he thought most expedient'. The chronicler gives us a blow by blow account:

> Upon 30 August 1644, he fully sets to destroy the Bishop's house and began to raise the pavement of the hall and break the great joists and stately timber work, hewn door and windows, with the haill slates and caused carry them down to the college. November 1644, now begins to tirr (strip) slates off that matchless roof. It is true, this house, yards and precincts were given him by the Estates whereof he might have made a more godly use.

The last stones were carted off by English soldiers in 1651 for their fort at the Castlehill.

The only building standing in this final leg of the Chanonry in Gordon's time, and for long after was the Chaplains' Court or Chambers, Dunbar's 'fair palice' containing chambers for 'twenty chaplains, some say more', at the south end of the bishop's garden. At that time its ranges still formed a courtyard, with a pend giving access from the Chanonry. The building had been converted into a divinity college by Bishop Patrick Forbes and its students would have swollen the numbers of those not included in the 1636 census. John Forbes and James Reid his servant are specifically noted in the census. Dr Forbes, Professor of Divinity at King's College was the son of Bishop Patrick and one of the outstanding intellectuals of his day. He had bought a lodging within the Chaplains' Chambers where he lived himself, (he was a widower), and which he mortified for the use of future Professors of Divinity. Gordon, in his Plan, does it the honour of a number, 20, 'Professor of Divinitys h. at ye Chappellans'. It was Forbes who, praised for

The south-west wing of the Chaplains' Court in the late nineteenth century. Bishop Dunbar's arms were displayed below the dormer, but the roll-moulded arched pend which gave access to the courtyard has been obliterated. It was later handsomely restored.

his open-handedness in Old Aberdeen, also mortified another lodging within the Chambers for the use of the master of the Music School of Old Aberdeen, and sure enough we find noted in the census Mr Gilbert Ross the music master, with his wife two bairns and a servant. David Anderson, a later Professor of Divinity made improvements there including 'a house where the chaplains' kitchen stood'. Unfortunately it was burned down. Anderson also had 'a little garden in the close, well dyked and an outer gate'.

Though by Orem's time the music master's house and other parts of the Chaplains' Court were in ruins, some sections were still habitable. He writes breathlessly of an attractive development by Alexander Molyson, a merchant in the north end of the city who purchased the north-east tower and restored it:

> He hath built a new yard-dyke at the back of the north side of the said chaplain's chambers anno 1714, and planted the other side of the said dyke, twenty-nine trees anno 1719 which were given out of the minister's yard of St Machar, and also the Bishop's Dovecot Green round about with young trees, November 1722.

One range of the Chaplains' Court still stands to this day at No 20 The Chanonry, the oldest inhabited house in Aberdeen.

Bailie Logan's Lodging.

We have reached the end of the Chanonry. It enjoyed a new lease of life after the Reformation with some canons staying on, and genteel families with large families moving in and enjoying the spacious feus. By Orem's time, as must be obvious from these last few paragraphs, there were difficulties. The political situation was volatile and instead of a thriving area which could have accommodated the High Street overspill, we find a few property owning speculators but no major developments. The mood of the time was uncertain, many buildings were ruinous, the atmosphere was gloomy. A combination of desperate events, the principal of which was Civil War had sounded the death knoll for the old Chanonry. Gilbert Ross had been ejected, Scroggie cast out, Bellenden fled, Dr Forbes gone into exile, Cluny put to the horn and Huntly beheaded. To these momentous events we must return in Volume Two.

To end on a cheerful note. The last name on the 1636 census is that of Mr Thomas Lillie, a notary who lived with his wife, his mother-in-law, his two brethren, his two bairns and two servants, not in the Chanonry but round the corner in the Seatongate. In 1604 his father Alexander had acquired forty roods of land there, described as on the east side of the road leading from Old Aberdeen to the Bridge of Don (Balgownie) formerly possessed by Sir Thomas Gordon of Cluny. It was perhaps Thomas Lillie or a successor who sold this landholding to one of the bailies of Old Aberdeen, William Logan. Here in 1676 Logan and his wife Janet Moir had a fine house built, Bailie Logan's Lodging which stands to this day and is now No 20-22 Don Street.

Appendix 1

Abirdene, Aberden, Aberdon:
A Troublesome Place Name

'It has long been recognised that the name of the present town of Aberdeen means the aber (mouth) of the Don'. So wrote William Alexander in *The Place Names of Aberdeenshire*, Third Spalding Club, 1953. This bold statement tends to halt in their tracks those like myself brought up in the belief that Aberdeen meant the mouth of the Dee, or, in more recent years, of the Denburn. But the theories of William Alexander and his successors are treated with respect. Aber, a Pictish word meaning river mouth survived into the North East's Gaelic speaking era which began around 900AD, after the Gaels' conquest of the Picts. (From the early twelfth century onwards, Gaelic itself was gradually ousted by 'Inglis' the Northern English form from which Scots developed).

It was at the beginning of Gaelic era that our rivers received their names. The Don was Deathan, or Dé'n, pronounced 'dane', giving us 'Aberdane', a sound midway between Aberdeen and Aberdon. The Dee in Gaelic was Dé, pronounced 'tshay' giving us something quite different. The Dee flowed south of the town and though Torry lay at its mouth and other early settlements were thought to have been established upstream, there is no linguistic evidence of the existence of an 'Abertshay' or even a later 'Aberdee'.

Aberdeen is thus A Pictish-Gaelic place-name, translating into English as 'Donmouth'. Where exactly was that? This volatile river has shifted its course over the centuries, curving in earlier times through the low-lying meadow land of the present Seaton Park, then turning south to flow along the Links and round the Broad Hill to enter the sea at Cunnigarhill, near the east end of Urquhart Road where the City Hospital stands, at least at time of writing. The Aberdeen Council Registers from the 1520s to the 1540s, make several interesting references to the 'North Watter', the old name for the Don, 'besyd the Cunnigar Hills', an area which would have offered primitive settlers shelter, a refuge from flooding, good vantage points for spying out land and sea, and food in the form of fish and shell fish, though the cunings, the coneys or rabbits themselves were not introduced until after the twelfth century. The nearby Powis Burn would have been a source of fresh water. Did the settlers follow it inland to the Loch of Old Aberdeen, and build crannogs there, for security? Did they build settlement at what became Seaton?

By the twelfth century, two forms, early versions of 'Aberdon' and 'Aberdeen' had come into use. A papal Bull of Pope Adrian IV of 1157, provides several variations of both forms. The Bull confirmed earlier grants made by the Kings of Scots to the *ecclesiam de Abbirdein*, the Church of Aberdeen, St Machar's Cathedral, which also appears as *abbirdonensem ecclesiam*. This Latin form, is still with us. We are Aberdonenses, Aberdonians, not Aberdeenians. The Bull mentions the King's teind (tenth part) of the *burgo Abbirdon*, the burgh of Aberdeen, and the church of St Nicholas of Abbirdone, as well as the town of Abirden, all of them today's Aberdeen.

Some years later, in the charters of William the Lion, the royal burgh is both Ab(er)doen and Aberdon. Then the balance begins to shift towards the 'Aberdeen' version. In the first volume of the *Register of the Great Seal of Scotland* which covers the years 1306-1424 there are eleven variations on Aberdeen, (Abirdene Aberden and the like) and only six on Aberdon. In the second volume, from 1424 to 1513, Auld Abirdene makes an appearance and by the mid sixteenth century, Aberdene or Aberdein had taken over, for both towns. 'Old Abirdene is again sore vexed,' the chronicler John Spalding moaned in 1641. The Old Aberdeen Burgh Records between 1603 and 1758 have numerous variations but prefers the abbreviation, Old Abd. By 1689, the current spelling, 'Aberdeen' makes its appearance in the Council Register, though the earlier forms were still in use. 'New' Aberdeen was brought into use at this time to distinguish it from Old Aberdeen, though this form dropped out of use by the nineteenth century. In conclusion two points can be made. Firstly, Aberdon is not a correct version for Old Aberdeen. Secondly, Old Aberdeen can be considered as a simple placename in its own right rather than an indication of being older than somewhere with a similar name.

DM

Appendix 2

The Belltower of King's College Reconsidered

The quholl fundation of this colledge being builded in a marrish ground, is underlayed with great rafters of oake, which behoved to be great coast and travell.

A Description of the two tounes of Aberdene, Parson James Gordon, 1661.

The belltower of King's College Chapel, focal point of the university, its surrounding community and immediately recognisable motif, has an aspect which has never been fully understood. The first tentative explanation of its peculiarities has come to be accepted as fact despite neither certain evidence nor any alternative explanation being considered. It is to be suggested here that Dr William Kelly (1861-1944), the scholarly Aberdeen architect, was wrong in his interpretation in 'Scottish Crown Steeples' in *A Tribute to William Kelly*, 1949. He argued that the tower had been 'stretched' whilst still under construction; that whilst originally intended to be 24 feet 10 inches square (7.6m), it was enlarged to an oblong 28 feet 3 inches (8.6m) along its east and west sides to accommodate the new bells. In this respect it is unlike the otherwise closely comparable towers of the same period, such as St Giles High Kirk in Edinburgh and St Nicholas Church in Newcastle, which are square.

The tower is located at the south-west angle of the chapel, partially engaged with its south wall but otherwise free standing to the west, south and east. The chapel gable is symmetrical with the west door, great west window, clerestory widow and roof ventilator all of which are aligned centrally above each other below the apex of the crow-stepped triangular gable. At the extreme northern angle of the chapel there are buttresses to west and north. These, however, are not echoed at the south end of the west facade where the comparable buttresses are related to the tower instead, as shown on page 120. That to the north (no. 1) emerging from the chapel whilst the southernmost buttress of the west front of the tower (no. 2) is located 17 feet (5.1m) from its companion. It is the adjacent south buttress (no. 3) extending a further 10 feet (3.0m) which imparts the asymmetrical effect. It would seem, therefore, that Kelly, confronted with the architectural conundrum of an oblong tower unsuited to receive a square crown steeple, conceived the idea of an enlargement of the original scheme whilst it was under construction. This explanation has since been accepted by Dr Richard Fawcett, 'The Medieval Building' in Geddes (ed), *King's College 1500-2000*, page 41, although, like Kelly, he is unable to produce any structural evidence to substantiate the theory.

No building can be satisfactorily analysed from its elevations, the plan must also be considered, that in D. MacGibbon and T. Ross, *The Ecclesiastical Architecture of Scotland* (1897), III, 289, Fig. 1208, provided by Mr J. C. Watt, architect, Aberdeen, being the readiest available whilst the originals are reproduced in Fawcett, 'The Medieval Building'. As this consideration is confined only to the bell tower, and in view of the small scale of the Watt plan (1:1250) the plan of the tower has been redrawn to 1:200. This highlights the considerable variations in the thicknesses of the four walls of the tower. The north wall, although an integral part of the 4 foot (1.2m) thick south wall of the chapel is increased to 7 feet (2.1m); the west wall is again 4 feet (1.2m); the east wall is 5 feet (1.5m) whilst the south wall is a massive 9 feet (2.7m). The ground floor chamber is 16 feet (4.8m) west to east by 13 feet (3.9m) north to south, with a window to the west and a doorway to the east. (These dimensions are approximate but the proportions are correct.)

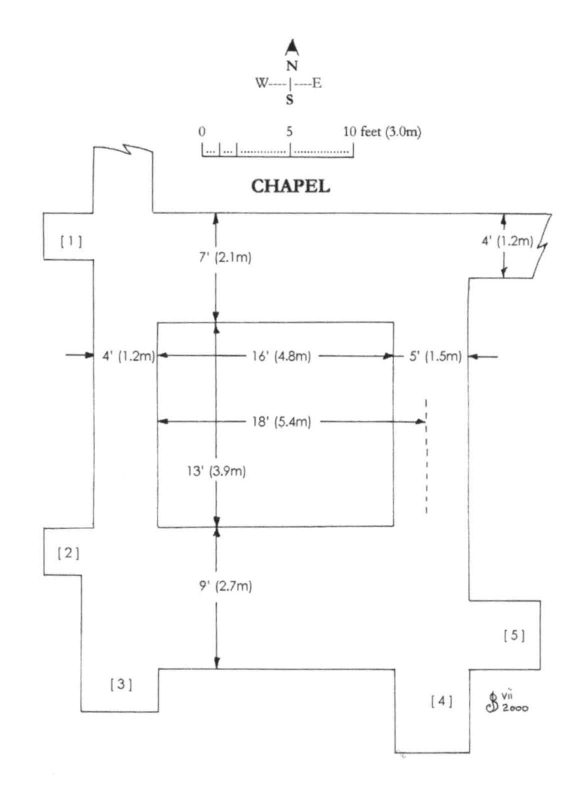

The location of the buttresses is equally irregular. The second west buttress (no. 1) is aligned with the interior wall of the chapel so symmetrically placed to echo the chapel's north-west buttress but the south-west buttress of the tower (no. 2) is aligned with its south interior wall. Then the south buttress (no. 3) commences and, because of the greater thickness of the tower's south wall, is necessarily extruded so much further south that it results in the asymmetrical aspect of the west front. It is also important to note that buttress no. 3 not only advances south but is slightly projected to the west, its base 'proud' of the otherwise continuous line of the lowest plinth running along the entire west front. This additional thickness is continued upwards and it is only in the vicinity of the uppermost off-set of the south buttress on the west front (no. 2) that it finally retreats into the wallhead below the corbel course which supports the parapet of the crown.

Why then were the north and south walls thickened and the south-west buttress further reinforced to the west? The short answer would seem to lie in Parson

Gordon's comment quoted at the outset, that the foundations of the college had to be laid on oak beams. That in turn raises the question of why Bishop Elphinstone selected a marshy site at some distance from the Chanonry at a time when the southward area was still undeveloped.

One possible explanation is that site had been selected and the new buildings already begun with the erection of the principal's lodging, a two storey block running along the line of the king's highway. Whilst substantial enough, such a building would not result in serious structural problems. We may further speculate that this first stage was the work of local masons, skilled enough at domestic construction but who had failed to appreciate the greatly increased loads which would later be involved with the more sophisticated work of the chapel and, still more, of the tower. By the time that factor began to emerge it was too late to alter the position hence the 'great cost and trouble' which was incurred.

Yet the nature of the area is apparent on Gordon's map which shows the chapel tower reaching towards the south where, until the courtyard was built and terminated by a buttressed round tower, it would be built on increasingly softer ground as it advanced towards the north bank of the Powis Burn. A stretch of ground which was to be long left undeveloped, a south facing slope reserved only for the college gardeners as late as 1661.

Two further clues are to be found in Geddes, 'Appendix: The Proportions and Solomon's Temple' and 'Post-reformation building' in her *King's College 1500-2000*. She comments that 'The side and angles of the apse [of the chapel] are considerably rebuilt due to subsidence.' (This was also noted by Kelly.) And still more significantly 'By the 1960s a serious crack had developed down the north-east corner of the tower, the only angle without a buttress. The repairs... involved inserting reinforced concrete collars inside the tower, tying a phosphor bronze band around the parapet, and pressure grouting the masonry. The cause of this damage, and presumably so much more in the past, was failure of the mortar pointing, in soft sandstone exposed to the full fury of North Sea weather.' But once again the cause may be otherwise, the imperceptible subsidence of the tower to the south set up the stresses which caused the fracture to appear in the north-east at the sole unbuttressed angle, the weak link in the chain. This possibility does not seem to have been given any consideration but structural engineers might grudgingly praise the inherent strength of the tower and conclude that the entire structure had moved diagonally from the north-east angle. Here then we have the reason for the offending oblong shape, the extruded buttress and the asymmetrical facade - extended foundations standing on rafters of oak. When considering a medieval building of the early 1500s we must neither look for nor expect the strict regularity of the classical; a degree of balance certainly, but at that period use still took precedence over uniformity.

J C Watt's cross section of the tower in Fawcett, 'The Medieval Building', Fig. 4.4, shows the bell chamber as being 18 feet (5.4m) west to east, indicated on my plan by broken lines. This thinning of upper walls is perfectly acceptable. Indeed in castle building it was normal, to relieve the weight of masonry and provide increased space for accommodation. Here the enlargement also had the further purpose of accommodating the bells.

The argument that, because other towers are square then King's should have followed the same pattern, is also open to question. Fawcett's assumption that it was possible that the final plan was modified while work was in progress is evidently derived from Kelly but is not in any way substantiated. Nor is it correct, at ground level at least, to say that the internal space is square despite the overall oblong plan because that space is oblong and from west to east so on the opposite axis to the supposed north to south 'stretching' as might be expected. He also observes that 'towers of oblong plan were by no means unusual in Scotland' and cites Stirling Holy Rude Church and Dysart Church, Fife. But the location of these towers in relation to the church which they serve to enhance is significant. The tower at Stirling is located at the west end of the nave whilst at St Self's, Dysart, the six storey tower of 1500 is integrated with the nave and south aisle. Reference is also made to the square towers of St Giles, Edinburgh and St John the Baptist, Perth, but their forms were dictated by their location over the crossing of nave, chancel and transepts whilst at Linlithgow, like Stirling, the square tower again shares the west wall of the nave. (see Mike Salter, *The Old Parish Churches of Scotland* (1994), pages 8, 9, 51 for plans).

Nor are his comments on the buttresses 'set well back from the angle they abutted' convincing. As will be apparent from the elevations and the plan, the only buttress at King's which does not abut an angle is that which is common to both chapel and tower. In the other cases cited there is no consistency as some, like buttress no. 1 at King's, are aligned with the inner rather than outer wall face of the nave.

There is a school of thought which considers that the medieval builders would have regarded a too strictly balanced facade as the offence because 'Only God is perfect'. So the fact that the south buttress was something of a maverick, strengthening a corner at a point where the solum was less than satisfactory, far from being a fault, may have been regarded as a virtue, a Gallovidian *desideratum*.

If the bishop, by now Dunbar, or his man of business, still Galloway, wanted a crown then that could be arranged later; as Kelly rightly notes the final upper courses had to be very precisely laid out to receive such a complex structure, but the tower had to be established first, even if on unfavourable ground which dictated its irregularities. One which was to have to bear the weight of the masonry of a structure 63 feet (19.2m) to the top of the battlements and 99 feet (30.1m) to the cross above the crown, together with the additional tonnage of five great and seven lesser bells.

So the oblong shape was not a choice but a necessity, dictated by the particular circumstances of the site. Were there protests from bishop and parson which were overruled by the master mason; sensible discussions or heated arguments? The records are silent on this as on much else. But no evidence has emerged from this study of the tower to indicate that the original ground plan was altered in any way. They were men faced with a problem which had to be resolved as best they could. It may be assumed that the 'footprint' of the bell tower of King's College off the High Street of Old Aberdeen is that which was laid out on the first day and which has served well ever since.

Ian B D Bryce

Select Bibliography

Books consulted
Anderson P J (ed) *Officers and Graduates of King's College, Aberdeen, 1495-1860,* New Spalding Club, 1893
Breviarium Aberdonense 2 Vols, Bannatyne Club, 1854, 1855
Boece, Hector, *Lives of the Bishops of Aberdeen, etc* New Spalding Club, 1894
Burnett, J G (ed) *Powis Papers, 1507-1894,* Third Spalding Club, 1951
Cullen, Walter, *Chronicle of Aberdeen*, Miscellany of the Spalding Club, 1842
Douglas, Francis, *A General Description of the East Coast of Scotland,* Paisley, 1782
Eeles, F C, *King's College Chapel, Aberdeen,* Oliver & Boyd, 1956
Geddes, Jane, (ed) *King's College Chapel, Aberdeen 1500-2000,* Northern Universities Press, 2000
Cuickshank, J, (ed) *Logan's Collections,* Third Spalding Club, 1941
Innes, C (ed) *A Description of both Touns of Aberdeen,* James Gordon, Spalding Club, 1842
Innes, C (ed) *Ledger of Andrew Halyburton,* Edinburgh, 1867
Innes, C (ed) *Registrum Episcopatus Aberdonensis,* 2 Vols, Spalding Club, 1845
Keith, Alexander, *A Thousand Years of Aberdeen*, Aberdeen University Press, 1972
Macfarlane, Leslie J, *William Elphinstone and the Kingdom of Scotland 1431-1514,* AUP 1985
Marren, Peter, *Grampian Battlefields,* AUP 1990
Meldrum, Edward, *Aberdeen of Old*, 1986
Munro, A M (ed) *Records of Old Aberdeen 1489-1903* , 2 Vols, New Spalding Club, 1909
Orem, William, *Description of the Chanonry etc,* J Chalmers, Aberdeen, 1791
Rait, R S ,*The Universities of Aberdeen: a History,* J G Bisset, 1895
Simpson W D (ed) *A Tribute to William Kelly, LLD, ARSA,* The University Press, 1949
Slezer, John, *Theatrum Scotiae,* London 1693, (1814 edition)
Smith, John (ed) *Old Aberdeen, Bishops, Burghers and Buildings,* AUP, 1991
Spalding, John, *Memorialls of the Trubles etc 1624-1645* . (2 Vols) Spalding Club, 1850
Stevenson D, *King's College, Aberdeen, 1560-1641,* AUP, 1990
Dennison E P & Stones J, *Historic Aberdeen: Scottish Burgh Survey*, Historic Scotland, 1997
Stuart J, ed, *Extracts from the Council Register of the Burgh of Aberdeen 1398-1570,* (1844): *1570-1625,* (1848): Spalding Club
Walker, William, *The Bards of Bon Accord,1375-1860,* Edmund & Spark, 1887

Booklets , Articles
O Boyle, Colm, 'St Machar: Some Linguistic Light? *Friends of St Machar's Cathedral, Annual Report*, 1998
Occasional Papers 1 - 12. Friends of St Machar's Cathedral
Simpson, W D, *The Origins of Chrsitianity in Aberdeenshire*, 1925

Index

Aberdeen Breviary, 7, 45, 60, 82-3
Anderson, Principal Alex, 140, 146, 151, 153, 166
Anderson, John, & family, 203
Angus, Thomas, 189, 190, 241
Arbroath, Declaration of, 23
Arbuthnot, Principal Alex, 159-60, 161, 163-5
Arran, Earl of 134, 136
Balbegno Castle ceiling, 110-1
Balgownie, (Don) Brig of, 3, 23, 33, 134, 254-5, 263
Baliol, John, 23
Barbour, John, 7, 26, 28-9
Barrow, Geoffrey, 24
beadsmen, 115- 59, 174
beggars, 184-5,187
Birnie, Wm, 157
Bishop, Archibald, scourger etc, 184, 256
Bishops, (Aberdeen) Bellenden, 217, 263; Benham, 18, 22, 34; Blacader, 39, 44; de Cheyne, 22, 23; de Lichtoun, 32, 34, 35; de Lindsay, 35, 36, 37, 39, 63, 107; de Pottock 17; Edward, 16; Forbes of Corse, 261; Gordon, Alex 101-2; Gordon, Wm, 136, 137-9, 140, 143-4, 145, 151, 231; Kininmund I, 23-4; II, 25, 26, 30, 31; Nectan, 15-16; Spens, 37, 38-9; Stewart, Wm, 131, 134, 136, 231, library, 133, pulpit 131-2
Bishop's Lodging, 214, 221
Bishop's Palace, Fetternear, 24; OA, 4, 25, 27, 37, 38, 105, 239, 261
Bisset, Principal, John, 139, 142
Blinseile, Provost Robert, 44, 48, 58
Boece, Hector *(Lives) passim*, as principal, 67-9, 76-7, 105, 136
Bogdan, Nicholas, 24
Bogforth, etc 27, 38, 259
brewers, 176, 218-9, 233
Brousterland, 31, 34
Bryce, IBD, 124
Buchans, of Auchmacoy & Cairnbulg, 260
bulls, (1157), 17; (1495) 50-2, 53 (1498); 49, 53-4
Buruel, John, 84
Candlemas ceremony, 234-5, 236
Caprastoun, (Hilton), 169-171
Castlehill, fort at, 255, 261
census, 1636, 184-5, 187, 212, 218
Channel/Water Draught, 253
Chanonry, 2, 20, 25, 34, 48,49, 249-63; smithy & alehouse, 34
Chanonry houses: No 3, 26; No 8, 22; No 10, 22; Nos 11, 12, (Tillydrone House,) 22, 111; Nos 13-16, 20; No 13, (Chanonry Lodge), 22; No 15, Castleton House, 22; No 16, 22
Chaplains' Court, 106, 261-2
Chepman & Myllar, 82-3
church lands, 17, 138
Cluny's Garden, 250
Cocklarachie, goodwife of, 204, 253
College Bounds, 54, 193-203, 253
Comyn, John, 23
Congregation, Lords of, 142, 144, 147
Crombie & Johnston Halls, 1, 55, 199
Corrichie, Battle of, 154, 156
Crosses, Girth, 40-1, 54; Market, 215, 230, age 231, arms, 230-1 celebrations at, 234, punishments at 233-4, removal of 247, repairs, 234, vandalism of, 146, 232,
Cruickshank Botanic Gardens, 26, 31, 250
Cruickshank, George, & Lodging, 254
Cullen, Walter, chronicler, 159, 161, 166
Cumming, Dr James, 73

Cumming Wm of Inverallochy, 73
Cunnigar Hill, 54, 57
Dee, Bridge of, 81, 105, 118-9, 125, 127
Discipline, 1st Book of, 152, 184, 2nd, 163-4
Dods, Simon, 62-3
Don, River, 2, 16
Don Street, see Seatongate
Douglas, Archbald, 174, 223
Dransart, Penny, 24
Drummer, 180-1
Dunbar, Bishop Gavin, 123, 129, 130, early career, 102-3, KC ,104-6, Bridge of Dee, Chaplains' Court, Hospital, St Machar's Cathedral, see separate entries; 106, 114-5, death, 117;
Dunbar's Hospital, 34, 111, 114-5, 259
Dunbar Street/East Back Gate, Road, 229,
Dunbar, Wm (poet), 63
Elphinstone, Canon John 135-6, 139, 250
Elphinstone Road, West Back Road, etc 229
Elphinstone, Bishop, Wm, early career, 42, 44, 50, +Ross, 44, +Aberdeen 44-5, foundation of King's College, 45-9, 58-9, 61, as statesman, 44-5, 50, death, 81; See also, KC, St Machar's Cathedral
Elphinstone Wm Snr, 42
Epistolare, 106
Erskine, John of Dun, 142, 159, 163
Fairs, Skyre Thursday & St Luke's, 49, 61, 180, 189-91
Fendour, John, 65, 79-80, 92-3
Fetternear, 24
Forbes, James of Corsindae, 134-5
Forbes, Dr John, 261, 263
Fordoun, John of, 27, 30
forestalling & regrating, 232-3,
Framper Tom, 254
Franch, Thomas, 115, 117, 118-9, 125-6 156-7,
Fraser, Alex of Powis, 203, 222, 244, 245, 253
Friars, 47, 146
Galloway, Alexander, 20, 60, 67, 75, 88, 98, 109, 111, 125, 131, visitation, 139-40; 206, 233
Garden, Alex, of Banchory, 255
Garden, Alex (poet etc), 221
Garden, Robert of Blairton, 173; Thomas, 255, 260, 263
Gelly, Albert 245-6
Glenlivet, Battle of, 254
Gordon, Alex of Birsemoir, 172, 250, 252, 255-6
Gordon, Sir Alex of Cluny, 172, 184, 215, 245, 250, 251, 263; Sir Thomas, 169, 172, 251, 263
Gordon, Alexander of Strathavin, 254
Gordon, James of Seaton, 242, 254, 258, 259
Gordon, Dr Wm, 182, 195, 201, 203, 204-9, 253
Gray, Andrew, 200, Lawrence, 200
Grays, (masons), 125
Guild, Dr Wm, 197, 238, 239, 240, 261
Halyburton, Andrew, 57-8
Hamilton, Patrick, 129-30
Hay W, 69, 136,
Heriot, Master Adam, 147, 151, 156, 159
High Street, (Middle Toun), 49, 211, 221
Hills, Broom, 2, 222, Fir, 222 Glebe, 2, 221, 222, Hermitage, 222
Hilton, 35
Humanity Manse, 71, 196
Huntly Castle, (Strathbogie), 145, 155
Huntly, **2nd** Earl, 56, **3rd,** 101, **4th**, 131, 136, 143, 146, 151, 153, 154, 155, **5th**, 156, 157, 161, **6th & 1st** Marquis 161, 204, 254, **2nd,** 220, 250-1, 263
Innes, Berold etc, 173, 205, 224-5
Inventory, (1542) 74, 78, 97
Jaffrey, George, 247
Keith, (Master) John, 214, 235
Kelly, Dr Wm, 60, 121, 123, 124
Kettle Hills, 2, 22
Kilgour family, 257-8, Geo, 258, Harry, 257, John Jnr 257, Patrick, 257-8
Kings: Charles I, 206-7, 209; David I 6,7; Edward I 23; Edward III 25, 33; James I, 32; James III 44; James IV, 45-6, 50, 56;

James V, 77, 126; James VI, 156, 164 Malcolm Canmore, 15-16 Malcolm 1V, 16 , Robert I 23; Robert II, 28
King's College: accommodation, 74-7, armoury, 133, building, 64-5, courses, 70-1, description, 64-5, Foundations, New, 162, 164, 165, Old, 162, founding, 52, at Fraserburgh, 186, kitchen, 78-9, library, 133, staff, students, 67, 74-5,
KC Chapel 63, choir, 94, consecration crosses, 84, 87, exterior, 84-9, flèche, 89, interior 89-91, music, 94-8, 99-100, nave 90-1, royal arms, 87-8, stalls, 94-7, subsidence, 58-9
KC Crown Tower, (Belltower) 121, 124-5, 128, bells, 123-4, 266
Knowles, Janet , 137, 143
Knox, John, 144, 152, 159, 163
Laings, economuses, Geo, 212, 244, Wm, 212
Lanes, see Wynds
Lawson, Subpr. James, 160, 161
Leech, Master David, 220
Leslie, Alex of Wardes, 249, John, 251
Leslie, Bishop, John, 103, 151-3
Leslie John of Balquhain, 146, 157
Lichtoun's (north) aisle, 35, 251
Lillie, Alex, 173, 263, Thomas, 263
Lindsay, Sir David, 130
Linlithgow Palace, 115, 126,
Lochs, Goul, 18, 19, 24; Bishop's/Dean's/Old Aberdeen, 2, 34, 176, 233, 241, 250
Logan, Bailie Wm's Lodging, 263
Lundie, John, 179, 182, 188, 195, 201, 207, 238, 253
Luther, Martin, 129, 130-1
Macfarlane, Leslie, 36, 71, 73
Manses, Chanonry, furnishings, 36; Auchterless, 22, 260; Banchory-Devenick, 22, 37, 253-4; Belhelvie, 22, 37, 251, 291; Birse, 22, 36-7, 260; Clatt, 22, 254; Cruden, 22, 254; Daviot, 20, 251, 259; Deer, 20, 54 254; Ellon, 26-27 253, glebe, 27, 259; Forbes, 26, 251; Invernochty, 34, 55, 62, 249; Kincardine o Neil 26, 253; Kinkell, 111, 256; Kirkton of Seaton, 20, 36, 260; Lonmay, 26; Methlick, 250; Monymusk, 34, 256, 259; Mortlach, 22, 111, 255; Oyne, 22, 254; Philorth; 26, 251; Rayne; 22; Tullynessle; 27, 34, 252, 256, 259; Turriff, 34, 25; Westhall; 34, 259
Manses, King's College, 72- 3, 194 196, 199-200, 203
Mar, John Earl of, 62
Marischal College, 59, 165, 231
Marischal, Earl, 154, 164
market, 232-233, change of day, 233, flesh, 247
Melville, Andrew, 160, 162, 164, 165
Melville, James, 71, 162
Menzies, Provost, Thomas, 129, 131, 136, 137, 145, 147
Mercer, Bailie Thomas 173, 179, 212, 220, 239
Middleton, Geo, 252-3
Middleton, Col John, 259
Mitchell's Hospital, 22, 27, 252, 254
Moray, Earl of, 144, 154 ,157,159
Mortlach, 15,16,17
Mote Hill 3, 4, 6, 16, 26, 32,
Mowat, John, clockmaker, 246-7
muckster, (John Volum), 178-9, 219
Muir, Dr Andrew, 175, 209
Mutray, Alex Bailie, 173, 209
oatcake sellers, 183, 199, 218
Old Aberdeen, burgh of barony, 49, 54-5; customs, (dues), 175-6; expenditure, 178; fines, 177; houses, 213-216; new Council House etc 239, 243-4, 244; name, 3, 264: occupations, 213, 216, 221; road repairs, 82, 178; rural nature of, 213, 219, 244 259; quarters, 183; taxes 175; tolbooth, 244-5; topography, 1-3
Pantons, 174, 259
plague, 159, 186
Popes, Adrian IV, 17, 22, Alexander VI, 50-1, 53, John XXII, 23
Ports, Bishop's 33, Chanonry, 56, Market 33, 36, 61, Chaplains' 131
Powis Burn, 1, 2, 54, 193, 195, 253

Queens, consorts, regents, Elizabeth I, 147, Margaret Tudor, 87-8, 89, Mary of Guise, 77, 134, 136, 142, 144, 147; Mary Queen of Scots, 78, 134, 142, 153, 156, St Margaret, 15
Reformation, 129, 130, 134, 142, 146-7, 150
Rough Wooing, 134-5
St Machar's Cathedral, 9, 32, 35, 80; builders +Cheyne, 23; +de Lichtoun, 32-3; +Dunbar 115, heraldic ceiling, 106-110, 112-3, twin towers, 106; +Elphinstone 79, 80; +Kininmund II 25-26; +Nectan? (Norman), 16; clergy, 17, 22, 30-1;
St Machor, (poem) 7-11
St Nicholas Kirk, 39, 45, 92, 130, 146,
Saints: Columba, 7,9,11, Devenick 10, Kentigern 12-13, Mochrieha etc 11-12, Martin of Tours, 11, Moluag, 15, Ternan 10
Schools, Cathedral, 22, 236; Grammar, 141-2, 234, 244; Sang etc 236-7, 244; fees, 238; new building, 239, 244; visitations, 241
Schoolmasters, Christie Wm, 243, 244, Cooper, Alex 242, Cumming, Wm 242-3, Hay, George, 241, 242, Wm Jnr 241, Snr 241, Lindsay, Wm, 233, 237 Logan, Wm 240, 241, Ross, Gilbert, 237-8, 262, 263, Smith, Wm, 242, 243, Wilguis, Alex 238-40;
Sandilands, James, elder, 204; younger, 194, 201
Scroggie, Master Alex, 260-1, 263
Seaton Park, 3, 13, 16, 27
Seatongate, 22, 27, 263
Seaton Stone 13-14
Shand, Borrow, peatman, 245
Simpson W D , 4,11, 14, 31, 106,
Skene, Dr Gilbert, 159, 201
Snow Kirk *(St Mary ad Nives)*, 60, 63, 70, 150, 196-9, 235, 239
Spalding, Alex, 188, 215
Stewart, Lord James see Moray
Stewart, Theophilus, 136, 141, 159, 200-1
Stocket, Forest of, 171
Tillydrone, (Donydronis etc), 2-3, 4, 221
Tillydrone Roundabout, 2, 250
Trades of OA, 191, 194, 217, 238
Thomson, George, mason, 206-7, 208-9
Twelve Roods, 201, 203, 222, 253
Turnbull, Bishop Wm, 42
Udney, Peter, 116-7
Vaus, John, 70, 83, 136
Watson, Master John, 139, 140
Warbeck, Perkin, 56
witchcraft, 209
Wynds, Bedford/Broomhill/College/Doctor's/Meston, 209, 210, 221-222; Beverlay's 227; Cluny's, 54, 191, 223-4, 250; Douglas, 223; Berold's/Brewery; 224-6; Reid's, 227; Wagril's, 226.